Cyber Security

For our families

Cyber Security

Economic Strategies and Public Policy
Alternatives

Michael P. Gallaher

RTI International
Research Triangle Park, NC, USA

Albert N. Link

University of North Carolina at Greensboro
Greensboro, NC, USA

Brent R. Rowe

RTI International
San Francisco, CA, USA

Edward Elgar
Cheltenham, UK • Northampton, MA, USA

Published by
Edward Elgar Publishing Limited
Glensanda House
Montpellier Parade
Cheltenham
Glos GL50 1UA
UK

Edward Elgar Publishing, Inc.
William Pratt House
9 Dewey Court
Northampton
Massachusetts 01060
USA

A catalogue record for this book is available from the British Library

Library of Congress Cataloguing in Publication Data

Gallaher, Michael P.
  Cyber security : economic strategies and public policy alternatives /
Michael P. Gallaher, Albert N. Link, Brent Rowe.
     p. cm.
  Includes bibliographical references and index.
  1. Computer networks–Security measures. 2. Business
enterprises–Computer networks–Security measures. 3. Computer
security–Government policy. I. Link, Albert N. II. Rowe, Brent, 1980- III.
Title.
  TK5105.59.G347 2008
  005.8–dc22

                                                                        2007039429
ISBN 978 1 84720 355 7

Printed and bound in Great Britain by MPG Books Ltd, Bodmin, Cornwall

Contents

Figures

Tables

Acknowledgments

We thank many individuals and organizations for contributing to the research and preparation for this book. We are pleased to acknowledge support from the Department of Homeland Security (DHS), the National Institute of Standards and Technology (NIST) and the National Telecommunications and Information Administration (NTIA); these three organizations commissioned several studies from which this book was derived. We also appreciate the support of RTI International and the University of North Carolina at Greensboro during the preparation of the final manuscript. In addition, the book has benefited from the comments of Dr Doug Maughan at DHS and Dr Greg Tassey at NIST, as well as the suggestions received during presentations of preliminary results at the Western Economic Association 81st Annual Conference, the 2006 Workshop on the Economics of Information Security, the 2006 Financial Information Systems and Cyber Security Conference and the 2005 Statistical and Applied Mathematical Sciences Institute National Defense and Homeland Security Workshop.

And finally we would like to acknowledge the gracious support and patience of our families and friends through out this process. Dr Gallaher would like to thank his wife, Robin and daughter, Kate; Dr Link would like to thank his wife, Carol; and Mr Rowe would like to thank his wife, Stacy.

PART 1

Technical and Economic Framework

1. The Cyber Security Imperative

INTRODUCTION

Cyberspace, or the nation's information technology (IT) infrastructure, is the nervous system of the USA. It links our nation's critical infrastructures across both public and private institutions in sectors ranging from food and agriculture, water supply and public health, to energy, transportation and financial services. This information control system is composed of hundreds of thousands of interconnected computers, servers, routers, switches and fiber-optic cables that allow our critical infrastructures to work.[1] As described by the National Science and Technology Council (2006, p. iii):

> The Nation's [IT] infrastructure – the seamless fabric of interconnected computing and storage systems, mobile devices, software, wired and wireless networks, and related technologies – has become indispensable to public- and private-sector activities throughout our society and around the globe. Pervasive, cost-effective communication enables a vast, constant flow of information that has transformed work environments and processes in government, business and industry, and advanced research, health care, and many other fields.

This IT infrastructure supports many other critical infrastructures in our nation.[2] Thus, according to the National Science and Technology Council (2006, p. iii): 'safeguarding the Nation's IT infrastructure and critical infrastructure sectors for the future is a matter of national and homeland security).'

In a 2005 report to President George W. Bush from the President's Information Technology Advisory Committee (PITAC), the security of the Nation's IT infrastructure was emphasized (2005, p. iii):[3]

> The [Nation's] IT infrastructure is highly vulnerable to premeditated attacks with potentially catastrophic effects. Thus, it is a prime target for cyber terrorism as well as criminal acts. The IT infrastructure encompasses not only the best-known uses of the public Internet – e-commerce, communication, and Web services – but also the less visible systems and connections of the Nation's critical infrastructures such as power grids, air

traffic control systems, financial systems, and military and intelligence systems. The growing dependence of these critical infrastructures on the IT infrastructure means that the former cannot be secure if the latter is not.

Cyber security threats – and by cyber security we are referring to measures for protecting computer systems, networks and information from disruption or unauthorized access, use, disclosure, modification or destruction[4] – are defined by the National Science and Technology Council (2006, p. ix) as 'asymmetric, surreptitious, and constantly evolving – a single individual or a small group anywhere in the world can inexpensively and secretly attempt to penetrate systems containing vital information or mount damaging attacks on critical infrastructures).' Preventing this from happening, or least mitigating the likelihood of events, is what is referred to as the cyber security imperative.[5]

Fundamental to an understanding of economic strategies and public policy alternatives for cyber security is an appreciation of the evolution of the Internet and the role played by the federal government in its development. In the past, the federal government has taken a lead role in supporting the research structure of our nation – a theme that is revisited in Chapter 7 and Chapter 12 of this book – and as such the federal government has helped to maintain and enrich our IT infrastructure. The importance of this supporting role was reiterated by the President's Information Technology Advisory Committee (2005, p. 13) as well:

> [T]he Federal government has a vital, irreplaceable role to play [in cyber security]. As at earlier stages of the digital revolution, Federal investment in fundamental research is required to fill the pipeline with new concepts, technologies, infrastructure prototypes, and trained personnel needed for the private sector to accomplish its cyber security mission.

This chapter provides an overview of the development of the Internet and public sector involvement in cyber security.

THE INTERNET[6]

The Internet is a general purpose technology. General purpose technologies have broad applications and productivity-enhancing effects in many downstream sectors. They induce dramatic economic changes by creating new industries and rejuvenating existing sectors.[7] A general purpose technology has the following three characteristics: pervasiveness, an inherent potential for technological improvements and innovational complexities that give rise to increasing returns to scale.[8]

The term 'Internet' refers to a global network of computers, while the 'World Wide Web' refers to the software that allows these computers to communicate with each other. The Internet has resulted in the creation of new industries including the following examples: Internet service providers (ISPs) such as America OnLine (AOL); producers of network communications equipment, such as Cisco Systems; and service/software providers, such as Oracle, that produce software and provide consulting services to help organizations use the Internet to enhance their efficiency.[9]

It has been asserted and documented that the Federal government and other elements of the US national innovation system played a key role in the creation of the Internet.[10] For instance, the Department of Defense and the National Science Foundation financed much of the research that resulted in the development of key infrastructure technologies, especially the creation of computer networks.[11] In addition to direct funding from federal agencies, policy instruments used included initiatives to foster R&D cooperation, targeted subsidies and bridging institutions to stimulate the development of the infrastructure technology. Also, several university spin-offs, such as Sun Microsystems from Stanford University, also played a key role in the development of this technology.

There were three distinct periods in the creation of the Internet and the World Wide Web.[12] The first period, which began in 1960 and ended in 1985, was characterized by the early development of computer networks. Two innovations that facilitated the formation of these networks were digital packet-switching, the technology used to link computers, and the development of standards and protocols that facilitated the communication of information across networked computers. The first version of the Internet, called ARPANET, was funded by the Defense Advanced Research Projects Agency (DARPA) of the US Department of Defense. In the mid-1970s, universities and other defense research organizations were added to the network.

The key standard developed during this initial period for communication via the Internet was the transmission control protocol/Internet protocol or TCP/IP. TCP/IP was primarily created by DARPA-funded engineers. TCP/IP is an open standard, which means that complete descriptions of it, as well as the rights to use this protocol, are publicly available. Significant network externalities were generated when the National Science Foundation adopted TCP/IP in forming its network of computers with universities and other research institutions.[13]

Other key events that occurred during this period were the development of e-mail – the first security-prone application for networks – and the development of Internet self-governance institutions. The latter refers to organizations, initially sponsored by the National Science Foundation (NSF) and the Department of Defense (DoD), which managed what became known as the Internet. The key institutions were the Internet Configuration Control Board, which later became the Internet Activities Board. As the system grew, it became difficult for the Internet Activities Board to manage the network while relying exclusively on government financing. Therefore, a public–private partnership, the Internet Society, was established in 1992 to oversee the growth of the network and the continued development of open standards.

The second period in the development of the Internet and the World Wide Web occurred between 1985 and 1995. During these years, there was rapid growth in network infrastructure in the public and private sectors. In 1990, the public sector transitioned from ARPANET to the NSF-funded next generation, NSFNET. In the private sector, there was a large increase in the demand for corporate computer networks, as organizations and consumers became heavy users of personal computers and organizations developed 'local area networks'[14] to allow these computers to communicate with each other.

Since 1995, the world has been in the third period of Internet development, characterized by a rapid increase in use of the Internet for commercial purposes and by individuals and organizations. Continued cost reductions and the evolution of wireless capabilities will continue to stimulate demand and support the development of new applications.

It is important to note that until 1991, the Internet was strictly a device for research and communication and not a device to be used for commercial purposes, as mandated by the NSF, which controlled the network. After lobbying by commercial interests, the NSF decided to abandon this policy. By 1995, management of the network had been completely transferred to four private companies: Ameritech, Sprint, MFS and Pacific Bell.

A fundamental factor in the growth of the World Wide Web was the development of the Hypertext Markup Language (HTML) document format and the associated Hypertext Transfer Protocol (HTTP) document retrieval protocol. HTML and HTTP facilitated the creation and dissemination of multimedia documents. That is, these innovations made it quite simple for firms to create 'web pages' with text, pictures and graphics and also enabled consumers to access these files easily. Furthermore, with HTML it was easy for Web page authors to provide links to other documents and this greatly facilitated the value and use of the network. The combination of HTML and HTTP essentially transformed the Internet into the World Wide Web.

A key tool in using the World Wide Web is the Internet browser, which allows a user to access and read HTML files at the click of a mouse. One of the first browsers, called Mosaic, was created at the National Center for Supercomputing Applications, an NSF-funded research center at the University of Illinois, by a graduate student named Marc Andreessen. Mosaic was ultimately developed into the Netscape web browser, which was the dominant browser in use until the development of Microsoft's Internet Explorer browser began to compete for commercial dominance. Microsoft literally gave away its browser, including the browser in its Windows operating system.

The widespread, rapid diffusion of technologies that enabled consumers and firms to gain speedy access to the Internet and the World Wide Web was fueled by several factors. These included precipitous declines in inflation-adjusted computer prices and the cost of information transmission, along with a concomitant increase in speed of information delivery through high-speed communication networks. Consumers purchased computers to gain access to information and entertainment that was being transmitted to them via the Internet. Over time, consumers became reasonably confident about purchasing items online, resulting in a substantial increase in e-commerce. Global e-commerce generated nearly US $13 trillion in revenue in 2006.[15]

PUBLIC SECTOR INVOLVEMENT IN CYBER SECURITY

In January 2001, the Bush administration initiated a broad-based review of information systems and cyber security. On 16 October 2001, in the aftermath of 9/11, President Bush issued Executive Order 13231: Critical Infrastructure Protection in the Information Age. According to the Executive Order:

It is the policy of the United States to protect against disruption of the operation of information systems for critical infrastructure and thereby help to protect the people, economy, essential human and government services and national security of the United States, and to ensure that any disruptions that occur are infrequent, of minimal duration and manageable and cause the least damage possible.

The Executive Order established the President's Critical Infrastructure Protection Board, thus providing the framework for executive branch oversight of activities that affect cyberspace security.[16]

Table 1.1 overviews the agencies responsible for monitoring our nation's infrastructures.[17] This table highlights the fact that, in general, security functions and responsibilities are quite disaggregated. Although cyber security crosses all of these areas, the decentralized nature of the Internet has prevented the establishment of a central organization responsible for supporting and coordinating cyber security.

Executive Order 13231 is important from a legislative perspective, but it should not be overlooked that from an economic perspective the federal government has a social responsibility to support fundamental research for the private sector to accomplish its cyber security mission. This responsibility stems from the public-goods nature of the knowledge that comes from fundamental or basic research that is generally conducted in colleges and universities and in federal laboratories. Because of the public-good nature of knowledge per se, organizations will underinvest in its creation from the perspective of society because they cannot appropriate all of the benefits of, or returns to, their investments.[18] Cyber security investments suffer from the same problems, a point revisited in Chapter 7.

ECONOMIC IMPACTS

Cyber security breaches are costly in terms of both direct damages and future lost opportunities associated with stifling innovation. While there are no consistent estimates of the annual cost to the private sector or the public sector from security compromises, the Computer Security Institute's 2006 'Computer Crime and Security Survey' found that a sample of 313 US organizations (from the 5000 US organizations surveyed) incurred $52.5 million in losses from IT breaches in that same year. For purposes of generalization, if the 5000 firms surveyed represent 90 percent of the private sector organizations with compromisable IT, then the losses reported by the 313 organizations could be representative of the losses incurred by the population as a whole. In 2006 cyber security breaches could thus have accounted for nearly $1 billion in the United States.

Table 1.1 Critical infrastructure lead agencies

Lead agency	Sectors
Department of Homeland Security	Information
	Telecommunications
	Transportation (aviation, rail, mass transit, waterborne commerce, pipelines and highways)
	Postal
	Shipping
	Emergency services
	Continuity of government
Department of the Treasury	Banking and Finance
Department of Health and Human Services	Public health (including prevention, surveillance, laboratory services and personal health services)
	Food (except meat and poultry)
Department of Energy	Energy (electric power, oil and gas production and storage)
Environmental Protection Agency	Water
	Chemical industry
	Hazardous materials
Department of Agriculture	Agriculture
	Food (meat and poultry)
Department of Defense	Defense industrial base

Source: White House (2003), p. 16.

Regardless of the assumptions in the above extrapolation, there is reason to believe that the $1 billion estimate is low. The $52.5 million reported by the 313 organizations is a gross underestimate of the total costs to the private and public sectors. The costs accounted for by the Computer Security Institute's (CSI) survey are direct costs to the organizations (for example, IT staff labor to resolve problems). Often there are external costs to customers who are affected by the breach. These costs are varied, ranging from simple downtime of an organization's computer network, which inconveniences staff and/or customers, to identity theft, which requires households to incur many hours of work to resolve. In addition, cyber security breaches in the public sector are rarely made public, but certainly agency offices incur similar categories of costs and the sum may well exceed a $1 billion per year.

A billion here, a billion there ... soon it starts to add up to real money, and soon it has an impact on the economy beyond the immediacy of the cyber security breach.[19] Organizations that incur such costs to respond to cyber security breaches pass those costs on, in total or in part, to consumers. In addition, organizations and consumers modify their behavior in light of the threat of security events – mostly likely, spending time on less desirable activities – and the potential lost benefits of foregone opportunities are almost impossible to quantify.

From an economic perspective, the incursion of these costs increases an organization's marginal cost and hence the price it charges for goods and services. This increase in price reduces consumer surplus, everything else remaining constant. From a macroeconomic perspective, these increases in marginal costs will eventually decrease aggregate supply (of goods) and will be observed as a higher rate of inflation, everything else remaining constant.

OUTLINE OF THE BOOK

This book represents, to the best of our knowledge, the first systematic analysis of the economics of cyber security issues and the role the public sector should play in supporting and protecting the infrastructure. Herein we draw primarily on case-based information and on focused survey data to help to explain the economic strategies that private sector organizations adopt to secure their IT infrastructure. Based on our understanding of these strategies, meaning their strengths and limitations, we propose several public policy responses that go beyond those that have come from recent policy reports.

Chapter 2 discusses the prevalence of cyber security breaches from a national perspective. We review the few efforts to collect organizational-specific information on aspects of cyber security, and we summarize a number of their findings in graphical form. From our review, which we believe is exhaustive, we emphasize a number of yet unanswered questions related to investment and research and development (R&D) strategies. The remaining chapters in the book offer what we believe are some of the first systematic efforts to address these questions from both a conceptual perspective and a case-based empirical perspective.

Chapter 3 builds from the general descriptive information in Chapter 2. We describe the goals and motivations of attackers and the tools and activities they use to achieve their goals. We also summarize general tools, processes and activities that IT security administrators and users employ to prevent breaches; and discuss technical performance issues of cyber security technologies and emerging threats. The decision-making and related investment processes concerning IT and computer security are based, in part, on the ongoing conflict between hackers and computer security administrators. These conflicts involve a variety of motivations, goals and security tools and procedures. The goals and motivations for hackers and the tools and activities they use are discussed in this chapter, and administrators' responses are then discussed in Chapter 4.

Chapter 4 presents an overview of what we call cyber security investment and implementation strategies. The information that underlies our model comes from 100 US organizations that we identified with input from the US Department of Homeland Security (Gallaher et al., 2006). This population represents six composite groups: financial services, health care providers, manufacturing, universities, small businesses and other organizations. We make the distinction within our frameworks between analyses that organizations conduct as part of an investment strategy and analyses conducted as part of an implementation strategy.

In Chapter 5 we present quantitative findings from detailed interviews we conducted with information security officers (ISOs). The interviews investigated how organizations determine their level of investment to address cyber security concerns and how they select specific solutions in terms of the models introduced in Chapter 4. Detailed formal survey interviews were conducted with 36 organizations and our results are summarized in this chapter.

Qualitative discussions about five specific stakeholder groups – financial service providers, health care providers, manufacturing firms, small businesses and universities – are discussed in Chapter 6. Financial service providers and manufacturing firms generally have the same outlook on cyber security, aside from regulation-specific impacts. However, health care providers, small businesses and universities have very unique challenges and perceive cyber security investment differently.

Chapter 7 discusses the public-good nature of cyber security and anticipates the discussion in Chapter 12 by suggesting several public policy recommendations aimed at helping organizations meet their cyber security imperative. The policies proffered follow from economic theory and relate to the provision of information by the public sector.

Chapters 8 to 11 contain case studies summarizing public sector activities supporting cyber security research and implementation. The case studies focus on activities undertaken by the National Institute of Standards and Technology (NIST). The NIST is a federal laboratory with a mission to promote US economic growth by working with industry to develop and apply technology, measurements and standards. As a group, these represent infrastructure technology, and we argue in Chapter 12 that the provision of infrastructure technology is an important role for government with regard to the cyber security imperative.

In Chapter 8, we investigate data encryption standards (DES). Encryption standards promote the diffusion of encryption products in order to provide the information security needed for Internet applications. We conclude that the NIST's role in establishing and updating DES has had measurable and significant social benefits.

The case study in Chapter 9 investigates security issues associated with the transition to Internet protocol version 6 (IPv6). This Internet protocol (IP) significantly influences the security of the interconnections that link the global network of computers, and this chapter focuses on the potential threats associated with 'IP' attacks (for example, intercepting information and spoofing). This chapter also identifies the activities needed, and estimates the costs associated with, transitioning to the new Internet protocol.

The case study in Chapter 10 reviews the testing of computer software and its impact on security. The software that underlies and communicates through the World Wide Web is comprised of millions of lines of code where vulnerabilities are constantly identified. This case study investigates the potential benefits of enhanced software testing tools (infrastructure technologies) in terms of software development costs and fewer disruptions to software users.

In contrast to Chapters 8, 9 and 10 which focus on external threats to the operation of the Internet, Chapter 11 investigates the human factor in cyber security. Internet users are not only subject to external attacks, but are increasingly vulnerable to internal security breaches perpetrated by 'spies' or disgruntled employees. This chapter investigates the potential benefits of an emerging access control mechanism supported by the NIST, role-based access control (RBAC), to streamline the management of employee access to sensitive information and processes. Again we conclude that the NIST's role in developing and promoting RBAC has had measurable and significant social benefits.

Finally, Chapter 12 concludes the book by offering a number of public policy recommendations to help organizations meet their cyber security imperative. Specifically, the government could: help fund the collection, analysis and dissemination of both reliable and cost-effective information related to cyber security for benchmarking purposes; provide guidelines for evaluating the effectiveness and efficiency of potential cyber security solutions; underwrite both the research and implementation costs for organizations that are pilot testing new innovations; and design mechanisms that redistribute the costs associated with a security breach to better provide incentives for individual organizations to enhance their cyber security.

NOTES

1. See White House (2003).
2. These infrastructures include, according to the National Science and Technology Council (2006, p. iii), 'those that supply our food, water, energy, financial transactions, and transportation, as well as public health, emergency response, and other vital services. The interconnectivity that makes seamless delivery of essential information and services possible, however, also exposes many previously isolated critical infrastructures to the risk of cyber attacks mounted through the IT infrastructure by hostile adversaries. The exposure to critical infrastructures to cyber-based attacks is expected to increase, as convergence of network and device technologies accelerates, and as systems increasingly connect to the Internet to provide added functionality or greater efficiency'.
3. The President's Information Technology Advisory Committee (PITAC) is appointed by the President to provide expert advice on how to maintain America's pre-eminence in advanced IT. IT leaders in industry and academia with expertise relevant to critical elements of the national IT infrastructure are members of the PITAC. The committee's studies help guide the administration's efforts to accelerate the development and adoption of information technologies vital for American prosperity in the twenty-first century (President's Information Technology Advisory Committee, 2005).
4. This definition of cyber security comes from the National Science and Technology Council (2006, p. 3). The council uses the terms 'cyber security' and 'information assurance' together, but herein we simply abbreviate this concept to 'cyber security'. The council (p. 3) states that 'the purpose of cyber security and information assurance is to provide for integrity – protection

against unauthorized modifications or destructions of systems, networks, and information, and systems of information authentication; confidentiality – protection again unauthorized access to and disclosure of information; and availability – assurance of timely and reliable access to and use of systems, networks, and information'.

5. A recent National Research Council report (Wessner, 2005) quoted US Congressman Sherwood Boehlert as saying that homeland security has to be a primary focus of activities across the federal government, and cyber security is one of the critical areas to address in homeland security science and technology efforts. The report goes on to say that the Federal government has to be involved because 'improving cyber security requires more basic research, and will require greater support for students in order to attract new people to the computer security field' (p. 10).

6. This section draws on Link and Seigel (forthcoming) and the references therein, especially Mowery and Simcoe (2002).

7. General purpose technologies include, for example, the steam engine, the electric dynamo and lasers.

8. See Bresnahan and Trajtenberg (1995).

9. Many examples of innovation complementarities and the rejuvenation of existing industries associated with the use of Internet are in Litan and Rivlin (2001).

10. Mowery and Simcoe (2002) have presented an articulate in-depth historical analysis of the development of the Internet and the World Wide Web. Much of what follows draws from their scholarship.

11. Technology infrastructure supports the design, deployment and use of both individual technology-based components and the systems of such components that form the knowledge-based economy. Following the logic of Martin and Scott (2000), the main mode of innovation for the Internet was decentralized development of what they term a complex system.

12. Mowery and Simcoe (2002) make the case for these three time periods, and we follow here their timeline of activities

13. Network externalities involve the change in an economic agent's benefits from consuming a good when the number of other economic agents consuming the good changes.

14. Local area networks are sets of connected computers directly connected to one another with cables or wirelesses. Such networks may or may not be connected to the wider Internet.

15. See CCID (2007).

16. This board is similar in scope, but not in motivation, to the National Infrastructure Assurance Council established by President Clinton under Executive Order 13130 on 14 July 1999.
17. This table comes from the White House (2003), p. 16.
18. This basic economic concept underlies government's support of research at colleges and universities, and it underlies the R&E Tax Credit of 1981 in the United States.
19. The late US Senator Everett Dirksen used to say of federal budgets: 'A billion here, a billion there, pretty soon it begins to add up to real money.'

2. Cyber Security Trends and Issues

INTRODUCTION

One of the policy recommendations that we make in Chapter 12 in response to the empirical and case-based analyses presented and discussed throughout the book is for the establishment of a national database related to cyber security. That recommendation is not offered casually, but rather it is one of the implications from our analyses. This chapter provides an understanding of the facts and extant data that underlie this recommendation.

In this chapter we summarize and discuss extant quantitative information related to trends and issues on cyber security. As will be seen, limited information is available. The paucity of such quantitative information underscores just how little is known about this topic in general. In addition, the paucity of such quantitative information also underscores the inherent difficulty in formulating public policies to address what we called in Chapter 1 the 'cyber security imperative': preventing cyber security threats – efforts by a single individual or a small group anywhere in the world attempting to penetrate systems containing vital information or mount damaging attacks on critical infrastructures.

The next section briefly overviews three data collection efforts to obtain descriptive information on cyber security issues.[1] In the following section we focus exclusively on selected information compiled by the Computer Security Institute (CSI) from the 'CSI/FBI Computer Crime and Security Survey'. Our emphasis on the CSI/FBI survey comes from the fact that more historical data are available from it than from the other two survey sources. In the final section we raise several issues that are suggested by the CSI/FBI data that have yet to be systematically investigated and that are critically important from a public policy (and public security) perspective. This section motivates our analyses and discussion in subsequent chapters.

SELECTED DATABASES RELATED TO CYBER SECURITY

E-Crime Watch Survey[2]

CSO magazine conducts an annual survey of security executives and law enforcement personnel. The survey, known as the E-Crime Watch Survey, is administered in cooperation with the United States Secret Service,[3] Carnegie Mellon University Software Engineering Institute's CERT® Coordination Center and Microsoft Corporation. The third annual survey was in 2006, and 434 individuals were surveyed. Key findings of the 2006 report include:

- mean company IT security spending was $20.2 million and median information technology (IT) security spending was $414 000 in that year;
- mean company losses from unauthorized computer system breaches were $740 000 and median company losses were $45 000;
- the number of security events has continued to decline over the past several years, and the impact of these incidents in terms of financial and operating loss has steadily increased; and
- insider threats are increasing in number, with over half of organizations that experienced a security event reporting one or more per year.

Global Security Survey[4]

The Deloitte Touche Tohmatsu (DTT) Global Financial Services Industry (GFSI) group has conducted a security survey in the financial services industry each year since 2003. Participants are financial institutions with a worldwide presence and with head office operations in one of the following areas: North America, Europe, the Middle East, Africa, the Asia Pacific and Latin America and the Caribbean. Among the sectors included in the survey are banking, securities, insurance and asset management. Regarding data collection, survey responses were mostly obtained through face-to-face interviews with the chief information security officer or chief security officer (CISO/CSO) or their delegate.

Of the many interesting findings reported in the 2006 report, some of them more relevant to our discussion include that IT security budgets have been increasing over time in the financial industries, and that the main reported reason for this trend is the significant increase in compliance costs to comply with regulations. In addition, CISOs are increasingly reporting directly to upper management, and corporate boards are now being mandated to evaluate cyber security issues – generating a demand for data and quantitative analysis.

CSI/FBI Database[5]

The 11th Annual CSI/FBI Computer Crime and Security Survey, conducted in January 2006, collected information on company activities in the year 2005.[6] As reported in final report of survey results (CSI, 2006), data are coded in terms of the year of the report. For example, reference to 2006 in a figure refers to the year of the survey; the information being summarized relates to 2005.

The CSI, with assistance from the San Francisco Federal Bureau of Investigation's (FBI's) Computer Intrusion Squad, surveyed 5000 information security practitioners throughout the United States. The following industrial sectors were included in the 2006 survey, and in parentheses are the percentages of organizations from each sector:[7] financial (17 percent), consulting (14 percent), information technology (11 percent), manufacturing (9 percent), educational (8 percent), federal government (8 percent), medical (7 percent), telecommunications (9 percent), local government (3 percent), state government (3 percent), utility (3 percent), legal (1 percent), retail (1 percent), transportation (1 percent), and other (11 percent).

Of those responding to the 2006 survey, most represent moderate- to large-sized organizations, 26 percent of the respondents were from organizations with 1500 to 9999 employees and 16 percent were from organizations with 10 000 to 49 999 employees. One-third (34 percent) of the respondents were from organizations with over $1 billion in revenues in 2006.

The CSI/FBI database is certainly the most comprehensive of the three databases described in this chapter.[8]

TRENDS AND ISSUES

Here we present selected CSI/FBI descriptive information which was collated from online CSI/FBI reports from 2002 to 2006. Information for years prior to 2002, when available, came from these reports. Selected data are summarized graphically and discussed in this section in Figures 2.1–2.12.[9]

These twelve figures form the basis for this section. While these figures are developed from survey data from CSI/FBI reports, it is important to offer a word of caution about generalizing from the trends and issues identified from the primary summary data and from our interpretations of those trends. In many instances the CSI realized less than a 10 percent response rate, and when the response rate to particular survey questions was greater than 10 percent it was greater by very little. In the absence of access to the primary data, weighted summary statistics could not be calculated and as a result no adjustment for response bias could be made in the summary figures. Caveats aside, the CSI/FBI report nevertheless represents, in our opinion, the best public information (that is, in terms of breadth and historical data for comparison) about cyber security spending and attack trends.

Figure 2.1 shows for the years 1999–2006 the percentage of respondents (616 US respondents out of 5000 US organizations surveyed in 2006) who reported at least one computer system incident or breach per year. To the extent that the respondents in each year are representative of the survey population, and to the extent that the survey population is representative of a constant proportion of the national population of organizations susceptible to an unauthorized computer system breach, it can be inferred from these data that there has been a declining trend in computer system breaches since 2000, with the single exception of 2005. In 2006, about one-half of the responding companies (52 percent) experienced a computer system breach. That was the lowest percentage reported during the period from 1999 to 2006.

Figure 2.2 shows for the years 1999–2006 the percentage of respondents (341 out of 5000 in 2006) who reported ranges for the number of unauthorized computer system breaches. It appears from the survey data that there has been a modest increase over time in the number of organizations experiencing 1–5 breaches per year, but at the same time, there has been a decrease in the number of organizations experiencing more than five breaches per year. Perhaps these trends indicate that once a breach occurs, organizations respond promptly to protect against further similar intrusions. In addition, with the automation of virus creation tools the number of different attacks may increase but the sophistication (innovativeness) may be decreasing, contributing to fewer repeat breaches.

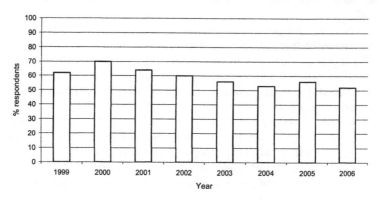

Note: There has been a slight downward trend in the percentage of organizations experiencing security breaches.

Figure 2.1   Organizations encountering at least one unauthorized computer system breach

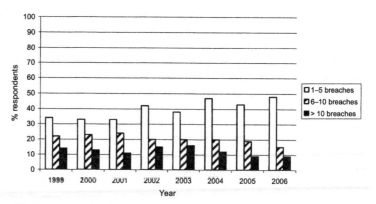

Note: The frequency of breaches greater than 5 has been on the decline over time, indicating that organizations are being responsive and that reactionary activities are effective.

Figure 2.2 Number of incidences of unauthorized computer system breaches

The extrapolated data in Figure 2.3 are nevertheless consistent with our generalization.

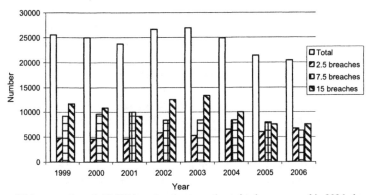

Note: Of the approximately 20 000 breaches that are estimated to have occurred in 2006, there is a slight increase in the number of organizations experiencing a relatively small number of breaches.

Figure 2.3 Estimated number of incidences of unauthorized computer system breaches

To provide some insight into the magnitude of this problem, we extrapolate the findings in Figure 2.2 onto the US population as a whole. The CSI/FBI reports state for each mean summary statistic the corresponding number of respondents to each survey question. As referenced above, for example, 341 of 5000 organizations responded to the question asking the number of unauthorized computer system breaches (within in a range) that were experienced in 2006. Based on the number of respondents each year, an annual response rate can be calculated. Thus, each mean summary statistic can mathematically be extrapolated to a 100 percent response rate for the survey population assuming that the respondents are representative of the survey population. Figure 2.3 is so based on Figure 2.2.

For the construction of Figure 2.3, respondents reporting 1–5 breaches per year are assumed to have experienced 2.5 breaches per year; respondents reporting 6–10 breaches per year are assumed to have experienced 7.5 breaches per year; and respondents reporting greater than ten breaches per year are assumed to have experienced 15 breaches per year. The figure also assumes that the survey population of 5000 organizations represents 90 percent of the national population of organizations susceptible to a computer system breach. Thus, Figure 2.3 shows a total of over 20 000 unauthorized computer system breaches in 2006. There has been a slight overall decline in the total number of unauthorized computer system breaches since 2002, with a noticeable decline from 2004 to 2006. As suggested from the trend of summary data in Figure 2.2, there seems to have been a slight increase in organizations experiencing a small number of breaches (for example, 2.5 breaches per year) over time.[10]

In response to the propensity to experience unauthorized computer system breaches, organizations reported that they reacted in a number of ways including the formulation of an investment strategy and a corresponding purchase of relevant software and hardware to meet their cyber security imperative. As shown in Figure 2.4, over the years 2004–2006, about 40 percent of the responding organizations allocated dollars equivalent to less than 2 percent of their IT budgets to cyber security, but in 2004 and 2005 about 50 percent of the responding organizations allocated 1–5 percent of their IT budgets to cyber security.[11]

An aggregate percentage of IT budgets allocated to cyber security was estimated for the national population of organizations investing in cyber security, using a weighted average of the percentages underlying Figure 2.4.[12] See Figure 2.5. In 2006, for example, the estimated percentage of an organization's IT budget allocated to cyber security was 3.9 percent.[13] According to the US Census Bureau (2006), in 2006, aggregate organizational expenditure on IT totaled $154 billion.[14] Assuming that the expenditure pattern of responding organizations mirrors that of all organizations, an approximation of total organizational investments in cyber security was about $6 billion in 2006.

Figure 2.6 shows the per employee estimated computer security expenditures – including capital investment expenditure plus operating expenditures – segmented by organizational size measured in revenues, for the years 2004–2006.[15] Over the three-year period, smaller-sized organizations (for example, less than $10 million in revenues) have increased their per employee expenditure, especially from 2005 to 2006, whereas in other companies there is less variation across years.

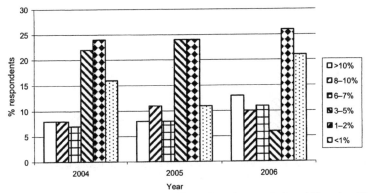

Note: The share of an organization's IT budget allocated to cyber security is variable and could be influenced by current events or the timing of system upgrades.

Figure 2.4 Percentage of IT budget allocated to cyber security

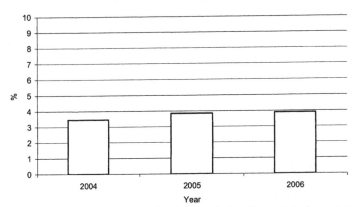

Note: Total organizational investments in cyber security have been relatively constant, and they are estimated to be about $6 billion in 2006. The sum of the percentages for each is less than 100 because a portion of the respondents did 'not know' the percentages.

Figure 2.5 Estimated percentage of IT budget allocated to cyber security

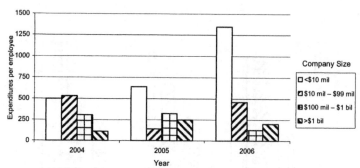

Note: Smaller-sized organizations have seen their per-employee expenditures of cyber security increase dramatically over time.

Figure 2.6   Average computer security expenditures (capital investment plus operating expenditure) per employee by size of organization (revenues)

Functions related to cyber security can be performed internally or they can be outsourced, or a combination of the two may be employed. As shown in Figure 2.7, 61 percent of the 609 respondents in 2006 stated that computer security functions were not outsourced but rather were administered internally. This percentage has been relatively constant over the three years shown despite research that suggests a growing managed security service provide (MSSP) market and potential social benefits stemming from outsourcing some security activities.[16]

Computer security breaches can originate from a variety of sources. The CSI (2006) lists 13 such sources: virus, laptop or mobile theft, insider abuse of Internet access, unauthorized access to information, denial of service, system penetration, abuse of wireless network, theft of property information, financial fraud, telecom fraud, misuse of private Web application, website defacement or sabotage. Four types of attack are summarized in Figure 2.8; these are among the more commonly reported types as measured by the percentage of respondents identifying the type of attacks or misuse. The percentage of respondents reporting any of these four types clearly declined, albeit moderately, from 1999 to 2006.

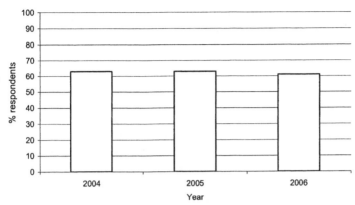

Note: Outsourcing of cyber security has been relatively constant over time.

Figure 2.7 Organizations with all computer security functions done internally

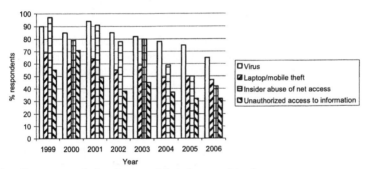

Note: Computer security breaches can originate from a variety of sources.

Figure 2.8 Type of unauthorized computer security breach

As stated above, total organizational investments in cyber security in 2006 may have totaled over $6 billion. The question is: Is it reasonable for organizations to be investing such an amount? While a private damage estimate of $1 billion cited in Chapter 1 does not seem to warrant this level of investment, profit-maximizing organizations continue to be concerned and experts warn of the consequences of underinvestment.

We discuss investment strategies in Chapter 4 and we point out that even with the safeguards that these investments engender, organizations are still reporting sizeable monetary losses caused by unauthorized computer security breaches. Figure 2.9 shows the reported dollar losses ($ thousands) for each year from 1997 to 2006. However, these data come from a small percentage of the survey population – just over 6 percent of the organizations responded to this CSI/FBI question in 2006. As a result it is probably misleading and it should not be inferred from the primary data summarized in Figure 2.9 that losses increased from 1997 to 2002 on a national basis, and then decreased in 2006. Reported losses followed this pattern, but the number of survey respondents also varied from year to year, and that is captured in the dollar trend. As will be discussed in Chapter 12, this highlights the need for enhanced data collection.

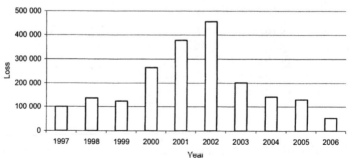

Note: Issues with low response rates and selection bias can lead to misleading results as shown in this figure where it appears that losses due to breaches have significantly declined in recent years.

Figure 2.9 Loss caused by unauthorized computer security breaches ($ thousands)

Figure 2.10 is an extrapolation of the data in Figure 2.9 to the national population of companies.[17] As suggested by Figure 2.9, losses have declined since 2002, but in 2006 they still totaled an estimated $1 billion at the national level.[18] However, it is unclear how comparable the available data are over time because of year-by-year differences in response rates and response biases.

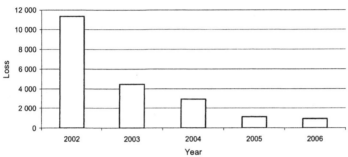

Note: Losses appear to have significantly decreased since 2002.

Figure 2.10   Estimated aggregate loss caused by computer system security breaches ($ millions)

To prevent unauthorized computer security breaches, organizations invest in a number of technologies. These technologies include – as carefully identified in the CSI/FBI survey – firewalls, anti-virus software, anti-spy software, server-based access control lists, intrusion detection systems, encryption for data in transit, encryption for data in storage, reusable account and login passwords, intrusion pre-emption systems, log management software, application-level firewalls, smart care and one-time password tokens, forensic tools, public key infrastructure, specialized wireless security systems, endpoint security client software and biometrics (CSI, 2006). The relative use of four of the more frequently utilized security technologies purchased to prevent breaches is shown in Figure 2.11. The percentage of respondents reporting that they use firewalls has increased slightly since 1999; the same is true for intrusion detection and data encryption. As will be discussed in Chapter 5, whereas almost all companies apply firewalls and anti virus software, the effectiveness of such measures varies greatly due to configuration, maintenance and staff expertise.

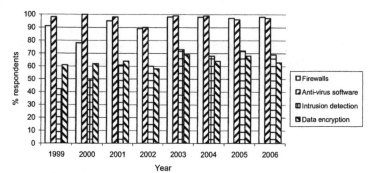

Note: The percentage of respondents reporting that they use firewalls has increased slightly since 1999; the same is true for intrusion detection and data encryption.

Figure 2.11   Technologies used to prevent unauthorized computer system security breaches

Finally, Figure 2.12 illustrates that a sizeable percentage of the CSI/FBI respondents did not report unauthorized computer security breaches to law enforcement. In 2006, 30 percent of the 385 (out of 5000) responding organizations incurred an unauthorized computer security breach but did not report it. Perhaps it is the case that organizations do not report unauthorized breaches because they do not want any public disclosure of the fact that their IT systems are insecure. In fact, in 2006, 48 percent of the respondents cited as a reason for not reporting unauthorized breaches that the associated negative publicity would adversely affect their image and their stock price, and 36 percent cited that competitors would use such information to their advantage (CSI, 2006).

UNANSWERED QUESTIONS

A number of questions come to mind from the graphical overview of cyber security trends illustrated in this chapter. First, with regard to the incidence of unauthorized computer system breaches described in Figures 2.1, 2.2 and 2.3: Why do computer system breaches occur? Whereas we overview the vulnerabilities of cyber security technologies in Chapter 3, the psychological motivation for such actions is very important for a complete answer to this question and this is beyond the scope of this book.

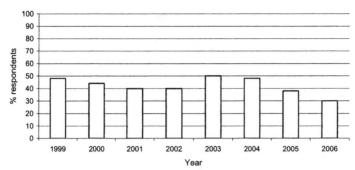

Note: A sizeable percentage of the CSI/FBI respondents did not report unauthorized computer security breached to law enforcement.

Figure 2.12 Organizations that did not report computer system breaches to law enforcement

Figures 2.4, 2.5 and 2.11 relate to an organization's investment strategy in cyber security; thus a relevant question is: How are cyber security budgets determined within organizations? Are scarce resources allocated rationally for such protection? Once allocated, how is the strategy funded by these investments implements? Figure 2.7 suggests, at a first-order level, that many strategies are implemented in-house without the assistance of outsourcing. But, as discussed in Chapters 4, 5 and 6, investment and implementation strategies are more complex than the summary data in this chapter illustrate.

Given the magnitude of the losses associated with unauthorized computer security breaches, as inferred from Figures 2.9 and 2.10, an appropriate question is: Does the public sector have a role in promoting cyber security, and if yes, then: What is the nature of that role? These questions are the topic of Chapter 7. Chapters 8, 9, 10 and 11 are case studies that validate the argument for the public sector having a role in promoting cyber security and in assisting organizations in attaining adequate cyber security. Chapter 12 reiterates this theme, and others, through specific policy recommendations.

And finally, a review of the available data reveals inconsistencies across studies and across time. It would be very useful to analyze how individual company actions (inputs) – such as level/type of outsourcing, use of firewall or change in spending – affects the number of breaches they experience. However, today poorly defined metrics, small sample sizes and self-reporting bias all make the underlying information supporting policy analysis in the area of cyber security suspect. This highlights the need for the establishment of a national database related to cyber security issues.

NOTES

1. There are other data sources on cyber security trends besides those discussed in this chapter. The National Institute of Standards and Technology's (NIST) Computer Security Resource Center maintains the ICAT Vulnerability Database at http://icat.nist.gov. This is a public, searchable index of vulnerabilities sorted using the common vulnerabilities and exposures list (CVE) at http://cve.mitre.org.

    The SANS Institute and the Center for Internet Security are membership-based organizations that charge fees for selected research, tools and training services, but which also make available to the public general guides, white papers and statistical counts and descriptions of recent attacks and current vulnerabilities.

    The PREDICT Project, funded by the Department of Homeland Security (DHS) and hosted by RTI was established, according to its website (www.predict.org) with three goals in mind: 'provide a central repository, accessible through a Web-based portal that catalogs current computer network and operational data; provide secure access to multiple sources of data collected as a result of use of and traffic on the Internet; and facilitate data flow among PREDICT participants for the purpose of developing new models, technologies and products that support effective threat assessment and increase cyber security capabilities.' Although PREDICT is currently accepting applications for data, at this date they have not released data based on privacy concerns.

    Other organizations that distribute information on patches and general security include Internet Security Systems (ISS), X-Force, Security Focus, BugTrack.com, NT Bugtraq and various industry Information Sharing and Analysis Centers (ISACs).

2. This section draws directly from www.cert.org/archive/pdf/ ecrimesurvey06.pdf.

3. The USA Patriot Act of 2001 (Public Law 107-56) mandates that the Director of the United States Secret Service 'take appropriate action to develop a national network of electronic crime task forces ... throughout the United

States for the purpose of preventing, detecting, and investigating various forms of electronic crimes, including potential terrorist attacks against critical infrastructure and financial payment systems)'.

4. This section draws directly from Deloitte (2006).
5. This discussion draws directly from CSI (2006).
6. We are using the term 'organization' to refer to respondents from the private and public sectors, though the vast majority are from private sector companies.
7. The number of respondents varies by survey question: 615 of the 5000 surveyed responded to the survey questionnaire, but not to each of the questions asked.
8. In fact, the CSI/FBI database is more comprehensive than the database that we analyze in subsequent chapters and from which we proffer public policy initiatives. That said, because we do not have access to individual respondent information from the CSI/FBI database, we conducted our own survey.
9. 'CSI offers the survey results as a public service' (CSI, 2006, p. 26).
10. 'Estimated' in the title of Figure 2.3 refers to the method we used to extrapolate from the survey population to the national population. Our assumption that the survey population represents 90 percent of the relevant national population is somewhat arbitrary, but it is in our opinion a conservative extrapolation factor.
11. Data prior to 2004 could not be assembled from the online CSI/FBI reports.
12. For this calculation, organizations that reported greater than 10 percent of their IT budget being allocated to cyber security are assumed to allocate 12 percent; organizations reporting less than 1 percent are assumed to allocate 0.5 percent; and organizations reporting in all other categories are assumed to allocate at the mid-point of the percentage range (for example, organizations reporting 8 percent to 10 percent are assumed to allocate 9 percent).
13. 'Estimated' in the title of Figure 2.5 refers to the method we used to weight responses to calculate a national average.
14. US Census Bureau (2006) reported total information and communication technology capitalized expenditures in 2004 at $139 335 million. Inflating that amount at a 5 percent annual rate yields a 2006 estimate of $153 617 million.
15. Data for earlier years were not available.
16. There are conflicting data on the trends in the growth of security outsourcing. Market research has shown that the outsourced security market continues to grow each year; however, survey research, such as the CSI/FBI surveys, has not shown an increase in outsourcing of security. If the security market is growing, it would imply that more companies are outsourcing, although maybe not those being surveyed. Furthermore, outsourcing habits have changed, as

firms seem to be becoming more selective about what processes and activities provide the most net benefits.

In a recent working paper, Rowe (2007) suggests that there may be social benefits (in addition to any private benefits) of one organization's decision to outsource security. Private firms do not consider spillover effects when they consider whether to outsource their security or how much to spend on security; however, many firms are deciding to outsource security operations because they are able to see private net benefits in the form of cost savings or security improvement per dollar of investment. But, even if a firm does decide to outsource, it may not invest at the socially optimal level since the resulting external benefits (externalities) will be shared with other firms and individuals.

Government may have a role to play to ensure that organizations consider the social benefits of outsourcing security when making their decision. This might include some form of subsidization of outsourcing – organizations could get a tax benefit for certain types of IT security outsourcing, if they spend the same amount of money on security. However, additional research on the effects of outsourcing – spending (costs) and security (benefits) – on firms that decide to outsource and other firms and individuals is needed.

17. The CSI/FBI reports do not report the number of companies responding to their survey for the years 1999–2001, thus no extrapolation is possible.

18. In contrast, Computer Economics Inc. (CEI) reports much higher estimates of the financial costs of past major virus attacks. According to the Congressional Research Service (CRS), CEI's cost estimates include the costs of recovery, clean-up after attacks, lost productivity, lost revenue from downtime, and the costs of public disclosure (financial market impacts, reputational effects, litigation and liability concerns, fear of job loss, and so on) (Cashell et al., 2004). CEI's worldwide economic impact estimates were $3.3 billion in 1997, rising to $13.5 billion in 2003. The associated reports, as well as CEI's consulting services, are available for purchase.

The British firm Mi2g reports much lower impact estimates. Mi2g publishes numerous economic impact estimates for viruses and worms as well as the number of incidents reported monthly and annually by organizations around the world. In 2005, Mi2g estimated the total economic damages from all attacks around the world to be just over $500 million (Mi2g, 2005a). CRS criticizes the 'black box' in which Mi2g calculates their impact estimates (Cashell et al., 2004).

3. Vulnerabilities and Cyber Security Technologies

INTRODUCTION

Organizations' investments in information technology (IT) security stem from the ongoing conflict between attackers and security administrators. They reflect the wide variety of motivations and goals of all players, as well as the security tools and procedures available. Hackers are only one type of unauthorized user. Criminals, disgruntled employees terrorists and hostile nation-states are other types of attackers. The distinction is important in terms of motivation, and resources available to finance the attack.

In this chapter we build upon the information in Chapter 2 by describing the goals and motivations of attackers and the tools and activities they use to achieve their goals. We also summarize general tools, processes and activities that IT security administrators and users employ to prevent breaches; and we discuss technical performance issues of cyber security technologies and emerging threats.

VULNERABILITIES

The Internet and computing infrastructure used by private and public organizations and individuals can be viewed as consisting of three categories of resources: (1) computing resources, such as central process units (CPUs) and memory, used to run applications; (2) storage resources, such as disk drives and storage area networks (SANs), used to store data; and (3) network resources, including routers, wireless access points and hubs, which connect multiple storage and computing resources together. Because physical security breaches are typically well defended under lock and key, network components must be compromised for an attacker to access any computing or data storage resources. Thus, network components are the most common target because they provide access and allow the attacker to threaten applications, operating systems or storage or computing resources once inside. The following discussion provides insight into the potential goals of attackers and the tools and methods they use to attack specific resources.

Goals of Attackers

In general, attacks on the cyber security infrastructure can be identified as pursuing one or more of the following broad goals, all of which can inflict economic damage on the target. Goals are defined differently from, but interrelated with motives. Goals are technical objectives. Motives are human objectives and include financial gains, inflicting malicious harm or furthering national or ideological interests.

Goal 1: Damaging or diminishing the effectiveness of vital cyber security infrastructure components

These attacks generally cause one or more vital pieces of a network's infrastructure either to become inoperable or to operate at a diminished capacity. Examples include denial of service (DoS) and distributed DoS (DDoS) attacks, or attacks that may cause a vital router or server to reboot or go offline. These attacks could be directed at a specific organization or individual, or intended to disrupt service for a large number of hosts (that is end-users) or networks.

The attacker could disrupt service for a large number of hosts or networks through worms or viruses that can infect a host and propagate to other connected hosts. Important data on the infected hosts could be destroyed in the process as a by-product or direct consequence of the virus activity.

Another widespread application of this goal is spam, or unsolicited commercial e-mail (UCE). A large number of spam messages originating from or sent to a single e-mail server can crash it or, at the very least, degrade its performance, which causes delays in the delivery of important e-mail messages.

Goal 2: Gaining unauthorized access to the target's sensitive information

Most businesses are vitally dependent on their proprietary information, including new product information, personnel data and/or client records. An attacker may derive direct economic benefits from gaining access to and/or selling such information, or may inflict damage on an organization by impacting upon its reputation. Attacks may be preceded by worms and viruses that create back doors in the target's infrastructure (for example, Blaster worm) for an attacker to enter and collect information. Other ways of gaining confidential information include: sniffing vital information from the network traffic originating from or intended for the target; guessing or cracking passwords on the systems of interest to gain access to the system; or causing a privilege escalation, in which an insider working in the organization uses security holes to increase their access level.

A special example of such attacks is phishing, in which the attacker attempts to extract private confidential information from targets by crafting forged e-mails or websites that pretend to originate from or belong to an entity the target may trust (for example, a bank, a health provider). Such e-mails generally attempt to solicit credit card numbers, social security numbers, bank account numbers or other private information from their targets for further resale or misuse.

Furthermore, once access has been attained, attackers can not only extract and use or sell private information, but they can also modify or delete sensitive information, resulting in significant consequences for their target(s).

Goal 3: Gaining unauthorized access to cyber resources for illegal use

Anyone – from an individual owning a computer attached to the Internet via a broadband connection to an employee of a large enterprise with multiple sites networked together – may possess resources that an attacker could take utilize. The most likely types of resources to become the targets of an attack are storage and network resources. For example, disk space resources are used to store illegal images of DVDs, MP3s and videogames. Attackers also very frequently use specific compromised hosts to originate spam and DoS attacks directed at other sites.

Furthermore, hackers may break into systems to get free services, such as free access to the Internet using a corporate or personal wireless access point. Another example is attacks on the billing infrastructure of cellular providers with the purpose of receiving free or reduced-fee access to the cellular networks. Cellular providers tend to be more vulnerable to these attacks compared to fixed-infrastructure carriers because of the rapid evolution of cellular technology. The convergence of digital and voice services on a single network allows attackers to introduce attack packets into the network more easily. In addition, the fact that newer cellular networks usually have a direct connection to the Internet makes them more vulnerable to attacks from the Internet.

As mentioned above, hackers typically attempt to take advantage of their victims' storage and network resources. In comparison, attacks in which the attacker gains access to computing power have been theorized in the literature; however, they remain relatively rare.

Combining Goals

An attacker pursuing one of the goals described above may in fact go through several steps, which include one or more of the other goals, before the final goal is achieved. An example of such behavior may be an attacker who first scans a portion of a network to find any vulnerable hosts, then uses an exploit to gain access to a number of personal computers with broadband connections (Goal 3) to perform a DoS attack on part of a target's infrastructure (Goal 1), such that the attack disables the protective infrastructure of the target and the attacker may gain access to the target's confidential information (Goal 2).

Such scenarios are not uncommon. The Blaster worm that targeted hosts running MS SQL server applications took control of the vulnerable hosts (Sophos, 2005). Its goal was a DoS attack on the Microsoft website that was scheduled to start on a specific day, when all of the infected hosts would begin generating bogus traffic intended to disrupt Microsoft's infrastructure. Disrupted service appears to have been the final goal of this particular attack; however, as stated above, more sophisticated multistage attacks are possible.

Recent information indicates that spammers and virus writers are finding benefits in cooperation: up to 86 percent of spam contains viruses that may take control of an infected host and use it as a relay to distribute more spam (*InformationWeek*, 2004). This new and troubling development elevates spam from the level of a nuisance to a serious cyber security threat.

Information Gathering by Attackers

Most cyber attacks are preceded by a phase during which attackers gather as much information about the target (for example, an organization, individual or network component) as possible. When a specific organization or individual is targeted, the methods involved in gathering information include: network scans to determine the topology of the target network; information about the target from open sources (for example, the Internet, print or other types of media); and social engineering, which involves holding conversations with employees, usually under an assumed identity (for example, a subcontractor or an employee from a remote company site). A common type of attack today that pursues this goal is wardriving, where vulnerable wireless access points are identified and mapped using wireless laptops equipped with a global positioning system (GPS).[1]

Furthermore, information gathering can be directed at specific network components, hardware or software. For example, an attacker may work to find a bug or hole in an operating system or application that is widely used so that an attack can easily be made on many individuals and/or organizations at the same time. In all cases, the information-gathering phase helps identify weaknesses in the target infrastructure that can later become a target of direct attacks.

Types and Methods of Attacks

As indicated in the previous section, cyber security attacks can be broadly classified as pursuing one of three goals. The means by which these goals may be pursued differ depending on the scale of the attack, the type of resource involved and the final goal (in the case of a multi-stage attack).

Table 3.1 is one tabulated breakdown of the major types and methods of attacks observed in today's Internet along with the possible intended goals of the attack.

Table 3.1 Types of cyber security attacks and associated goals

Attack type	Description	Goal(s)[*]	Method(s)	Notes
Network probing/ scanning	Primary goal is to glean as much information as possible about the target infrastructure, network topology, operating systems and applications in use that could allow identification of weaknesses for further exploitation	[**]	Network-mapping tools like nmap can be used to determine how many hosts are attached to a network within a specific address range, what operating system (OS) version and patchlevel they are running and what network applications are available.	Usually causes no direct damage

Table 3.1 (cont'd)

Attack type	Description	Goal(s)	Method(s)	Notes
Distributed DoS	Large number of hosts with broadband connections begin generating bogus traffic targeted at a single site in a coordinated manner, disrupting the service provided by the site	1	Packet or connection generator capable of producing large amounts of legitimate-looking Internet traffic	The attacking hosts must be compro-mised prior to the attack through other means, like worms or trojans
Other DoS	Any other direct attack on the infrastructure that causes degradation or failure in performance	1	Sending malformed packets that cause a router to reboot. Misconfiguring pieces of infrastructure like routers and firewalls to which the attacker may have gained access through other means	
Spam	Although usually not intended to directly harm the recipients, can nonetheless cause damage to the vital infrastructure by overloading e-mail relays and security tools associated with them	1	Software capable of sending out e-mail at the same time to a very large number of recipients. Recipient lists are gleaned from Web sites, newsgroups, Internet Relay Chart (IRC) channels; probed from poorly configured mail servers and resold to spammers	

Table 3.1 (cont'd)

Attack type	Description	Goal(s)	Method(s)	Notes
Traffic analysis/ sniffing	Packet sniffing is performed using special software capable of intercepting copies of packets. It may pursue probing to find out more about the target as well as attempting to sniff (e.g., cleartext login passwords or other types of sensitive information for further misuse)	2	A packet sniffer installed on a compromised host on a network to which the target directly attacks, or the network that the target's traffic traverses. The job of a hacker becomes significantly easier if wireless infrastructure is being attacked, because it makes it simpler for the hacker to listen in on the traffic	
Appli- cation/host compro- mise	Host or application compromise can be achieved in a number of ways: exploiting bugs in applications running on the host remotely or locally and gaining unauthorized access by using information gained from probing or through a back door installed by a worm or a virus	2, 3	Worms, viruses and trojans can be used to compromise a host or an application running on a host. Also, illegal privilege escalation (e.g., to administrative privileges) can be achieved locally if the attacker has a non-privileged login to a host running a vulnerable application	

Table 3.1 (cont'd)

Attack type	Description	Goal(s)	Method(s)	Notes
Account/ identity/ informa- tion theft	The pursued goals could be gaining access to more private information and gaining access to resources for further misuse	2, 3	Methods vary from phishing and social engineering to recovering sensitive information from stolen or discarded equipment. Cross-site scripting is another example in which malicious is code injected into Internet bulletin boards or websites that may steal identities of people logging in later	This type of attack overlaps with traffic sniffing, because information gleaned from the passing traffic can be used to forge identities
Zero-day attacks	Attacks of unknown nature and goals	1, 2, 3	An example is when first victims of a new virus are identified. The nature of a virus, its mode of propagation and the extent of the damage it causes may be unknown until it is analyzed by security tool vendors or the Computer Emergency Readiness Team (CERT)	Some network security tools are capable of detecting that something out of the ordinary is happening without being able to pinpoint exactly what is happening. This requires a high degree of human involvement

Notes: * Goals 1, 2 and 3 are defined earlier in this chapter; ** This is a precursor to most types of cyber attacks and associated goals.

COMMON CYBER SECURITY TOOLS AND PROCEDURES

Currently available security tools vary widely in the type and number of attacks they address, and in their effectiveness, cost and complexity. Some are created for a specific, very narrow purpose, such as virus scanners, network traffic or file encryptors. Others are more general purpose, capable of monitoring the health of an entire corporate network with multiple agents distributed throughout, or are tasked with preventing attacks of multiple kinds (for example, intrusion detection and prevention systems). In many instances, several activities can be combined to become more effective at restricting or minimizing the number of successful attacks.

Table 3.2 provides an overview of the common types of security tools and activities currently employed by organizations. The categories of tools and activities include firewalls, content filters, intrusion detection and prevention systems, access control, strong user authentication, cryptography, hardening, auditing, end-user and administrator training and insurance. The coverage in Table 3.2 is broader and more detailed than the excerpted data summarized in Figure 2.11. But it should be viewed as complementary information. Table 3.2 describes each tool type, gives examples of the type of tool and describes the type(s) of attack(s) the tool is capable of addressing by either detecting or preventing it. Finally, some disadvantages and performance metrics for each tool type are indicated. A more detailed description of these security tools and activities is provided later in this chapter.

Some of the same tools can be used by both an attacker and a security administrator for conflicting purposes. For example, a careful administrator uses a penetration testing tool to check for any loopholes into the network. An attacker uses the same tool to identify the same loopholes before attacking the network.

Note that the tools and security methodologies listed in Table 3.2 are not all independent of each other; they represent a common set of tools, without any attempt to create a seamless organization. Most of the tools work as a combination of hardware, firmware and software components. Generally, higher-performing enterprise-level tools tend to have a higher proportion of hardware components as compared to small business or personal tools, which are mainly designed to run on the individual personal computers inside the network.

Table 3.2 Common security tools and methodologies

Type of tool/ security method- ology	Types of attacks addressed	Disadvantages	Performance metrics
Firewalls	Capable of addressing a wide range of attacks by stopping the malicious traffic from penetrating the protected network. May address DoS, probing/scanning, host compromise, zero-day attacks	Create obstacles to network traffic. May make it difficult or impossible to run certain types of applications (e.g., video-conferencing or other peer-to-peer applications). May limit network performance by becoming the bottleneck	Measures of network throughput. Many vendors advertise 1Gbps interfaces on their firewalls, but they are not capable of sustaining traffic at those speeds
Content filters	Viruses, worms, trojans, spam. Some types of network-based intrusions that include sending malicious code or data directly into vulnerable applications can also be filtered out if integrated into the firewall solution	May impose performance limitations on the servers running the content filters (e.g., mail servers equipped with spam and virus scanners). Can be labor-intensive to customize and maintain	False-positive rate, frequency and availability of updates

Although performance metrics for each tool are available, in general assessing the effectiveness of any specific system containing multiple components is difficult because the proof of its effectiveness lies partly in the absence of security incidents. Some comparative analysis could be performed based on the number of incidents discovered and prevented before and after the introduction of a new system or component.[2] Better

Table 3.2 (cont'd)

Type of tool/ security method- ology	Types of attacks addressed	Disadvantages	Performance metrics
Intrusion detection/ prevention systems (IDS/IPS)	Cover the broad range of known and unknown attacks. Capable of responding in real time to specific threats by, for example, partitioning affected networks, real-time filtering of traffic, raising alarms and identifying affected hosts and networks. Response is governed by enterprise-wide sets of policies	Similar disadvantages as firewalls. Require a knowledgeable staff to maintain. Costly at the enterprise level	False-positive rate, measures of network throughput

inferences could be made if information about numbers and types of security incidents were available within a particular business sector so that organizations can compare their results to other organizations engaged in a similar line of business. However, this presumes better reporting of incidents by everyone involved than is commonly observed. Improvements in security tool interoperability could also in part help solve this problem by providing a common base for reporting security incidents.

The following sections link the common categories of tools and activities to the appropriate enterprise, small business and personal network environments.

Table 3.2 (cont'd)

Type of tool/ security method- ology	Types of attacks addressed	Disadvantages	Performance metrics
Access control	Makes unauthorized privilege escalation more difficult. Allows creation of more flexible access control schemes that provide for a minimally necessary level of access to users at a fine-grained resolution (e.g., per-application, database). Chapter 11 discusses in detail one approach known as role based access control (RBAC)	Must be carefully administered. May require a centralized policy repository and a knowledgeable staff	Ease of administration
Strong user authenti-cation	Makes identity theft more difficult either by making it more difficult to steal the necessary credentials (passwords) or by making the credentials harder to forge (biometric solutions, magnetic swipe cards, public key infrastructure – PKI certificates)	Additional expenses required to enable and administer. Requires a knowledgeable staff	Cryptographic strength in PKI certificates, cost, ease of administration (in biometrics and card-based access) and maintenance

Table 3.2 (cont'd)

Type of tool/ security method- ology	Types of attacks addressed	Disadvantages	Performance metrics
Crypto- graphy	Provides mathematical methods for protecting the confidentiality of communication channels and establishing and assuring identities of communicating parties. Thus, makes it difficult to forge identities and eavesdrop on communications channels	Cryptographic techniques usually carry performance and/or economic costs. Performance and economic costs have a trade-off in that higher performing (hardware based) cryptographic solutions carry a higher cost of introduction	Cryptographic strength, cost, ease of administration and maintenance

Security Tools and Methods

This section provides a more detailed description of the major categories of security tools and methods. These tools and methods provide security through a combination of hardware and software products. This is then followed by a discussion of administrators' user security practices and activities.

Firewalls

A firewall is a combination of hardware and software mechanisms that allow for the isolation of a segment of a network from the rest of the Internet. Typical firewall functions include traffic filtering[3] and network address translation (NAT). Firewalls can be stateless (for example, traffic filtering) or stateful;[4] stateful firewalls create more flexible and less restrictive access policies. The sets of rules and policies governing the

Table 3.2 (cont'd)

Type of tool/ security method-ology	Types of attacks addressed	Disadvantages	Performance metrics
Hardening	Addresses all types of attacks by making the cyber infrastructure inherently more difficult to attack by reducing the number of vulnerabilities	Requires knowledgeable staff and investment of time. Conflicts between OS patches and applications are not uncommon (e.g., a specific application may run only with specific sets of patches and adding a new patch may break an application). Hardware hardening carries a higher economic cost because it may require replicating resources or keeping critical infrastructure lightly loaded to allow for bursty load spikes	Availability of patches, measure of application problems related to frequent patching, percentage of critical patch coverage, monitoring how well the system has weathered spikes in load (natural or attack related)

firewall behavior can be static or dynamic, capable of responding to threats in real time. Regardless of the scope of deployment (enterprise, small business or personal network), firewalls perform similar functions. Differences lie in performance, ability to respond to detected attacks and the proportion of hardware elements. Enterprise firewalls typically are dedicated pieces of hardware capable of isolating a network consisting of thousands of computers. Firewall performance is scaled down for small business environments in which weaker, less complex firewalls are more

Table 3.2 (cont'd)

Type of tool/ security methodology	Types of attacks addressed	Disadvantages	Performance metrics
Auditing	Addresses all types of attacks by uncovering known vulnerabilities and detecting intrusions based on anomalies in audited logs. Auditing may also look for anomalous accesses to data or resources from both inside and outside the organization based on log and access control information, thus addressing hacker attacks as well as insider attacks	Time-consuming if done manually (it can be automated), requires knowledgeable staff	Time invested vs. number and seriousness of uncovered problems
End-user and administrator training	All types of attacks	May be costly and time-consuming. Data on vulnerabilities and ways of dealing with them are constantly updated, requiring continuous education, which requires training to be a continuous ongoing process	Time invested vs. number of security incidents, speed with which the incidents are handled

commonly used. In personal network environments, a firewall can be an embedded hardware device or a piece of software installed directly on a home computer. Furthermore, some firewalls are dedicated to filtering a specific type of traffic, such as isolating cellular general packet radio service (GPRS) networks[5] from the Internet.

Content filtering

Content filtering comprises a number of approaches and mechanisms. The commonality lies in their ability to scan network traffic in real time and either alert the recipients to the possible malicious nature of the traffic or block the traffic from getting to its destination completely. This function is similar to traffic filtering, commonly performed by firewalls, but in content filtering the content of the traffic is inspected.

In the enterprise environment, examples of content filtering include mail gateways equipped with virus and spam filters that either place questionable e-mail messages in quarantine or mark them as containing questionable content. In small business and personal network environments, similar tools can be deployed as part of the e-mail client solution.

Firewalls may also be capable of content filtering. This is an advanced firewall function typically available in enterprise-level systems. These devices are capable of scanning network packets passing through them for signatures of known intrusion methods, such as viruses or worms.

Intrusion detection and prevention systems (IDS/IPSs)

An intrusion detection and prevention system is a combination of hardware and software mechanisms capable of alerting system administrators to an intrusion (in real time or after the fact) and, in some cases, capable of responding by preventing the spread of intrusion.

In the enterprise environment, IDS/IPSs are complex systems, consisting of multiple components and management stations. IDS/IPSs are capable of monitoring the state of the hosts connected to the network and real-time monitoring and filtering of network traffic. They usually absorb the functionalities of firewalls, content filters and virtual private networks (VPNs) into a single solution.[6]

In small business environments and personal networks, an IDS may be as simple as a file system integrity checker, capable of detecting alterations of vital executables (for example, system-level files that are part of essential applications or the operating system) made by an intruder and alerting the system administrators to that fact. Another type of host-based IDS may monitor the traffic entering and leaving the host and alerting the user to anomalous behaviors (for example, ZoneAlarm[7]).

Strong user authentication[8]

Strong user authentication implies establishing the identity of a user through multiple methods that are difficult to circumvent. This may mean that a user identity is established through a password,[9] using his or her biological attributes (for example, palm or fingerprints or retinal images), or a system in which a user possesses a secret that is impossible to guess or calculate (for example, public key infrastructure, PKI,[10] certificates).

At all levels of deployment, strong user authentication can take the forms of encrypted passwords, smart cards, biometric access devices, PKI, Kerberos[11] and other secure access methods and tools.

Cryptography

Cryptography provides for a set of techniques that allow people to conceal data and establish its integrity (that is, lack of unauthorized modification) and/or authenticity of communications channels through mathematical transformations. The complexity of transformations usually directly relates to cryptographic 'strength'; thus, stronger cryptographic techniques require more complex transformations as opposed to weaker ones. Cryptography can provide the following:

- Data confidentiality, intended to conceal the data from eavesdroppers. Data confidentiality is achieved through a process of encryption – a transformation of what is referred to as 'clear text' data into a form that cannot be understood without reversing the transformation. The transformation is performed using one or more keys. Such a key can be a secret shared between the sender and receiver (symmetric) or use of a combination of public (known to everyone) and private (known only to the owner) keys (asymmetric). Examples of symmetric key encryption algorithms are DES (data encryption standard) and AES (advanced encryption standard). An example of asymmetric encryption algorithm is RSA.
- Data integrity, intended to prevent unauthorized modification. Data integrity assurance is achieved by computing a short (compared to the data) message digest of the data and transmitting the digest along with the data. The recipient can then recompute the digest and compare it to the received one to verify that the data have not been verified in transit. Depending on the desired level of security this function can be

achieved by applying a one-way hash function to the data, which does not require possession of any keys to be computed and thus does not provide good security, since an attacker can alter an intercepted message and then replace the digest in the message with the new recomputed value. Another way to guarantee data integrity is to pass the data through either an HMAC (Hashed Message Authentication Code) or a CBC-MAC (Cipher Block Chaining Message Authentication Code). Both require existence of a pre-agreed secret key between the sender and the receiver. The sender uses his copy of the key to compute the message digest and transmit it along with the message; the receiver uses his copy of the key to verify that the computed digest matches the received one.

- Data authenticity, intended to ensure the identity of the originator of the data. Data authenticity can be guaranteed by computing a signature of the message and transmitting it along with the message, similar to the digest in the data integrity function. The crucial difference is that this time the signature is computed using a secret key known only to the sender (private key), while the receiver uses a different key (public key), usually known to everyone and associated with the identity of the sender, to compute the signature and compare the results.
- Non-repudiation, making it impossible to deny that a party has sent or received specific data. The non-repudiation function is generally related to the authenticity function in that the presence of a message signature that was computed from a private key known only to the owner guarantees that only the owner of that key could have originated the message.

Some or all of these can be applied to communications channels or data in general (for example, files) depending on the requirements and policies of the organization. Many security tools include cryptographic functions as part of their processes. Virtual Private Networks (VPNs) are a common example: they frequently provide all four of the functions described above to create a private network within a public network, so that access to it is tightly controlled and communications are confidential. It is becoming more and more common to see VPNs built on top of suite of protocols standardized by the Internet Engineering Task Force (IETF[12]) as IP Security, or IPSEC, as opposed to earlier solutions that tended to use weaker semi-proprietary protocols.[13] Cryptographic functions are also commonly built into Web browsers in the form of implementations of the protocols standardized by IETF TLS/SSL – Transport Layer Security (TLS) and its predecessor, Secure Sockets Layer (SSL). They help secure the communications that occur between Web browsers and Web servers in a course of, for example, a session between a bank and its client. Chapter 8 provides more discussion on data encryption standards.

Security Practices and Activities

The tools described above require a certain amount of maintenance and updating, and all staff (including both IT staff and users) have important roles in implementing a secure network. This section briefly describes several specific activities that help improve the relative security level of an organization.

Hardening

Hardening means taking reasonable measures to ensure the security of the cyber infrastructure. This activity usually includes keeping the applications and operating system up to date with available updates offered by vendors and restricting access to vital infrastructure elements both through the network through cryptographic means and by fine-tuning access controls, as well as by protecting physical access to critical pieces of infrastructure.

An example of hardening that is common at all deployment levels is patching, or promptly applying security updates issued by the operating system or application manufacturers. This process results in the reduction and mitigation of vulnerabilities in the infrastructure, thus making the infrastructure as a whole more secure and reliable. Patching may be manual or performed using automated tools.

At the enterprise and small business levels, hardening may also mean physically restricting access to critical pieces of equipment, such as routers and servers.

Hardening firmware may mean keeping up with the latest firmware updates from equipment manufacturers. Hardware hardening may take the shape of using well-established vendors for critical pieces of equipment, maintaining hardware homogeneity for the purposes of quick replacement and replicating important functions in multiple instances of hardware to cope with spikes in load either occurring naturally or caused by malicious activity.

Access control

Access control refers to a methodology that allows system administrators to assign access rights to users (that is, login, read, write, modify, view, execute and so on) in a flexible fashion. It allows the designation of a minimal set of rights needed by users to perform their functions. Such assignments create environments that are intrinsically more secure as compared to those in which users find themselves in possession of rights that are not necessary for their day-to-day activities, and thus open possibilities for abuse. Implementations of flexible access control are operating system (OS) and application specific. Examples include access control lists (ACLs),[14] controlling access to files or databases, boot passwords and application-level passwords. Chapter 11 provides a more in-depth discussion of access control and describes the potential impact of role based access control (RBAC), a set of access control procedures developed by NIST.

Auditing

Auditing implies automated or manual scanning of logs and verification of system compliance to company security policies by, for instance, checking access lists against the policy and checking system configuration settings.

An organization should possess a security policy to which all of the elements of its cyber infrastructure must adhere. The process of verification of this adherence may be manual or automated depending on the scale of the organization and the comprehensiveness of the security policy. This verification may include penetration testing, in which internal staff or contractors try to break into or find holes in the infrastructure to identify and expose weaknesses in the policy or its implementation.

Auditing also refers to periodic checking of available logs of users' activities and incoming and outgoing network traffic to search for anomalies that may indicate intrusions. Large enterprises may employ keystroke monitoring tools and packet sniffers to monitor their employees' activities.

End-user training and policies

End-user training may include certification training for the IT staff to ensure their proficiency with available security tools and proper understanding of incident reporting procedures or user training in common security precautions. Training may also include educating chief information officers (CIOs), chief executive officers (CEOs) and board members on security best practices, advantages of incident reporting and benefits of membership in information-sharing organizations such as Information Sharing and Analysis Center (ISACs)[15] for the purpose of improving the security environment in their organization.

Furthermore, users and IT staff should be directed by specific guidelines dictating their IT activities. For example, users should have specific policies to follow when accessing their network remotely, taking data 'off campus', making changes to their computer's applications or operating system, or engaging in other activities identified as potential security threats. Chapter 11 provides more discussion on the threat of insider attacks.

TECHNICAL PERFORMANCE ISSUES

Each type of security tool comes with its own performance limitations. However, performance metrics vary greatly across tools and methods, making comparisons difficult. The performance of firewalls is typically measured by the amount of traffic that an IDS or a VPN is capable of handling. For content filters, such as virus scanners, performance is measured in terms of time elapsed between the discovery of a new worm, virus or trojan and the availability of the mail server and the additional load they place on the mail server – this may be measured in terms of the number of e-mail messages processed on a hypothetical but common server configuration. Manufacturers generally advertise performance characteristics of their products and, if the results are favorable, those of a few close competitors. Publications like *InfoWorld* and *CNET* sometimes also perform independent comparisons of similar security products and make the results available to the public.

As the threats faced by corporate IT departments grow in their complexity and scale, so do the tools they employ to address those threats. Integrated systems combining individual components such as packet sniffers, firewalls and virus scanners are beginning to appear. These systems consolidate multiple functions into a single solution controlled by a single robust security policy. Some vendors are capable of offering an entire integrated solution in a single product. Frequently, however, a single enterprise-wide system can be put together out of components produced by different security tool vendors. One of the problems that these vendors have been dealing with recently is the ability of their tools to interoperate with tools of other vendors – that is, the ability of tools to describe detected vulnerabilities and attacks to each other and to report them in a consistent manner to operators or monitoring systems. For example, simple IDS systems capable of detecting network-based attacks on infrastructure components may need to report detected attacks to a centralized monitoring system so that proper automated or manual actions may be taken to address the new threat.

Having a common vocabulary and format for reporting these events is becoming increasingly important. Efforts have been made in the industry to create such standards, of which the three most common are: CVE (Common Vulnerabilities and Exposures) (CVE, 2005); IDMEF (Intrusion Detection Message Exchange Format) (IETF, 2005); and SDEE (Security Device Event Exchange) (ICSA Labs, 2005). CVE is essentially a dictionary of known vulnerabilities, in which each vulnerability has a unique name like CVE-1999-0006 and a short description. IDMEF and SDEE, on the other hand, are message protocols that describe how tools should communicate. IDMEF and SDEE messages have a way of including CVE names in them as one of the options, but they also allow tools to use proprietary naming schemes.

The development of CVE resulted in the creation of a common dictionary for describing security vulnerabilities in cyber infrastructure elements. CVE, partially funded by the Department of Homeland Security, was developed by a wide range of experts including security tool vendors, response team service providers, academic institutions and non-profit organizations. The CVE project hosted by the MITRE Corporation includes a continuously updated list of over 3000 entries currently describing commonly known vulnerabilities, each with a unique name. Each entry contains a brief description of the vulnerability and references to other sources of information (for example, Bugtraq or CERT databases) where more detailed descriptions can be found. The CVE list is freely available and allows security tools to use a common naming scheme when reporting detected vulnerabilities in the infrastructure. CVE-compliant tools are capable of either generating CVE names when vulnerabilities are detected or allowing users to search for specific CVE entries based on the CVE names. In short, CVE offers a common naming scheme that security tools and human operators can use to exchange information about vulnerabilities with each other.

An example of a system properly using CVE would be a network scanner capable of detecting known vulnerabilities in systems attached to the network and reporting those vulnerabilities using CVE names to a network monitoring system. This monitoring system may then display this information for the benefit of the network operator or take automated measures.

IDMEF (Intrusion Detection Message Exchange Format) is a protocol for communications between security tools. It was developed by IETF to standardize the automated reporting of vulnerabilities and attack alarms, so that disparate security tools may be able to communicate with each other in a common format. By its definition, IDMEF subsumes the functionality offered by CVE, which is just a dictionary of vulnerabilities. IDMEF messages can include CVE references, but it goes further by allowing references to other sources of information like Bugtraq and OSVDB (Open Source Vulnerability Database) for describing a detected vulnerability. It also allows security tools to describe attacks that may not have names in vulnerability databases and defines the language that describes the actions taken by the IDS/IPS in response to an attack.

Finally, a strictly vendor-based effort to define a protocol similar to IDMEF is called SDEE (Security Device Event Exchange) and is being defined by ICSA Labs. Cisco Systems appears to be one of its few large backers. SDEE is similar to IDMEF in many technical respects. The MITRE CVE Web site lists a large number of security tools that are partially or fully CVE compatible. Security tools compliant with IDMEF and SDEE are beginning to appear on the market as well.

In general, standardization and interoperability efforts such as the ones just described serve several purposes. First, they improve communications between different components of an organization's security system, which in this case does not have to purchase its entire security solution from a single vendor. Second, they encourage sharing of incident information with outside organizations like ISACs. Although it has yet to be mandated or become common practice among firms, the sharing of information on breaches and vulnerabilities would serve to improve the overall security environment by allowing organizations to benefit from shared information and experience and thus to detect and respond to new attacks more quickly.

CONCLUSIONS

Emergence of new consumer and business applications has led to a number of novel threats whose potential effects are not yet adequately understood. These innovations usually bring lower total cost of ownership (TCO) or increased ease of use, that is, improving an existing function such as telephony. However, decisions about their adoption are typically made without a detailed economic analysis of their security impact. The following are emerging technologies that bring along with them significant cyber security implications:

- Wireless technologies. Wi-Fi (802.11a/b/g), emerging WiMax (802.16), Bluetooth and cell phones are all examples of wireless technologies that allow for easier access to networked resources from home, the road and remote offices. All of them, however, have serious security implications, because by moving away from a fixed, physically secure infrastructure of land-based local area networks (LANs) and phone networks they allow hackers easier access to the same infrastructure. The threat introduced by wireless technologies must be assessed very seriously, and the convenience of wireless access must be weighed against the increased susceptibility to attacks on the infrastructure. The relative cryptographic weakness of the currently employed wireless security solutions (WEP, WPA-PSK and WPA-Enterprise) and lack of education among the public regarding the risks posed by running an improperly configured wireless network, as well as the increasing pervasiveness of wireless technologies, are a big part of the reason for why this threat will be with us for a while.
- Single-vendor security solution. Using a single-vendor solution for network hardware components, end-user host operating systems, and/or other applications lowers the TCO of security for an organization; however, this also increases the susceptibility of the infrastructure to a catastrophic failure, because all of the components of such infrastructures usually have common exploitable weaknesses. Thus, an attack by a worm, for example, may bring down the entire network instead of a subset of hosts. Decisions about adopting single-vendor approaches to cyber infrastructure must be carefully weighed against the increased susceptibility of this infrastructure to a single attack.

New types of attack methods are also increasingly complex, requiring IT security administrators to constantly develop new solutions to prevent attacks and/or mitigate the impact of breaches. The following are attack trends that are reshaping the effectiveness of past security approaches and associated investment schemes:

- Spam (UCE). Spam, as stated above, is increasingly becoming a significant security threat instead of a simple nuisance. The latest indications of collaborative efforts between virus writers and spammers suggest that spam must be treated with the same level of caution as other more common security threats, such as viruses, worms and trojans.
- Phishing. Phishing is becoming increasingly targeted and sophisticated, and is no longer strictly the domain of scammers. As recent incidents uncovered in Israel (O'Brien, 2005) have revealed, even large

companies are sometimes involved in phishing to steal their competitors' sensitive information.

- Spyware. Spyware (software installed on a computer without explicit knowledge or consent of the user, monitoring his or her actions and or taking partial control of the computer) is also becoming more sophisticated in avoiding detection and presents a problem even if the reasons for its installation were benign (that is, the recent SONY DRM incident). In this case, music CDs from SONY contained spyware software intended to prevent illegal copying; however, bugs in the software actually allowed hackers to abuse it and take control of computers running it. Thus, installing this spyware actually increased the vulnerability of the computer.
- Botnets: Robot networks or 'botnets' are networks of computers (frequently in disparate locations around the world) containing back doors known to a single hacker or group of hackers. These hackers can then use these computers to perform functions such as relaying spam or performing DoS attacks on a specific host or domain without the knowledge of the owners. Because of the relative homogeneity of home computers' operating systems (OS) – for example, use of Microsoft Windows – and the failure of owners to keep their OSs properly updated with new patches, hackers frequently use botnets to comprise large numbers of home computers attached to broadband Internet connections (for example, DSL [digital subscriber line] or cable-modem connections) and connected to the Internet 24 hours a day. These botnets present a serious problem to network administrators under attack because of their distributed nature.

NOTES

1. The following is an example scenario of wardriving: a hacker equipped with a wireless laptop and a GPS unit can walk or drive around listening for available wireless access points and map their locations based on the GPS data and the direction of the signal. This information can be used later to gain access to companies' or individuals' infrastructure, depending on the security mechanisms in place.
2. This approach, while in other security environments would likely be very successful, would be problematic in that cyber threats are so dynamic in nature that lack of incidents for one period of time, would not imply a future lack of or reduction in the number of incidents.

3. Traffic filtering refers to the ability of a network device to inspect incoming packets in real time and reject or accept them based on a set of rules or policies. Typical reasons to reject packets would be packets coming from the Internet and attempting to create a connection with a host inside the protected network to which connections are not allowed.

4. Stateful firewalls, or connection-tracking firewalls, go a step further than stateless firewalls by attempting to associate each packet with an existing connection and making decisions about accepting or rejecting packets based on this information as well. For example, if a Web session has been allowed to be established between a Web browser inside the firewall-protected network with an outside server, a connection-tracking firewall will accept follow-up packets going back and forth between the browser and the server based on the existing connection state.

5. GPRS networks allow cellular phone users to access the Internet and send short message service (SMS) messages from their phones. See Wikipedia for further information at http://en.wikipedia.org/wiki/General_Packet_Radio_Service.

6. According to Answers.com (2005), a VPN is defined as 'a private network that is configured within a public network (a carrier's network or the Internet) to take advantage of the economies of scale and management facilities of large networks. VPNs are widely used by enterprises to create wide area networks (WANs) that span large geographic areas to provide site-to-site connections to branch offices and to allow mobile users to dial up their company [local area networks] LANs.

7. ZoneAlarm is a firewall product. More information can be found at http://www.zonealarm.com/.

8. Strong authentication is also referred to as a two-factor authentication and is defined as containing two of the three following components: something a person knows, has or is. PKI certificates make user electronic credentials harder to forge by introducing strong cryptographic methods in credential verification. Biometrics verifies identity by analyzing unique physiological attributes (retinal pattern, finger- or palm print) that are difficult to replicate. Magnetic (or other type) ID cards require possession of the card to validate the identity.

9. In most enterprises, plain-text passwords (for example, johnSmith9!) are used at the host level; however, after a user enters his or her password at a computer, the operating system encrypts the password before checking with the necessary server for a user's permission.

10. According to Answers.com (2005), PKI is defined as 'a framework for creating a secure method for exchanging information based on public key cryptography.

The foundation of a PKI is the certificate authority (CA), which issues digital certificates that authenticate the identity of organizations and individuals over a public system such as the Internet. The certificates are also used to sign messages (see code signing), which ensures that messages have not been tampered with'.

11. According to Answers.com (2005), Kerberos is defined as 'an access control system that was developed at MIT in the 1980s. Turned over to the IETF for standardization in 2003, it was designed to operate in both small companies and large enterprises with multiple domains and authentication servers. The Kerberos concept uses a "master ticket" obtained at logon, which is used to obtain additional "service tickets" when a particular resource is required'.

12. IETF is a non-profit organization that is responsible for standardizing the vast majority of Internet protocols. See their website at www.ietf.org.

13. Internet Protocol version 6 (IPv6) was designed with security in mind and enables very simple adoption of the IPSEC standard. Chapter 9 provides further discussion of this benefit of IPv6 adoption.

14. ACLs are a matrix-like approach to assigning privileges to users. The rows include users, and the columns include permissions at very fine levels of granularity (for example, read, write, execute, access settings for files or folders). These lists can create management challenges because of the amount of information in such a matrix.

15. ISACs – see http://www.isaccouncil.org/about/ for more details.

4. Cyber Security Investment and Implementation Strategies: Theories

INTRODUCTION

Little is known about how organizations evaluate their cyber security investments, where organizations obtain information relevant to such investments, and how they assess the benefits and costs of such investments. Economic theory suggests that an organization should evaluate cyber security investments using the same fundamental tools as for evaluating any business investment. Private benefits should be weighed against investment costs, and the organization should then engage in increasingly stringent security activities until the marginal cost of an investment equals the marginal benefit from that investment.[1]

Determining this optimal level of cyber security investment requires information related to the efficiency of the investment and its marginal cost, as well as to the security returns from the investment and its marginal benefit. These factors are generally related to organizational and performance characteristics of the organization, such as its existing information technology (IT) characteristics, the compatibility of available cyber security technologies with current technologies, the security needs of the products and services the company provides, the capabilities and experience of its IT staff, and the preferences and perceptions of its customers. In addition, expectations of future threats or compromises, vulnerabilities and technical change influence the timing of investments, the costs incurred and the benefits received.

However, a volume of evidence suggests that most organizations do not view their cyber security investment decisions in the same way that they view other investment decisions. Rarely does an organization undertake a sophisticated or even semi-quantitative financial analysis (that is, cost–benefit or rate-of-return analysis) prior to investing or deciding on the investment level needed. In fact, it is common for organizations simply to react to a breach or compromise and give the appearance of addressing the existing problem.

Such real-world practices lead to inadequate or uninformed evaluations of security threats. Two barriers contribute to the lack of quantitative analysis limiting an organization's ability to determine its optimal cyber security investment strategy. The first barrier is a limited availability of reliable, cost-effective information needed to make informed investment decisions. The second barrier is the externalities and public-goods nature of cyber security knowledge that follows from cyber security investments. The first barrier could lead an organization to underinvest or overinvest in cyber security – both of which imply inefficiencies. The second barrier always leads to underinvestment in cyber security.

Because of a lack of reliable, cost-effective information, most organizations do not have the historical information needed to make informed investment decisions based on the likelihood of future attacks.[2] This lack of information is compounded by the fact that extreme cyber security events have a low probability of occurrence.[3] As a result, it is difficult, time-consuming and costly for an organization to assess the probability of a breach occurring, much less the related impacts. These impacts include, but are not limited to, potential downtime and remediation costs because of a breach and the overall reputational cost to the organization. Additionally, organizations lack the necessary information to assess cyber security technologies that are in-house or available from vendors and the implementation and maintenance costs of these technologies.

Relevant and accurate knowledge of the probability of being attacked and the associated costs of a breach are scarce. Consortia and trade associations established by public and private organizations encourage information sharing; however, the lack of economic incentives to participate and share information (that is, free-rider problems) has limited their success.[4] As a result, private organizations with incomplete information may not be able to calculate private benefits correctly. Or, some sections within an organization may not understand the IT road map sufficiently to realize that reactionary investments which are generally considered to be inefficient as compared to proactive actions in the long run.[5] In general, the lack of reliable information to inform the analysis may be the primary factor limiting the use of traditional economic methods for evaluating the efficiency by which cyber security investments are made.

Underlying these issues are the externalities and public-goods nature of cyber security. Any investments in cyber security made by an organization, particularly of a proactive nature, will generate social (indirect) benefits in excess of private (direct) benefits. And because an organization will not fully appropriate all of the benefits it receives from a cyber security investment (that is, benefits accruing to other organizations) it is likely to underinvest in cyber security. Cyber security investments lead to the creation of cyber security-related information – data or simply experience and understanding – that can have the characteristics of a public good.[6] It is well known that public goods are typically underprovided by private markets as compared to their socially optimal levels of provision (Stigliz, 1988).

This chapter presents an overview of what we refer to as cyber security investment and implementation strategies. The information that underlies our model comes from interviews and discussions with over 100 US organizations that were identified as a representative cross-section with input from the US Department of Homeland Security. This population represents six composite groups: financial services, health care providers, manufacturing, universities, small businesses and a handful of other organizations.

Within the cyber security decision process, we make the distinction between analyses conducted as part of an investment strategy and analyses conducted as part of an implementation strategy. Management and/or IT staff work on the investment strategy largely through two not entirely exclusive approaches: by setting a security budget (for example, a certain percentage of the total IT budget) or by determining the level of security they want to achieve and maintain. IT staff typically are solely responsible for the implementation strategy, in which they determine the most efficient approach to meet the organization's security needs, whether through a more proactive or a more reactive approach. In smaller organizations, the distinction between the investment and implementation strategies is blurred: the same staff are involved and analyses are intermingled. However, in larger organizations, organizational hierarchy often leads to compartmentalizing different phases of the decision-making process that determine the overall level of cyber security.

OVERVIEW OF THE CYBER SECURITY DECISION-MAKING PROCESS

Figure 4.1 presents an overview of an organization's overall cyber security decision-making process as introduced above. It begins with determining an organizational cyber security investment strategy and prioritizing anticipated cyber security needs. These organizational-level decisions in turn guide the implementation strategy where specific security solutions are evaluated and compared.

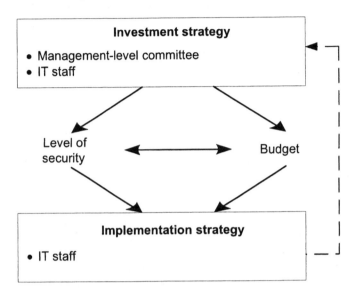

Note: Management and IT staff coordinate to determine an organization's implementation strategy and then IT staff are responsible for the implementation strategy.

Figure 4.1 Cyber security decision-making process

Conceptually in the literature, the optimal cyber security investment strategy is discussed in terms of the highest net present value (NPV) or the best cost–benefit ratio. Using such techniques, the costs of cyber security investment opportunities should be compared to the expected benefits, where benefits are represented as avoided damages expressed in terms of the probability and expected cost of an event occurring. NPV and cost–benefit analysis approaches are discussed below.

However, organizations are quick to point out that the inputs to this type of quantitative analysis are difficult, costly and, in many cases, impossible to obtain. As a result, when management staff are involved in cyber security decisions, they rely very heavily on qualitative assessments of their security needs, which are then compared to quantitative analyses of other (non-IT) needs and investment opportunities. Furthermore, during our informal interviews, organizations indicated that determining their cyber security strategy was driven by a range of internal and external factors, including regulations, client requirements, business requirements and reputational concerns. These drivers are discussed in more detail below.

We have defined organizations' cyber security investment strategies in terms of two dimensions. One approach is to identify security needs and priorities, and is referred to herein as determining a 'targeted level of security'. Essentially, this entails deciding on the optimal level of security for an organization (given other spending priorities, regulations, data sensitivity and privacy risks, and so on) and associated spending based on robust analysis. At this point in the strategic process, it may be difficult to quantify costs and benefits explicitly; thus, a qualitative assessment is made to determine which cyber security objectives and requirements are essential (and likely to be cost-effective) for the organization's operations.

A second investment strategy approach is to determine the level or share of resources an organization should (or has available to) invest in cyber security. In this scenario, cyber security activities and purchases are determined, within a budget constraint, to maximize security. This is a second-best approach in the sense that it may not explicitly identify cyber security needs as the basis for investment and could result in either an underinvestment or an overinvestment in cyber security. However, these needs are implicitly weighed against competing needs and investment opportunities when the budget is determined.[7]

Our interviews revealed that organizations frequently incorporate a combination of targeted level of security and budget constraint requirements when formulating their cyber security investment strategy. In contrast to the investment strategy, the implementation strategy is conducted almost solely by IT staff and involves collecting and evaluating information on specific cyber security solutions obtained from both internal and external sources. Organizations noted that deciding the extent to which their cyber security strategies focused on preventive and proactive solutions versus reactive solutions was the defining component of the implementation strategy.

Organizations with more proactive implementation strategies (for example, more labor and software and hardware focused on preventing new types of breaches) indicated that this approach led to fewer breaches; however, organizations' opinions differed on the relative costs and benefits of more proactive versus more reactive strategies.

CYBER SECURITY INVESTMENT STRATEGIES

Determining the optimal level of cyber security investments or deciding how much to invest in cyber security is a complex decision that is made based on differing levels of information and on various business and regulatory requirements. In general, neither individuals nor organizations use quantitative methodologies to determine the optimal level of cyber security investments. Instead, organizations tend to use a more qualitative approach, identifying and prioritizing security needs based on regulations, customer needs, specific network activities and historical experiences.

A business case including both proactive (preventive) and reactive (recovery) costs could allow more accurate planning and accountability exercises; however, based on informal interviews with organizations and our review of the literature,[8] organizational network differences and the multitude of security products and services make the business case approach generally unsuitable in this situation. The preventive costs are a function of labor and capital spending, which can be easily calculated (once the proper metrics are defined), but the incurred and estimated future recovery costs are much more difficult to capture. Several major problems exist preventing such estimates from being readily available:

- The future probability (prospective) of a cyber security breach is unknown. Differences in network topology and the dynamic nature of types of attacks and available solutions make any probability estimates inherently uncertain.
- The indirect and direct recovery costs (retrospective) of cyber security attacks are not known. No common metrics (and associated methodologies) have been agreed upon to estimate or measure the cost of cyber security attacks; however, an estimate of the costs should be much more certain than for the prospective case (probabilities) above.

Instead of trying to perform a typical cost–benefit analysis, many organizations hire external auditors to determine their optimal level of security based on International Organization for Standardization (ISO) 17799 or National Institute of Standards and Technology (NIST) 800 series guidelines or customized recommendations. Other organizations use internal audit procedures. In some cases, metrics and methodologies used for physical security cost analysis are used for cyber security, but unlike a physical attack, 'a cyber attack generally disables – rather than destroys – the target of attack' (Cashell et al., 2004, p. 30); thus, such an analysis approach is inherently flawed. Other commonly used methodologies include analyzing stock fluctuations, utilizing risk analysis techniques and following competitors' policies and procedures.

Investments in cyber security are typically more difficult to evaluate than other decisions made by organizations because the costs and benefits cannot be easily observed or estimated. The costs of securing a network include:

- hardware and software products, updates and installations;
- effort spent by IT staff to test and implement security technologies, monitor the status of network security (including updating), and respond to any problems; and
- time involved in defining the policies and procedures to be used by IT staff as well as (more significantly and possibly importantly) those to which all staff must adhere.

The hardware and software purchases are the simplest to quantify, but the time spent by IT staff on security as opposed to other IT issues and the time spent by regular staff reading and following security policies cannot be captured easily. Cost can vary significantly by organization because of specifics of business operations and legacy systems.

The benefits are even more difficult to quantify. The desirable benefit is that the network and any data therein remain secure. Austin and Darby (2003, p. 123) note that, particularly in an environment with high pressure to boost earnings, 'when there is uncertainty about the level of uncertainty – that is, when it's unclear whether the loss-making event will happen with 0.01 percent probability or 0.001 percent probability – it becomes even harder to justify spending a lot of money to avoid the loss'. A $1 million loss will only appear as a $100 loss in a financial calculation if it is predicted to have a 0.01 percent probability of occurrence; however, if that event does occur, the losses could be much larger than predicted because loss predictions could be similarly inaccurate. IT managers are commonly asked to use some type of financial assessment techniques to justify their funding on security to company executives, even though they are known to be questionably accurate. In most instances, empirical analysis focuses on labor resources (as opposed to value of data or lost sales). For example, Gordon and Richardson (2004) conducted an interview with an Oracle representative who stated that when they were considering when to replace an intrusion prevention system (IPS), they analyzed how many alerts they were getting, how many people were needed to track down and resolve these alerts, and how many of the alerts were false positives. When compared with their tests of the new system, this helped them decide to replace the system immediately.

Corporate Investment Theory

Corporate finance theory has been researched extensively for the past 50 or 60 years; however, much of today's commonplace corporate investment strategy is based on ideas first proposed in the 1950s. Although cyber security investing introduces particular complexities that were not present 50 years ago, the theoretical framework is helpful to review as numerous other factors have caused finance models trouble in the past.

Prior to the late 1950s, organizations made capital and R&D investment decisions largely based on anecdotal evidence and real experiences, but, in 1958, Modigliani and Miller (1958) proposed using a more mathematical approach. The theories they proposed were based on the assumption that markets operate efficiently, so economic models could be used to determine the viability of all investment decisions. In a working paper chronicling the historical development of corporate investment decision-making, Dempsey (1996) looks critically at the positive and negative aspects of qualitative versus quantitative decision-making practices.

The theory proposed by Modigliani and Miller lays the groundwork for modern neoclassical finance theory; in essence, it suggests that asset valuation models, which calculate an organization's value based on expected future net cash flows (including future investment decisions), should be used to determine how an organization should invest. If a positive net present value (NPV) is generated, the investment should be made. Other researchers (Ross, 1978; Ryan, 1982) modified this basic idea and created the capital asset pricing model (CAPM), in which investments are made based on their comparability to returns available from government bonds or other relatively safe investments. Other organizations began to calculate a project's NPV, based on discounted cash flow analyses (DCF), and to compare this NPV with a certain hurdle rate to determine whether an investment should be made.

However, these types of analyses, which according to Dempsey are still very pervasive in most corporate decision-making processes today, can lead organizations away from investments that cannot be easily quantified and ignore personal experiences and other more qualitative factors that need to be considered (Hayes and Abernathy, 1980). Hodder and Riggs (1985) and Hodder (1986) suggest that these issues do not reflect the deficiency of the NPV method, but rather an inappropriate application of NPV (for example, by using incomplete data); they suggest that NPV provides an invaluable tool to evaluate potential investments (Hodder and Riggs, 1985).

Corporate investment decisions today largely rely on NPV or return on investment (ROI) calculations; however, according to Hayes and Abernathy (1980), many companies in the United States have suffered by putting too much stock in such quantitative models. Many factors, such as increased staff skills, new product developments, increased security and changes in stock valuation cannot be accurately (or closely) captured in models. Therefore, these factors are often left out of investment decisions, causing some to say that organizations are generally too conservative.

As with these factors, cyber security activities (proactive and reactive) and the impact of breaches introduce additional costs that are very difficult to capture in a model. Consequently, organizations have largely relied on qualitative evaluations when comparing cyber security investments with decisions that can be more easily quantified. Unfortunately, many quantitative-minded executives tend to ignore or look unfavorably upon such information that can seem very subjective.

Cyber Security Risk Assessment and Investment Optimization Research

Over the past ten years, academics, vendors, government organizations and various consortia have conducted extensive research to determine the best methodology by which cyber security investments should be made. The Workshop on Economics and Information Security, held annually since 2002, has generated significant debate and publicity surrounding how economic methodology might be able to help refine investment decisions on security,[9] and numerous government bodies have produced metrics by which security can be measured and evaluated.

The NIST published a document in July 2003 intended to assist organizations in measuring three key factors: the implementation of security policies, the effectiveness and efficiency of the security policies and mechanisms in place, and the impact of any security events. The document, entitled 'Security Metrics Guide for Information Technology Systems', provided instructions on how to determine what metrics would be most useful to an organization and the best ways in which to use them. Although it does not identify the specific metrics that should be used (the authors suggest that this should differ depending on organizational priorities and activities), it does provide a set of questionnaires that could be very useful in assessing the current infrastructure – hardware, software, administrative practices, user policies and past occurrences, for example.

Other organizations such as the International Organization for Standardization (ISO), the SANS Institute, and the numerous CERT centers have published similar materials. Although these are useful, they do not help organizations directly quantify their relative state of security and develop an investment plan based on explicitly quantified costs (prevention, attack, and repair costs) and benefits (efficiency of the network and lack of costs).

Larry Gordon and Marty Loeb, economics professors in the School of Business at the University of Maryland, have written extensively on their efforts to analyze investment decisions and the costs associated with cyber security intrusions using economic tools. In their recent book (2006) aimed at cyber security administrators and financial analysts, they provide an overview of a variety of qualitative and quantitative techniques available for assessing the relative value of cyber security investments. However, the more rigorous analyses they present require the estimation of the probability and the impact of specific types of breaches, values that differ significantly among organizations and are very difficult to calculate.

In an article in *Network Computing*, Gordon and Richardson (2004) state that one-third of respondents to a survey the authors administered indicated that they were using NPV as a major factor in determining the level of IT security investment. Although the authors praise organizations using an NPV instead of a simple ROI calculation, they point out that externalities may cause an NPV decision to be flawed because it does not consider the effects that inadequate security may have on other organizations. Varian (2000) further suggests that computer security in practice is so poor because the risk involved is widely shared. Anderson (2001) suggests similar problems, analyzing the complexity of cyber security by using economic concepts such as network externalities, asymmetric information, moral hazard, adverse selection, liability dumping and the tragedy of the commons.

Soo Hoo (2000) and Schechter (2004) introduced novel ideas on how to best determine the appropriate level of security for an organization. In a working paper for the Consortium for Research on Information Security and Policy (CRISP), Soo Hoo (2000) discusses an econometric approach in which uncertainty and flexible modeling tools can be used with available data to determine appropriate security levels. In his doctoral dissertation, Schechter (2004) introduces the idea that a market could be created for vulnerabilities (in which they could be traded), and that the current price for a threat on a product could help consumers determine how secure it is.

Campbell et al. (2003) presented another analysis that looked at the effect of security scares on share prices. The authors find that a significant negative market reaction occurs following IT security breaches involving unauthorized access to confidential data. However, they did not find a significant change in the market if the breach did not involve confidential information.

Gartner, an IT consulting firm, has produced numerous reports on the use and value of quantitative and qualitative analysis of cyber security investment decisions. A November 2005 Gartner report, 'Use a Cost–Benefit Approach to Justify Security Expenditures' (Scholtz et al., 2005, p. 1), recommends that 'security teams should avoid basing information security expenditure requests primarily on non-defendable financial ROI projections, and instead exploit clearly articulated, balanced value propositions'. This is a theme that resonates with what we heard in interviews with many companies: IT security administrators are being pushed to quantitatively support their investments, and subsequently they are developing unrealistic analyses that are not well received by management. Qualitative analyses are more useful in most cases because of the lack of supporting data.

Finally, both Congress and the President have taken notice of the need for improved cyber security investing and the need for a better incentive structure to motivate optimal investing. The Subcommittee on Cyber Security, Science, and Research and Development of the US House of Representatives released a report in December 2004 that noted that the Y2K problem and the electrical blackout in the northeast could be used to help identify the cost of a cyber attack. Furthermore, the committee report suggested that the insurance and auditing industries would be best able to use past experience in developing cost methodologies for cyber security. Unfortunately, this advice has largely been ignored.

Further, the White House spent considerable effort in 2002 working to encourage the insurance industry to offer cyber security insurance as a way to incentivize them to improve their cyber security measures. The idea goes that companies would be required by insurance companies to achieve a certain level of cyber security before they could get insurance, which they would need either to comply with regulations or to ascertain business deals or individual customer relationship (Krebs, 2002).

According to the 2006 CSI/FBI Survey (see Chapter 2), 29 percent of organizations had reported that they acquired external cyber security insurance, up from 25 percent in 2005. Although there is a wealth of information advocating the potential value of cyber insurance (Gordon et al., 2003b), many companies are still not currently interested. The extensive audits required by security companies and the relatively expensive prices have been deterrents (D'Aqostino, 2003). Further, Ogut et al. (2005) pointed out that the interdependency of cyber risk results in an inefficient insurance market and that the imposition of legal penalties and increased information sharing were both needed in addition to any insurance to help achieve optimal investments.

Throughout the research conducted to date, many analysis techniques have been proposed, but no commonly held methodologies have been identified. However, all experts seem to agree that more information sharing could significantly improve security methodologies and consequently allow IT spending to be more in line with individual and organizational needs.[10]

CYBER SECURITY IMPLEMENTATION STRATEGIES

Based on our interviews, we found that organizations tend to characterize their cyber security implementation strategies differently, but the broad concept of a *proactive* strategy versus a *reactive* strategy resonates well in discussions of cyber security strategic planning (that is, in what specific products and activities to invest). That fact logically raises the question: What is the optimal strategic mix of proactive versus reactive cyber security activities for an organization?

Whereas a proactive strategy, in general, leads to fewer cyber security breaches, in some instances a reactive strategy may be more cost-effective. An analogy can be made as to how extensively a software programmer should test a new software product prior to installation. Most programmers attest to the fact that it is impossible (or prohibitively expensive) to develop error-free software code. Thus, programmers select a level of (proactive) testing and debugging activities, knowing that in the future some errors will be identified that require (reactive) fixes, patches and work-arounds. Experienced programmers implicitly conduct cost–benefit analyses based on history, experience and market pressures to determine the optimal level of effort that should be devoted to testing and debugging.[11]

Similarly, the optimal strategy mix of proactive versus reactive cyber security strategies for an organization depends on many factors. For example, some dimensions of a proactive strategy, such as staff training and adoption of innovative strategies in a timely fashion, can yield significant benefits at reasonable cost. However, trying to anticipate and block all forms of rapidly evolving viruses can be expensive and perhaps only marginally effective. Thus, under certain circumstances the most cost-efficient strategy could be a reactive one. Specifically, it may be most efficient (from a private perspective) to rely on existing, proven security technologies and then to be able to implement patches quickly when new viruses are identified.

However, the line between proactive and reactive investment strategies is not always clear, nor is the line necessarily reflective of specific technologies or practices. The definition of a proactive versus reactive technology changes over time as the technology becomes established and eventually obsolete. For example, at a basic level periodically requiring users to change their password, once viewed as a proactive policy, has fallen out of favor. Users who are forced to change their password periodically are more likely to write it down or reuse a password used elsewhere, risking a security breach. Similarly, employing a person to monitor an intrusion detection system could be proactive, but if the person is looking for trends with which they are already familiar, this technique may be reactive. In addition, hiring someone to break into a network could be proactive, but if the person is using a vulnerability scanner that uses only known vulnerabilities, the strategy is reactive.[12]

From our interviews, it was obvious that the adoption of a generally proactive versus reactive strategy has an impact on the level and type of IT expenditure as well as on overall business operations. Table 4.1 provides an overview of both IT impact and non-IT impact costs as they relate to being relatively more proactive or reactive. Proactive strategies have regulatory and reputational benefits, and because they are likely to lead to fewer events, they can reduce business interruptions. However, respondents in our interviews often said that proactive strategies can be restrictive. Close to one-third of the organizations we spoke with said that user convenience was equally, if not more, important than security, which led them to use reactive strategies in some instances. Proactive strategies also have external benefits that organizations cannot capture.

Below we discuss two conceptual approaches, introduced earlier in this chapter, that can be used to evaluate the optimal level of proactive versus reactive cyber security activities: cost minimization subject to a fixed level of output (that is, level of security) and output (that is, level of security) maximization subject to a fixed budget constraint.

Table 4.1 Comparison between IT and non-IT costs and benefits based on security strategy

Security strategy	IT impacts	Non-IT impacts
Proactive	Cost: Cutting-edge hardware and software (likely more expensive than well-established solutions) Cost: Information gathering, installation, debugging, and maintenance costs (labor)	Cost: User inconvenience
	Benefit: Decreased need for reactive labor	Benefit: Regulatory and reputation benefits Benefit: Fewer business interruptions
Reactive	Cost: Infrastructure (mostly labor) resources needed to respond quickly and effectively Cost: Resources (labor) needed to repair damaged systems and data	Cost: More events, and thus a likely increase in downtime Cost: Potential damage to reputation
	Benefit: Decreased investments in proactive (risky) solutions	Benefit: User convenience Benefit: Flexibility to accommodate diverse business environments

Note: Incorporating user costs is important to assess fully the costs and benefits of security strategies.

As shown in Figure 4.2, organizations indicated that they strive to identify an appropriate balance or combination of proactive (A) and reactive (R) cyber security strategies. Drawing from economic theory, we illustrate this trade-off between implementing a reactive strategy (vertical axis) and a proactive strategy (horizontal axis) in terms of a family of curves that are concave to the origin. These so-called 'iso-security curves' that are farther from the origin represent higher levels of cyber security.[13] In Figure 4.2, we also depict what is referred to as a budget line reflecting the monetary resources available to the organization to support or invest in cyber security.

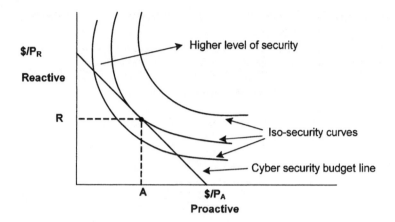

Note: Point (R,A) corresponds to the maximum level of security attainable subject to the budget constraint.

Figure 4.2 Selection of optimal proactive versus reactive strategy to maximize cyber security

For example, if the organization allocates all of its cyber security resources toward a proactive strategy, it would find itself at the point labeled $/P_A; alternatively, if it allocates all of its cyber security resources to a reactive strategy, it would find itself at the point labeled $/P_R, where P_A and P_R are conceptually the unit price of a proactive and a reactive activity, respectively.[14]

Maximizing Security Subject to a Budget Constraint

Although most organizations do not use solely a cost-minimizing or output-maximizing (budget constrained) approach, our interviews indicate that more organizations tend to rely on their budgets to drive the level of security that they have in place (rather than the inverse relationship). Cyber security staff frequently indicated that their budgets are basically fixed (or change modestly from year to year); as a result, they view their role as essentially maximizing the level of security that can be provided subject to a predetermined level of resources. This approach is similar to a production function economic model where output (in this case, security) is maximized subject to a budget constraint. As illustrated in Figure 4.2, if we take the organization's IT budget as given (fixed), the optimal strategy mix is at the point of tangency between its budget line (the slope of which is determined by the perceived relative cost of proactive and reactive activities) and the highest iso-security curve that can be attained. This optimal point represents the optimal mix of reactive, R, and proactive, A, strategies.

Cost-Minimizing Approach to Cyber Security

Organizations' risk management staff look to leverage a wide range of information and expertise when assessing cyber security threats and developing a cyber security investment strategy. Such capabilities enable organizations with a more holistic view of cyber security to determine the level of security or due diligence appropriate for the organization and then have the IT staff develop the most cost-effective implementation strategy. In this way, organizations seek to minimize costs while achieving a desired level of security. This strategy will include a combination of proactive and reactive measures. Investments in cyber security are costly, as are repairs from breaches. Thus, an organization will select a cyber security strategy that minimizes what it views as net costs. This can involve investing in both cyber security hardware and software and staff training, as well as modifying organizational operations that could increase day-to-day operating costs by restricting how IT systems can be deployed or how users can access and interact with IT systems.

As shown in Figure 4.2, the cost-minimizing approach is for an organization to identify the level of security that it determines is most appropriate for the organization, represented by the appropriate iso-security curve. This level is then taken as fixed, and the budget line is adjusted in or out (parallel shift) based on the total level of spending necessary to achieve the desired security and the perceptions of the cost of being more proactive or more reactive. The appropriate balance or combination of using a proactive and reactive strategy is then based on the determined level of security and the budget line that creates a point of tangency. This enables the organization to spend the optimal level of investment dollars on proactive and reactive strategies based on a specific desired level of security.

Conceptual Levers Affecting the Relative Use of Proactive Versus Reactive Strategies

The above models in Figures 4.1 and 4.2 focus on the private costs and benefits as they relate to private organizations. However, we support the body of research and security experts who claim that the private benefits implicit in these models are likely not to represent the total social costs and benefits if externalities are considered. Society therefore may benefit from a different mix of proactive versus reactive strategies than is optimal from a private perspective. As discussed earlier, the public-goods nature of cyber security may distort private investments from what is socially optimal for society as a whole. Market failures may lead to underinvestments in cyber security if not all of the costs are borne by the investing organization – if cost externalities of security breaches are incurred by other organizations in the network. In addition, the public-goods nature of information sharing and dissemination has generally led to limited sharing of information about threats and solutions, commonly referred to as free-rider tendencies.

Issues of cost externalities and information free-ridership also have implications for selecting a more proactive versus a reactive cyber security strategy. In general, a reactive strategy is more likely to lead to cost externalities imposed on organizations throughout the network because of the nature of the network. In contrast, a proactive strategy minimizes breaches and reduces cost externalities. In addition, proactive investments are more information-intensive and are affected more by free-ridership issues, where the reduced sharing of information increases the cost of evaluating and adopting proactive strategies.

Cost Externalities

Figure 4.3 shows how internalizing cost externalities affects the optimal proactive versus reactive cyber security strategy mix. Incorporating cost externalities of breaches (cost spillovers throughout the network) increases the price, P_R, of reactive cyber security solutions, which rotates the budget curve inward. In terms of the output maximization strategy, this reflects that for a given budget constraint, when all cost externalities through the network are considered, a lower level of social cyber security is actually being achieved. As shown in Figure 4.3, the maximum level of security is now achieved by decreasing the level of reactive cyber security solutions from R to R'.

With regard to the cost-minimization strategy, incorporating cost externalities incurred throughout the network increases the cost of reactive activities, which, in turn, affects the necessary budget to maintain the level of security desired. Because reactive activities have become relatively more expensive, the result is that when cost externalities of reactive measures are

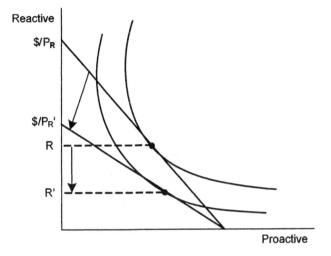

Note: As firms are required to internalize cost impacts born by third parties, the budget curve pivots making proactive solutions more attractive.

Figure 4.3 Internalizing externalities increases price of reactive options $(P_R < P_R')$

incorporated in the investment decision, the cost-minimizing solution is to shift toward a more proactive cyber security strategy to reduce the cost necessary to achieve the desired level of security.

Information Sharing

Cost-minimizing and output-maximizing analyses can also be used to portray the impact of information sharing on the selection of proactive versus reactive strategies. As shown in Figure 4.4, in aggregate, information sharing decreases the price, P_A, of proactive solutions.[15] This rotates the cyber security budget line outward. In the security-maximizing approach, this increases the amount of proactive solutions that can be implemented with the given budget constraint, thus leading to an increased level of proactive solutions at the tangent point of the budget curve and the iso-security curve – A to A'. The overall result is a higher level of cyber security (that is, a higher iso-security curve) achievable given the new budget constraint.

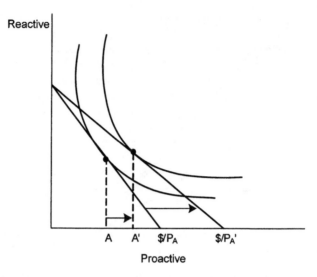

Note: Lowering the cost of proactive options also pivots the budget curve making proactive options more attractive.

Figure 4.4 Information sharing decreases cost of proactive options
$(P_A > P_A')$

The cost-minimization strategy is also affected by this shift. With the level of desired security held constant,[16] the necessary budget line could be shifted inward and more focus put on proactive strategies, while the same level of security is maintained at a lower overall cost.

CONCLUSIONS

This chapter offers a conceptual model of the cyber security decision process, which is comprised of both an investment strategy and an implementation strategy. To the best of our knowledge, the models presented herein are among the first to segment these strategic aspects of the cyber security decision process and, by so doing, to provide a framework for focusing on public policy issues.

The distinctions of where within an organization decisions related to cyber security are being made and by whom are important when evaluating public policy. For example, if barriers to the implementation of cyber security solutions are technical or infrastructural in nature then public policy should focus on the implementation process. Government is more likely to influence implementation strategies through the funding of R&D, promoting collaborations and research consortiums, and supporting testing and validation processes. These activities can lower the cost of adoption by providing key infrastructure technologies and promoting information sharing. In addition, public policy may want to promote research in technologies with the greatest social benefits (positive externalities). Our research suggests that more proactive strategies tend to have more social benefits; Chapter 5 provides a more robust discussion of this finding.

Alternatively, if barriers to cyber security are primarily associated with management's allocation of resources, then a clear understanding of investment strategies related to cyber security is essential for policy analysis. Further, from a systematic view, changes to the legal system could potentially influence financial investment analysis related to cyber security. For example, if one firm (Firm A) could be held liable for damage caused by attacks on other firms (Firms B, C, and D) when those attacks originate[17] from Firm A's network, then Firm A would have a greater economic incentive to invest in more proactive solutions that might prevent negative externalities imposed on other companies and individuals. Finally, the ability to document and quantify the probability of events and expected loss is important for communicating threat information with upper management; and this is also a potential area where public sector involvement could promote research.

NOTES

1. This is a conceptual approach and represents a simplification of the necessary steps needed to determine the optimal course of action; however, many organizations may implicitly use such a decision process every time they consider what investments (including those directed towards cyber security) they should make or request, even if they do not explicitly think about their actions and strategies in this way.

2. Many organizations, particularly small businesses, may not have encountered a significant attack or a breach at all. Thus, such organizations (and all organizations to some degree) base decisions only on the attacks and breaches they have observed, and the appropriate responses based on this information. As such, decisions are based on incomplete information.

3. After such events occur, they may actually have a higher probability of occurrence, especially when no easy remediation of the vulnerabilities and avoidance of the threats are possible.

4. This relevant and applicable knowledge is in part codified, but is also in part tacit. Because of its tacit nature, the activities of consortia and trade associations are important. But also because of its tacit nature, the effectiveness of any information sharing depends on the experiential knowledge of those doing the sharing.

5. See Neumann (2004) for discussion of the need for more long-term planning for computer system and security development.

6. Public good characteristics refer to a good being non-rivalrous and non-excludable. Classic examples include national defense and lighting of common areas

7. Seventy-five percent of organizations have a structured budget process. While this does not imply that they are given a fixed budget, it does suggest that most decision-makers must use some form of explicit or implicit metrics, either quantitative or qualitative, when receiving funding for cyber security.

8. Many articles mention and evaluate the inadequacy of business case approaches to evaluating cyber security investments. The Congressional Research Service (CRS) specifically discusses this dilemma in its report (Cashell et al., 2004).

9. The website for the Workshop on the Economics of Information Security, convened in Cambridge, England, in June 2006, is http://www.cl.cam.ac.uk/users/twm29/WEIS06/. Links to past and subsequent workshops are available at this website.

10. Gordon et al. (2003a) discuss the problems underlying the current lack of adequate information sharing. They further introduce a model that empirically supports the assertion that more information sharing would lead to improved security. Additionally, Gal-Or and Ghose (2005) find that increased information sharing has a greater positive effect on security for larger firms and in more competitive industries.

11. Chapter 10 provides a rich discussion of the optimal private investment level for software development and testing and the optimal social level. The economic impact of the difference between these two provides an estimate of the cost to society of socially-suboptimal investments.

12. Further, it is not clear that proactive versus reactive strategies are exclusive. While it is clear that those who are not proactive in their risk management will use purely reactive strategies, those who are completely proactive may also decide to adopt reactive strategies. The issue may not concern proactive and reactive strategies as much the reasoning that went into a decision. Further,

being proactive could mean applying best practices or adding more security measures; the terms 'proactive' and 'reactive' are thus not prescriptive.

13. We use the term 'iso-security curves' to describe different levels of security that organizations set out to achieve. This terminology is based on economic production theory which describes 'isoquants' in a similar way to show how two inputs can be combined in different ways to produce a given level of output.

14. Obviously, we are simplifying the trade-off. Of particular note is the fact that in reality the adoption of a reactive or proactive activity is likely to appear more like a step-wise function than a linear one.

15. This statement implies that if there is more information sharing occurs by all organizations, on average, then the cost of being more proactive will likely decrease.

16. Obviously, investing in a more proactive strategy versus a more reactive strategy imposes different risks on an organization. We assume that these risks are incorporated in the prices of the strategies.

17. By 'originate' we do not mean that Firm A knowingly attacked other firms. Instead, we mean that by not being secure, Firm A enabled hackers to use their network as a staging point from which to attack other companies and individuals. See Chapter 3 for information on botnets, which are commonly used by hackers for such purposes.

5. Cyber Security Investment and Implementation Strategies: Empirical Evidence

INTRODUCTION

In this chapter we present findings from the analysis of a small sample of organizations interviewed to collect information on how organizations determine their level of spending on cyber security and the explicit solutions they select.[1] As discussed in the previous chapter, 100 organizations were interviewed, and from those interviews the conceptual models in Chapter 4 were developed. In addition, detailed surveys were also administered, 36 organizations willingly provided empirical data as shown in Table 5.1. While we do not suggest that our subsample of 36 organizations is representative of the population of organizations that rely on the Internet and thus are affected by computer security breaches, we nevertheless present our analysis of these organizations as a template of the type of empirical analysis that is needed in the academic and professional literatures to understand cyber security issues better and thus to inform public policy better.

SURVEY FINDINGS

A general theme that emerged during our interviews was that many organizations are undertaking an extensive review of how cyber security impacts on their business operations, and many have begun or are planning to begin restructuring their processes. Specifically, there is a trend toward cyber security being treated very holistically; that is, organizations are beginning to realize that relevant information associated with cyber security issues includes much more than the concerns of the in-house IT staff.

Table 5.1 Survey respondents, by industry group

Industry	Participants
Financial services	6
Health care providers	6
Manufacturing	6
Small businesses	6
Universities	7
Other	5
Total	36

Note: Surveys were conducted with organizations in key sectors to collect detailed information on investment and implementation strategies. The Other category includes two electric utilities and three Internet Service Providers (ISPs).

Decisions related to the amount of resources allocated each year to hardware and software, and specific cyber security procedures and policies affecting users, should be informed by a variety of sources within each organization, including but certainly not limited to the IT staff's knowledge and expertise.

All parts of an organization are affected by IT-related decisions, and thus potentially can offer relevant views that could benefit the whole organization. Therefore, management staff at many organizations are beginning to realize that cyber security decisions should be evaluated in terms of risk management. Every organization is vulnerable to the risk of a cyber security breach, so protecting the privacy of organizational information should be a managerial issue of priority. Furthermore, many breaches can result in legal and human resources issues, so those administrative units are becoming more involved in decision-making, most often related to the development of user policies.

During the investment strategy phase, decision-making generally occurs within one of two organizational areas: either the IT department or a business strategy or management department or committee (for example, risk management).[2] Table 5.2 shows, by industry group, where cyber security priorities and budgets are primarily determined within the organizations with which we spoke. Financial service and health care organizations are more likely to have investment strategies set by management-level groups, whereas manufacturing and universities are more likely to determine their investment strategies within IT departments.

Table 5.2   Primary source of cyber security investment strategy, by industry group

Industry group	Within IT department (%)	Within management department (%)
Financial services	33.3	66.7
Health care providers	33.3	66.7
Manufacturing	83.3	16.7
Universities	60.0	40.0
Other	85.7	14.3
Total	60.0	40.0

Note: Small businesses are not included because investment decisions are intermingled. The table shows that financial service and health care organizations are more likely to have investment strategies set by management-level groups, whereas manufacturing and universities are more likely to determine their investments strategies within IT departments.

As shown in Table 5.3, organizations in which investment strategies determined within their IT department track relatively more information on breaches than do organizations with investment strategies made within management groups. Though the differences between the sources and across types of security compromises are not statistically significant, this was a particularly surprising result. Both types of organization also rely on external sources of information, with organizations in which investment strategies are determine with the management groups utilizing such information more.

Further, organizations with investment strategies made within a management department or group are on average much more likely to track incident metrics, such as the number of IT staff hours needed to respond to an event and the number of user hours impacted upon by an event.

Schematically, Figure 5.1 offers a diagram of the flow of decision-making and the information sources that act as inputs to this process. This figure is an elaboration of Figure 4.1, which introduced the relationship between the formulation of an organization's investment strategy and its implementation strategy. Cyber security investment decisions are influenced by both internal and external sources of information.

Initially, external influences (for example, regulations, client requirements) and internal information regarding business processes can act as drivers that, in combination with the budget process, largely determine an

Table 5.3   Percentage of organizations internally tracking security events,
           by source of cyber security investment strategy

Security compromise	Source of cyber security investment strategy	
	Within IT department (%)	Within management department (%)
Denial of service	82.4	66.7
Unauthorized access to information	76.5	83.3
Viruses, worms or spyware	88.2	75.0
Severe spam floods	88.2	75.0
Theft of proprietary information	88.2	75.0
Hardware theft	88.2	83.3
Abuse of the wireless network	64.7	66.7
Web site defacement	76.5	66.7
Misuse of public Web applications	76.5	66.7
Financial fraud	76.5	75.0
Eavesdropping on communications	64.7	58.3
Unauthorized modification of permissions	82.4	66.7

Note: None of the organizations with whom we spoke felt that they had all the relevant expertise in-house to make efficient, effective cyber security investment decisions. Thus, external sources of security-related information are critically important. This reliance on external resources is a major focus of our findings and analysis throughout this report. The table shows that organizations making their investment decision within their IT department were typically more likely to track internally security events.

organization's implementation strategy. Additional internal and external resources (for example, National Institute of Standards and Technology (NIST), International Organization for Standardization (ISO), and American National Standards Institute (ANSI), publications and vendor recommendations) are used to inform specific capital investment decisions and the structure of how policies and procedures are implemented. Subsequently, organizations make specific investment and management decisions concerning cyber security hardware, software, IT staff procedures (labor) and user policies. The overall output of this process, in large part, determines the nature and frequency of breaches that occur.

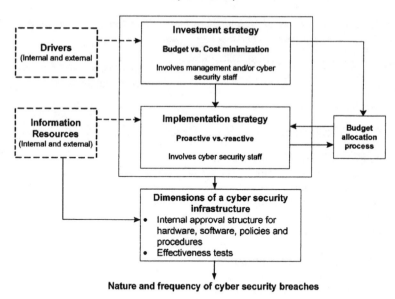

Nature and frequency of cyber security breaches

Note: Internal and external drivers impact upon investment strategies, while the availability of information resources impacts upon implementation strategies.

Figure 5.1   Diagram of cyber security investment decisions inputs and outputs

Table 5.4 provides a grouping of the major internal and external information sources that affect the cyber security investment decision-making process, either as drivers or as resources to cyber security practitioners or individuals responsible for approving cyber security purchases, policies or procedures.

In most organizations with which we spoke, the budgeting process is based significantly on the previous year's budget and, to a lesser extent, on regulations or forecasts of anticipated needs. Only a few organizations determined the budget for cyber security through a cost-minimization strategy, including a rigorous cost–benefit analysis and/or a risk management framework, based on a desired level of security. Thus, in Figure 5.1, the budgeting process is separate from the investment decision-making process. In some cases, there is feedback between an organization's strategy for security and the budget it sets for cyber security; this is

Table 5.4 Categorization of relevant drivers and information resources

Internal	External public	External private
Drivers		
Business process needs (i.e., strong business reliance on network) Major past breach	Regulations	Client demands Supplier demands
Information resources		
Internal audits Staff experience/training Internally collected/ calculated data (e.g., number of compromises, cost estimates) CEO/CTO/COO, etc. suggestions	NIST best practices ISO guidelines ANSI guidelines Security impact estimated (e.g., CSI/FBI survey) CERTS, SANS, etc.	Customer suggestions/ requirements Vendor suggestions/advice Conferences or trade publications Outside consultants Other organizations External audits

Note: Public sector drivers and information resources represent levers that the government can employ to influence investment and implementation decisions.

represented by the arrow from the implementation strategy to the budget allocation process.

Investment Strategy

Using the information resources listed above in Table 5.4, organizations must develop a process for cyber security spending; this includes the budgeting process, capital labor resource allocation and, subsequently, evaluation of spending.

Investment strategy: Cyber security budgets

More than 75 percent of organizations in our study indicated that they have a structured budget process. However, this process took a variety of forms: some organizations had a budget set once annually and others quarterly.

Further, the specific amount spent on cyber security varies significantly both across and within industry groups. The organizations with which we spoke, on average, allocate 5.7 percent of their IT budget to cyber security; however, based on our limited sample, there are differences among industries. Table 5.5 provides a comparison of cyber security spending by industry group for the surveyed organizations.[3]

Table 5.5   Average cyber security budgets as a percentage of IT budgets, by industry group

Industry	Average cyber security budget (as % of IT budget)
Financial services	3.3
Health care providers	6.2
Manufacturing	4.2
Small businesses	10.1
Universities	3.3
Other	8.5
Total	5.7

Note: Financial services reported a relatively low share of their IT budget being spent on cyber security. However, this sector's IT budget is large as a percentage of total revenue; thus this should not be interpreted as an indicator of under-investment.

Of the organizations with which we spoke, small businesses tend to spend a larger share of their IT budget on cyber security compared to other groups, while the financial services industry and universities tend to spend a smaller share, which is consistent with the findings from the CSI survey presented in Chapter 2. These differences across industries are likely to be reflective of economies of scale and the relative size of total IT budgets, as opposed to differences in the concerns with cyber security issues.

Whereas cyber security budgets are influenced by the factors discussed above, the cyber security officers with whom we spoke indicated that there was not always a direct link. Although our data indicated that slightly more than one-third of organizations view the previous year's budget as the primary determinant of their current cyber security budget, participants did imply that additional resources would be provided for perceived new threats. In addition, a main determinant of organizational budget change seemed to be the effect of new regulations. But in general, most IT departments viewed their task as to do the best they could to prepare for cyber security threats with essentially an exogenous security budget.

Investment strategy: Cyber security expenditure allocation

During our interviews, most organizations indicated that they perform ROI, IRR, NPV and/or cost–benefit calculations as part of their cyber security investment decisions. However, when asked for specific examples of calculations conducted and how they generated the relevant information for the calculations, few were able to provide any details. One example cited was by a university that implemented an automated password reset system, allowing the university to reduce their telephone calls to staff by 50 percent; for this they could compare the cost of the system to the labor savings. However, in no instance did any company provide us with an example in which it quantified the probability of an event or the associated expected damage. Two organizations, both in the financial industry, indicated that such analysis was being conducted internally, but they were unwilling to elaborate.

In many instances, the target level of security and/or the resulting share of the IT budget directed toward cyber security were dictated by external factors. For example, organizations indicated that regulations were by far the most significant factor affecting their investment strategy; on average, organizations indicated that over 30 percent of their cyber security activities and investments were motivated by regulations. Similarly, the second greatest external influence was client requirements; many clients, Visa being the most often mentioned, require certain cyber security hardware, software, policies and procedures and routine audits to engage in business relationships. Table 5.6 provides additional information on the relative importance of drivers motivating the level of security maintained by organizations that participated in these interviews.

The Implementation Strategy

Both internal and external information were found to be particularly important for IT staff involved in making implementation decisions. We offer for consideration that a regulation or a client requirement may influence an organization to take a more proactive approach to cyber security by forcing that organization to adopt more restrictive user policies and/or to purchase more state-of-the-art hardware and software technologies. Alternately, not having enough information available in the

Table 5.6 Cyber security drivers

Categories	Average % across organizations
Client driven	16.2
Regulation driven	30.1
Result of internal or external audit	12.4
Response to current events (e.g., media attention)	8.2
Response to internal security compromise	7.3
Network history/IT staff knowledge	18.9
Externally managed/determined	5.0
Other	1.7

Note: Regulations were most frequently identified as an important driver. This was followed by Network history/IT staff knowledge.

public domain could cause an organization to adopt a more reactive strategy, addressing cyber security issues only when they affect operating processes.

In this section, we focus on the use of information resources utilized by organizations when determining appropriate proactive and reactive implementation strategies. The inputs to this strategy decision help in understanding the possible ways to influence how organizations make decisions. Furthermore, these same resources are used when organizations make decisions related to the specific dimensions of their cyber security infrastructure, including the hardware and software they will purchase, and the user policies and the IT staff procedures they will employ.

Table 5.7 shows the overall rankings of reliance on information resources for hardware and software decisions and IT security procedures and activities. These numbers represent the percentage of organizations ranking each resource in the top three in terms of relative importance.

Internal information
The data suggest a heavy reliance on internal information resources for analysis. This includes the use of internal auditing; the relative involvement of the IT staff and in-house executives to determine the level of cyber security; and the tracking of internal IT information, such as the number of

Table 5.7 Importance of information resources

Resource type	Hardware and software (%)	IT security procedures/ activities (%)
Government regulations	18.1	44.4
Customer suggestions/requirements	16.7	12.5
Vendor suggestions/advice	30.6	8.3
NIST best practices	12.5	26.4
ISO guidelines	5.6	9.7
ANSI guidelines	5.6	5.6
Security impact estimates (e.g., CSI/FBI survey)	2.8	6.9
CERTs, SANS, etc.	6.9	12.5
Conferences or trade publications	22.2	12.5
Outside consultants	15.3	13.9
Other organizations	13.9	4.2
External audits	11.1	12.5
Internal audits	11.1	33.3
Staff experience/training	66.7	51.4
Internally collected/calculated data (e.g., number of compromises, cost estimates, etc.)	36.1	31.9
CEO/CTO/COO, etc. suggestion	11.1	5.6
Other	2.8	2.8

Note: Respondents were asked to rank each resource type on a 1 to 5 Likert scale where 1 = most important and 5 = least important. Shown in the table are the percentage of respondents ranking each information resource with a 1, 2 or 3. The table shows that staff expertise/training is the most important source of information. In addition, government regulations are a primary determinant of IT security procedures, and vendors are a key source of information for selecting hardware and software.

breaches, IT staff hours needed to resolve any problems and user time required to reach a solution.

Most internal information is built on previous knowledge and experience from IT staff members. Thus, the validity and completeness of this information is depended on the relative skill level of the staff.

Although our interviews did not attempt to discern the relative level of competence of the responding organization's IT staff, it is important to note that we did hear from numerous experts and industry members who indicated that the skill level of IT staff varies widely among and within organizations. Some staff failed to continue with self-education as technology changed, while others were not aware of the business repercussions of certain actions. Both inadequacies can cause significant security problems (although both inadequacies can be ameliorated through internal human resource expenditure).

Many different private and non-profit organizations, including Cisco and the Information Systems Audit and Control Association (ISACA), provide a variety of certification courses. There are certification programs for specific technologies, as well as more general programs. The certified information systems security professionals' certification program, accredited by the American National Standards Institute and ISO, seemed to be the most respected.

In addition to IT staff knowledge and ability, internal resources include the collection and use of certain internal data. Such information includes data on breaches – the number of breaches incurred by an organization of various types, the number of cyber security staff hours needed to resolve the attacks, the eventual solution and the number of user hours required for resolution – as well as resource utilization information (that is, how IT staff spend their time). Internally collected information can be analyzed to determine specific vulnerabilities and resource utilization as well as to estimate costs and probabilities of attack.

Most organizations with which we spoke were tracking at least some internal information, but many were not using it as part of their investment decision-making process. Organized into five breach categories, Table 5.8 shows how industries compare in their tracking of information.

Financial organizations tend to track the most information on breaches. As a group, the manufacturing organizations with which we spoke tracked the least amount of information, with small businesses not far behind.

Additionally, we gathered information on whether organizations track the resource utilization of their cyber security staff. Table 5.9 summarizes this information. While most organizations (approximately 60 percent) are collecting data related to their response to cyber security problems, fewer than half are collecting data on total resource (labor) use related to cyber security. In our discussions, several organizations indicated that they did not see the need for tracking the hours of their cyber security staff time. In a couple of instances, the reason given was that the organization was so small that they did not think it made sense to collect such data, while others indicated that they trusted the judgment of their staff. Two other organizations commented that they could not get approval to collect such resource allocation data.

Table 5.8   *Percentage of organizations that track at least one type of breach within each category*

Type of breach	Industries	Track number of incidents? (%)	Track IT staff hours? (%)	Track user hours? (%)
Denial of service	Financial	83	83	33
	Health care	67	17	0
	Manufacturing	50	17	0
	University	100	29	14
	Small business	50	17	17
	Other	100	100	100
Viruses, worms, spyware, and spam	Financial	100	100	67
	Health care	100	83	17
	Manufacturing	67	17	17
	University	100	29	14
	Small business	100	50	33
	Other	100	100	100
Unauthorized access/network abuse	Financial	100	83	50
	Health care	100	33	0
	Manufacturing	67	17	0
	University	100	29	14
	Small business	100	50	33
	Other	100	100	100
Web abuse	Financial	100	67	33
	Health care	67	33	17
	Manufacturing	50	17	17
	University	100	29	14
	Small business	50	17	17
	Other	100	100	100
Theft/fraud	Financial	100	83	50
	Health care	100	50	17
	Manufacturing	50	17	17
	University	100	29	14
	Small business	83	17	17
	Other	100	100	100

Note: Most organizations track the number of incidents. However, it is less common for organizations to track the impact on IT staff and relatively few tracked impacts on users.

Table 5.9   Percentage of organizations tracking cyber security resource allocation

Resource	%
Responding to IT security problems	58.3
IT security staff education	44.4
Monitoring IT security status	36.1
Testing IT security measures	33.3
Installing new IT security measures	33.3
Gathering information	25.0
Other	11.1

Note: Most organizations tracked time allocated to responding to security problems. Fewer tracked general cyber security support activities.

When we asked whether organizations were tracking the time spent by users on selecting passwords and receiving any cyber security training, executive-level involvement in security decisions or business unit managers' participation, most organizations indicated that they do not track such information. Fewer than 20 percent collect information on users, while only 5 percent track executive-level or business unit managers' time.

Comparison of information resources
We asked organizations about the external information resources they used. As presented in Table 5.10, external information includes both publicly and privately generated data and other information. Many organizations relied on vendor and customer suggestions to help them decide on the types of hardware and software to have in place. They similarly used NIST best practices[4] and relied on both external audits and outside consultants when making decisions on user policies and cyber security procedures.

Despite significant variation, organizations indicated that on average they depend more on internal than external resources. The relative importance of informational resources did vary across industry groupings and within industry groupings. Based on discussions, we coded the top three resources that each organization stated it used in determining its cyber security procedures and activities. The three most frequently mentioned resources were scored as 1 and the rest were scored as 0.[5] As such, a higher value implies that an organization valued a certain resource more highly than others.

In Table 5.10, universities are shown to be the least reliant on external information sources, reflecting in-house expertise as well as the diversity of their needs. The health care industry is the most dependent on external public sources of information, and small businesses are the most reliant on external private (vendors) sources of information.

Dimensions of a Cyber Security Infrastructure: Summary Results

Although often not explicitly discussed, organizations determine what specific hardware and software they will purchase and what user policies and IT security procedures they will employ based on:

- The organizational investment strategy. When we asked 'Is the Chief Information Security Officer (CISO) or Director of IT Security given a budget or does he/she work with a management committee to determine a target level of security and then spend the amount necessary to achieve that level?' most organizations indicated that they have both factors in play.
- The organizational implementation strategy. When we asked 'Does the organization take a more proactive versus reactive approach to security?' most organizations indicated that they have a blend of approaches.

Based on these factors, cyber security staff members are allocated resources (for example, capital and labor) toward a variety of activities. While in most instances organizations that we interviewed allowed cyber security staff to determine the best use of their time, responses varied on the type of security technologies purchased and on what vendors were selected.

Our interviews also included a discussion of what factors influenced organizations' decisions to adopt a specific security technology or to invest in the adoption of a new user policy or procedural change. The following factors were most often cited:

- Likelihood to improve security: this factor was, not surprisingly, most often cited. The ability of the product, policy or procedure change to improve security, either to meet internal security objectives or to satisfy a government regulation, was very important to almost all respondents.
- Ability to improve productivity: the second most important factor, cited by more than half of the interview participants, was the ability of the

Table 5.10 Types of information resources used, by industry group

Industries	Hardware and software	Procedures	Policies
Financial			
Internal	1.50	1.17	1.17
External public	0.33	1.33	1.17
External private	1.17	0.50	0.67
Health care			
Internal	0.83	0.83	0.50
External public	1.08	1.83	2.00
External private	1.08	0.33	0.50
Manufacturing			
Internal	0.80	0.83	1.00
External public	0.60	1.50	1.17
External private	1.60	0.67	0.83
University			
Internal	2.08	2.00	1.67
External public	0.58	0.50	1.00
External private	0.33	0.50	0.33
Small business			
Internal	0.83	1.33	1.17
External public	0.33	0.33	0.67
External private	1.83	1.33	1.17
Other			
Internal	1.90	1.80	1.80
External public	0.30	0.80	0.60
External private	0.80	0.40	0.60
Total			
Internal	1.32	1.31	1.20
External public	0.54	1.06	1.11
External private	1.13	0.63	0.69

Note: A higher index value implies relatively more importance of the information resource. The table shows that internal sources were the dominant source of information identified (with the exception of small businesses). Public information was used most in the areas of procedures and policies. See Gallaher et al. (2006) for details on how the index values were constructed.

procedure to improve the productivity of users and/or cyber security staff.

- Widespread industry use: approximately one-quarter of the organizations with which we spoke cited the use of the technology, policy or procedure by organizations in a similar market segment as a motivating factor.

At the bottom of the list of factors influencing organizations' decisions on when to adopt a new technology, policy, or procedure was cost – including both the immediate and the projected total cost of ownership, or TCO. Small businesses were the exception and did consider TCO a relatively important factor.

In addition to a discussion of the decision on whether to adopt a new technology, policy or procedure, we asked interview participants how they decided from which company to purchase a new technology solution. Not surprisingly, most respondents noted that the effectiveness of the product was the most important consideration. However, most of the other factors cited received about equal weight. These factors included cost (immediate and TCO), degree of homogeneity with the existing infrastructure, general interoperability of the product and reputation of the vendor or service provider. Our interviews revealed that:

- Approximately 75 percent of the security products in use come from large, well-established companies (as opposed to smaller organizations).
- Approximately 67 percent of these products are well-tested products (as opposed to being more innovative).[6]

It is important to point out that cost was important when organizations were deciding from which company to purchase the security product. When asked what usually caused organizations not to adopt technologies or make policy or procedural changes in the past, more than half of the respondents indicated each of the following factors (listed in order of the number of times each was mentioned, the first being the most frequent): disruption of user or cyber security staff productivity; expense of the product (immediate and TCO); too complicated or time-consuming; lack of a perceived threat (difficulty convincing management); and anticipated staff resistance.

Of particular interest is that disruption of user and/or cyber security staff productivity was cited most often by organizations as a reason why a certain technology, policy or procedure was not adopted. This indicates a major barrier to the adoption of adequate security processes and reflects and area where research is needed to lower the burden on users. Although organizations did not cite cost as an important factor when deciding to adopt a new technology, policy or procedure, it was mentioned as a reason why investments have not been made in the past.

Finally, organizations assess the effectiveness of their cyber security investments differently. Many rely on internal and external audits and vulnerability tests to assess compliance with regulations and customer requirements, as well as whether the investments satisfy internal security goals.

IMPLICATIONS OF THE SURVEY FINDINGS

In this section, we provide additional analysis of the relationships between organizations' strategies, information resource use and cyber security investments. We build on the conceptual frameworks underlying the investment and implementation decisions described in the beginning of this chapter.

Based on our interviews, we found that implementation strategies generally range from more proactive to more reactive, where a proactive strategy implies that security compromises are anticipated and safeguards are built into the IT system to prevent them, and a reactive strategy implies that an organization responds to known threats with typically established technologies so that security compromises can be addressed efficiently and effectively. We also gleaned from the interview process that fewer security compromises resulted when an organization or company adopted a proactive strategy as opposed to a reactive strategy, but the frequency and extent of such compromises – realized or averted – were not disclosed.

During the interview process, we asked respondents to characterize their cyber security activities and strategies in terms of proactive or reactive. In most cases, an organization employed a cyber security strategy with both proactive and reactive elements. Based on each respondent's characterization, we then asked about the extent to which the organization can adhere to its defined proactive strategy, where a response of 10 was 'always' and a response of 1 was 'never'. We also asked, using the same response code, about the extent to which the organization always adhered to its defined reactive strategy. From these responses, we constructed a proactive index for each organization; this index is the numerical difference between the extent to which the respondent stated that the organization always adhered to a proactive strategy and the extent to which the respondent stated that the organization always adhered to a reactive strategy.[7]

Figure 5.2 shows the distribution of proactive indices for the 36 responding organizations. The figure also shows that the majority of organizations (29 of 36) in the sample characterize themselves as relatively proactive (proactive index > 0). Only 7 of 36 characterize themselves as relatively reactive (proactive index < 0). Also, the figure shows that in most cases there is not a dominant pattern by industry; most of the organizations do not cluster by industry according to the value of their proactive index.

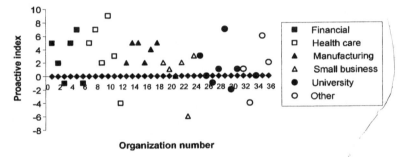

Note: The figure shows that most organizations viewed themselves are being proactive, with a few universities and in the financial service firms identifying reactive tendencies.

Figure 5.2   Distribution of interview responses, proactive versus reactive strategy, by industry group

However, by averaging the proactive index by industry group, some trends do appear. Table 5.11 shows the mean proactive index for each of the six broad industry groups. Universities and small businesses are relatively much less proactive than health care organizations, financial services firms or manufacturing businesses. Our Other category includes organizations that adhere to both more proactive and more reactive cyber security strategies.

Links between Information Sources and Proactive Strategies

Respondents indicated that a significant cost of adopting more proactive strategies was evaluating and testing new cyber security procedures and

Table 5.11 Mean proactive index, by industry group

Industry Groups	Mean Proactive
Financial	2.833
Health care	3.400
Manufacturing	3.833
Small business	0.333
University	0.200
Other	0.750

Note: On average the financial services, health care and manufacturing sectors indicated that they were the most proactive.

technologies. An organization's ability to obtain cost-effectively reliable information on the effectiveness of policies, procedures or new technologies influences its overall cyber security strategy. Based on this insight, it follows that industries that have more external public information available may pursue more proactive cyber security strategies. As a result, we looked for a correlation between an organization's proactive or reactive cyber security strategy and its reliance on external public information in its decision-making process.[8]

Table 5.12 shows the mean importance of external public resources for cyber security by industry group.[9] Health care organizations, financial service companies and manufacturing companies rely relatively heavily on external public resources. In contrast, universities and small businesses rely relatively little on external public resources.

Table 5.12 Mean external public resources, by industry group

Industry groups	Mean external public
Financial	1.333
Health care	1.600
Manufacturing	1.500
Small business	0.333
University	0.600
Other	1.000

Note: The financial services, health care and manufacturing sectors tended to rely the most on public sources of information.

Focusing on the use of external public resources and anticipating some of the policy conclusions in Chapter 12, Figure 5.3 shows the relationship between the proactive index and the use of external public information for cyber security resources.

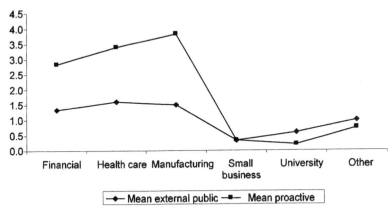

Note: In general, there is a discernable relationship between the use of public information resources and the more proactive the industry group.

Figure 5.3 Mean proactive index versus mean external public resources, by industry group (correlation coefficient = 0.93)

In general, there is a discernable relationship between the use of external public information resources and an increase in the proactive index of the industry group. While causation cannot be determined from Figure 5.3, our interview-based information suggests that causation does flow from informational sources to strategy adoption.

As the schematic in Figure 5.1 suggests, an organization's cyber security implementation strategy also influences dimensions of its investment decisions and the frequency of security breaches (about which no organization or company would discuss in any quantitative manner). Organizations were willing, however, as part of the interview process, to suggest the level of their cyber security investments as a percentage of their overall IT budget, as previously discussed. Some organizations were more precise about that percentage, while others were only willing to share that information in terms of a wide range of percentage values. We were nevertheless able to obtain an estimate of the percentage of the IT budget spent on cyber security.[10]

Figure 5.4 shows that there is a relationship between an industry group's spending on cyber security as a percentage of its IT budget, and its proactive strategy. It also shows that there is not a one-to-one relationship across the industry groups but, for example, small businesses, which are the least proactive, allocated the largest percentage of their IT budget to cyber security.

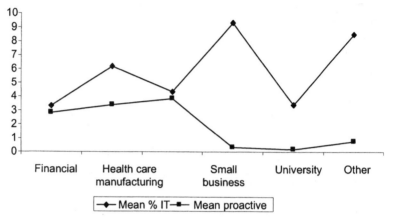

Note: The relationship between industry's mean % IT spending and the mean proactive index is not well defined.

Figure 5.4   Mean proactive index versus mean investment in cyber security, by industry group (correlation coefficient = – 0.42)

The matrix in Table 5.13 generalizes from the above findings in terms of a conceptual relationship between an organization's or company's proactive versus reactive cyber security strategy and its use of resources for cyber security.

This generalization, along with the interview information assembled, suggested that fewer IT resources are needed to achieve a secure IT environment in a proactive organization. This also suggests that from a policy perspective, public sector effort to decrease cyber security breaches could focus on increasing the availability and usability of public domain information.[11]

Table 5.13 Relative proactive versus reactive strategy by use of public and private external resources

	Reactive cyber security strategy	Proactive cyber security strategy
Use of external public resources for cyber security	Low	High
Use of external private resources for cyber security	High	Low

Note: In general, the use of external public resources tends to correlate with proactive strategies and the use of external private tends to correlate with reactive strategies.

Factors Influencing the Level of Cyber Security Investment

Based on interviewees' comments to the survey questions, discussions with numerous experts on cyber security trends and problems, and a review of the extant literature, we offer three hypotheses:

- *Hypothesis 1*: Organizations with structured cyber security budgeting processes will invest a larger share of their IT budget on cyber security.
- *Hypothesis 2*: Organizations that do not share security information will invest a larger share of their IT budget on cyber security.
- *Hypothesis 3*: Organizations that are more labor intensive in the creation of value will invest a larger share of their IT budget on cyber security.

The first hypothesis reflects our understanding of what takes place during a structured or systematic annual cyber security budgeting process. Such activities, within the organizations that we interviewed, are more deliberate and incorporate reasoned forecasts of security needs. These organizations are also relatively more proactive and anticipatory in their strategy toward cyber security.

Our second hypothesis comes directly from the theoretical analysis of Gordon (2003a), and postulates that companies that do not share information (and likely do not benefit from others' shared information) are less efficient and have spent a larger share of their IT budget on security. This follows logically from the theoretical and empirical literature related to efficiency gains in R&D from participation in research joint ventures (Hagedoorn et al., 2000; Hall et al., 2003).

Our final hypothesis reflects our understanding that many cyber security compromises originate internally from employees and that more labor-intensive industries (for example, financial services, health care and universities) may be impacted upon more heavily by cyber security problems. Thus, an organization with value being generated in a more labor-intensive way will require greater cyber security investments.

These hypotheses are tested using the following statistical model:

$$CSPct = f[Budget, ROIIRR, Emp, Coop, X] \qquad (5.1)$$

where: *CSPct* is the percentage of an organization's IT budget spent on cyber security in 2005; *Budget* is a binary variable equaling 1 if the organization has a structured process for deciding its annual cyber security budget and 0 if otherwise; *ROIIRR* is a binary variable equaling 1 if the organization employs either a quantitative return on investment (ROI) or internal rate of return (IRR) analysis when deciding to adopt new cyber security technology and 0 if otherwise; *Emp* equals the ratio of employment to sales; *Coop* is a binary variable equaling 1 if the organizations shares tracked security compromise information with other organizations and 0 if otherwise; and **X** is a vector of other organizational characteristics.[12]

Based on Hypothesis 1, our expectation is that the estimated coefficients on *Budget* and *ROIIRR* will be positive. Based on Hypothesis 2, our expectation is that the estimated coefficient on *Coop* will be negative. And based on Hypothesis 3, our expectation is that the estimated coefficient on *Emp* also will be positive. Fixed industry effects are accounted for in **X**.

The estimated ordinary least squares results from the model in equation (5.1) are in Table 5.14.[13] The results from the parsimonious specification in column (1) of the table confirm each of the three hypotheses.

Organizations with structured cyber security budgeting processes allocate a greater percentage of their IT budget to cyber security; the estimate coefficients on *Budget* and *ROIIRR* are positive and significant. Organizations that cooperate and share security information allocate less of their IT budget to cyber security; the estimated coefficient on *Coop* is negative and significant. Finally, organizations that are more labor-intensive also allocate a greater percentage of their IT budget to cyber security; the estimated coefficient on *Emp* is positive and significant. The overall fit of this specification is also significant.

Table 5.14 Ordinary least squares regression results, CSPct *dependent variable (t-statistics in parentheses)*

Variable	(1)	(2)	(3)
Budget	5.43	5.83	6.64
	(2.69)*	(3.03)*	(3.01)*
ROIIRR	3.09	3.08	2.79
	(1.82)***	(1.92)***	(1.40)
Emp	0.29	0.295	0.24
	(3.02)*	(3.26)*	(1.60)****
Coop	−4.31	−2.75	−2.79
	(−2.08)**	(−1.30)	(−1.25)
Service	—	−3.56	—
		(−2.04)**	
Financial	—	—	−3.26
			(−0.98)
Health care	—	—	−4.84
			(−1.30)
Manufacturing	—	—	−2.46
			(−0.74)
Small businesses	—	—	1.39
			(0.30)
Universities	—	—	−4.35
			(−1.10)
Intercept	−1.84	−0.73	−0.24
	(−0.85)	(−0.35)	(−0.07)
R^2	0.426	0.503	0.540
F-level	5.18*	5.45*	3.00*

Notes: * denotes significance at the 0.01 level; ** at the 0.05 level; *** at the 0.10 level; and **** at the 0.15 level.
'Other organizations' are captured in the intercept term in the specification in column (3).
Also note that each of our hypotheses is confirmed, to some degree, by the regression result.

The specification in column (2) includes a binary variable, *Service*, equal to 1 if the organization is a service organization (financial services, health care and universities) and 0 if otherwise. Its estimated coefficient is significant; service organizations allocate a smaller percentage of their IT budget to cyber security than do organizations in other industry groups.[14] However, *Service* is collinear with *Coop* and hence the significance of *Coop* declines although it remains negative as hypothesized.[15]

Finally, the specification in column (3) controls for the industry group of each organization. Little is gained from this more complete specification, and taken as a group, the industry variables are insignificant.

Although not hypothesized, we did include one additional binary variable in each of the three specifications that was equal to 1 if the organization's investment strategy is determined by the IT department, and 0 if determined by a management group. In no case was the estimated coefficient on this variable significant.

Caution should be exercised when generalizing from the results in Table 5.14, not only because of the small sample size but also because the statistical analysis is the first of its kind and there are no other studies for comparison purposes. That said, the findings do have organizational and public policy implications, which are explored below.

We assume that the actual level of investment in cyber security among the 36 organizations we interviewed are the optimal level given the information available to the organization; that is, these organizations are allocating resources rationally given their information set.[16] Our results therefore suggest, holding constant the level of compromises, that greater security information sharing among organizations, either individually or through consortia arrangements, increases internal security investment efficiency.[17]

We also consistently found a positive relationship between the structure of the investment decision-making process and the relative level of investment. This raises several issues, such as whether these investment decisions are made at the most appropriate organizational level (that is, IT versus management), and if so, whether traditional quantitative evaluation metrics are the most appropriate metrics to use for cyber security. On the one hand, many organizations today estimate such metrics to enable rough cost–benefit analyses; on the other hand, benchmarking information and standard guidelines could make that process more efficient.

While organizations view many dimensions of their cyber security process as proprietary and, as we found in this study, are reluctant to share investment information, companies that did not share information tended to allocate more of their IT budget to cyber security (possibly implying inefficiency). A broad-based confidential expenditure survey by a public sector or non-profit organization – perhaps patterned after the 'CSI/FBI Computer Crime and Security Survey' – could serve the public good by allowing benchmarking and analyses aimed at investigating the socially optimal level of cyber security investments. There is precedence that this can be done appropriately as evidenced, for example, by the Census

Bureau's handling of research and development (R&D) information collected on behalf of the National Science Foundation through its RD-1 reporting form.

And finally, our finding that more employee-intensive organizations allocate a greater proportion of the IT budget to cyber security suggests that there may be some internal security issues and concerns common across all industries. If so, then standardized protocols embedded within network support would benefit all organizations. And, if relevant information about such security needs could be assembled from organizations by a public infrastructure such as the NIST, such protocols could be updated on a timely basis.

CONCLUSIONS

Our descriptive analysis in this chapter provides what may be the first systematic empirical information on the investment and implementation strategies of organizations related to cyber security. Realizing the many caveats associated with any small-sample analysis – and viewing this analysis more as a template for future research than as prescriptive facts – several interesting relationships emerge that can cautiously inform the direction of public policy.

Of particular importance from the perspective of understanding investment and implementation strategies are the differences we discovered among organizations and across industry groups on the source of cyber security information relied upon and the relative importance of each source. Generally, organizations rely upon a mix of internal and external information sources. The availability and us vestment in this area. Thus, in the absence of reliable data, most (larger) organizations primarily relied on staff expertise and past experience to assess the vulnerabilities and the expected costs of security events.

Among the external sources, private sources are most important for hardware and software, as would be expected because those are proprietary products. However, there are obvious incentive issues associated with vendors being the primary source of information driving implementation decisions. This implies some role for the public sector in the development of common standard testing procedures to support unbiased comparisons of products and to verify product claims.

External public sources are most important in influencing security process and procedures. Publication by trade associations, the ISO and the

NIST provide best practice in complying with regulations and mitigating threats. Again this emphasizes a continued role for the public sector in gathering and disseminating sensitive information.

Of particular importance from the perspective of informing public policy is the relationship we suggest between organizations that rely on external public resources and the proactive nature of their cyber security strategy. Since pursuing a proactive strategy is likely to reduce computer system breaches, it follows that one important role for government is the provision of information on state-of-the-art technologies and procedures that promote proactive cyber security approaches.

NOTES

1. Research based on a report prepared for the Department of Homeland Security (Gallaher et al., 2006).
2. During interviews, all participants indicated that investments decisions involved IT staff and most had some upper-management involvement; however, all organizations were able to define their organization as making investment decisions in one framework more than the other.
3. Several organizations with cyber security budgets that did not come from their IT budget had to estimate how the cyber security budget compared to their IT budget. Further, small businesses obviously have very different IT budgets from those of other organizations that participated in our interviews. If we weight the responses based on company revenue (as a very rough weighting factor), we get an average of ~5.0 percent, which, as we would expect, is a slightly lower percentage than the total represented in Table 5.5.
4. The NIST has published more than 50 documents on a variety of security hardware, software, policies and procedures. See http://csrc.nist.gov/ publications/nistpubs/ index.html.
5. Hypothetically, if a respondent told us that NIST best practices documents (public external), customer suggestions or requirements (private external), and internal audits (internal) were the three most important resources, then that respondent's organization would have three informational indices with the following values: external public resources = 1, external private resources = 1, and internal resources = 1. If instead the respondent told us that vulnerability estimates from US CERT (public external), NIST best practices (public external), and ISO guidelines (public external) were the three most important resources, then that respondent's organization would have three information

indices with the following values: external public resources = 3, external private resources = 0, and internal resources = 0.

6. These figures are based strictly on participants in this study and should not be interpreted as statistically significant.

7. Theoretically, if an organization always adhered to a proactive strategy (score of 10) and never adhered to a reactive strategy (score of 1), we calculated a proactive index of 9 (10 − 1). Similarly, if an organization always adhered to a reactive strategy and never adhered to a proactive strategy, the proactive index was −9 (1 − 10). This proactive index is subjective in two ways. First, its construction is based on our interpretation of the respondent's characterization of the organization's cyber security investment strategy. Second, assuming consistency in this characterization, the index still reflects only one respondent's opinion; certainly, it is possible for other knowledgeable individuals within the organization to have differing opinions depending on the scope of their expertise in the cyber security area. Given these caveats, and given the extant literature on cyber security investments and strategies, we believe that its effort in this regard is the first to attempt to quantify this important dimension.

8. We compiled information on three types of information resources – internal, private external, and public external – and created an informational index for each.

9. A higher value implies that external public resources are utilized more by a certain industry group relative to other types of resources (external private and internal).

10. When reported as a range, the midpoint of the range was used in the analysis.

11. However, we also learned from its interviews that within an organization the optimal cyber security strategy is not totally proactive. Thus, in order to investigate a more statistically based conclusion, we used regression techniques to analyze our data.

12. Albeit a descriptive relationship in Figure 5.4, there is not a theoretical foundation for including a proactive/reactive variable in our model.

13. We present the ordinal least squares (OLS) results for ease of interpretation. Tobit is the theoretically correct estimation procedure because *CSPct* is a truncated variable; however, the distribution of *CSPct* has no observations clustered near either 0 percent or 100 percent and thus the implications of the OLS results are no different from the Tobit results (not reported but available upon request).

14. Note that the IT budgets of service organizations are likely larger than those of non-service organizations.

15. When *Coop* is deleted from this specification, the level of significance of the coefficient on *Service* increases.

16. Gordon and Loeb (2002) proffered a model for the optimal level of cyber security expenditure. Their model assumes a performance variable, such as potential loss from a compromise. Unfortunately, no performance information is in our dataset.

17. Infrastructures to facilitate security information sharing are conspicuously absent from the Cyber Security Research and Development Act, P.L. 107-305. The White House (2003) acknowledged government's role in cyber security when transaction costs related to prevention are high, and efforts such as PREDICT, which is intended to enable the sharing of computer transactions data, are helping in that regard. However, such more effort is needed. The transaction costs associated with intra-organization information sharing are indeed high because of the public-good nature of information per se.

6. Industry-Specific Cyber Security Investment Decisions

INTRODUCTION

In this chapter, we provide qualitative information on the investment processes of the five industry groups discussed in Chapter 5: financial services providers, health care providers, manufacturing companies, small businesses and universities. Based on our interviews, financial services providers and manufacturing companies have generally the same outlook on cyber security, aside from regulation-specific impacts. However, health care providers, small businesses and universities all have very unique challenges and perceive cyber security investment very differently.

Our discussion of each industry group parallels the cyber security investment model offered in Figure 5.1. In particular, we highlight important drivers and information resources by industry, as well as describing institutional, environmental and regulatory factors affecting cyber security investments.

We also discuss cyber security investment and implementation issues faced by electric utilities, ISPs and home users. Although very few members of these groups were surveyed, in-depth interviews were conducted to investigate their security decision processes.

FINANCIAL SERVICES

Although the financial services industry receives the third highest number of attacks, behind only the government and the manufacturing sector (IBM, 2005), several expert and industry interviews suggest that the level of security is not as high as the public might believe. The financial services industry includes banking, investment and insurance institutions, which have similar missions; however, small and medium-sized banks and credit unions operate very differently from national and multinational corporations.

We conducted interviews with banking institutions, insurance companies, investment firms and a Federal Reserve branch. We contacted 34 organizations, had informal discussions with 12 people and completed six survey interviews. Generally, the organizations with which we spoke had a similar focus and strategy related to cyber security; differences we observed seemed to be related to staff rather than to business differences. Compared to the other industries with which we spoke, financial companies viewed security as less important than both the performance of the network and convenience to users (internal non-IT staff). As one representative of a medium-sized local investment company commented, 'security always takes a backseat to business.' One US regional bank executive was very open about his past experience as an industry consultant. He indicated that his experience caused him to characterize much of the industry as making very inadequate cyber security investments. During his first six months in his current position, as CIO, he doubled the cyber security budget for his organization based on his consulting experience.

Drivers: Motivational Factors

All financial institutions with which we spoke indicated that regulations, specifically the Gramm–Leach–Bliley Act (GLB) and the Sarbanes–Oxley Act (SOX), had caused their cyber security budgets to increase and in many cases had forced company executives to give cyber security issues more attention. Some companies, however, who did not given adequate attention to compliance with regulations, have paid a price. For example, according to the Federal Trade Commission (FTC), which monitors compliance with the GLB, in August 2004 Nationwide Mortgage Group and Sunbelt Lending Services, Inc., were charged with failing to comply with GLB security requirements (FTC, 2004).

Furthermore, as of August 2007, 39 state laws have been passed that require organizations to inform consumers when their personal information might have been compromised (Consumers Union, 2006). Quite a few financial institutions have had breaches that required such disclosure.[1] As a result of both federal regulations and state disclosure laws, many financial institutions have begun to spend more money on cyber security, and many have recently created separate IT security departments.

Information Resources

Most financial institutions rely on qualitative information to make their investment decisions; however, most do track information on breaches and use of IT staff time. Several even try to track the value of attacks by a combination of IT staff hours, users' time and impacts on current and/or prospective client relationships. All financial institutions with which we have spoken track the effect on their network of an application going down because of a cyber security breach, whereas only two-thirds of other types of organizations track this information.

Although most members of the financial industry indicated that they do not provide any statistical data to consortia, they were among the most active organizations in providing information to a small peer group and/or participating in best practice sharing groups, such as the Financial Services Information Sharing and Analysis Center (FS-ISAC). However, one large insurance provider indicated that it is not a member of the FS-ISAC because of the $75 000 annual membership fee.

Additionally, the Gartner Group seemed to be a particularly important resource for decision makers in this industry. Several organizations mentioned Gartner as one of their most important resources for informing and shaping cyber security investment decisions. The chief information security officer (CISO) of a southeast US banking institution indicated that if Gartner recommends a certain technology solution, management always approves the solution.

Impact and Opinion of Regulations and Standards

As mentioned above, the GLB and the SOX have a significant impact on the relative level of security in the financial services industry. In most cases, people seem to believe that the impact of these regulations has been positive, though several mentioned a very high (and potentially inefficient) compliance cost. However, there was no consensus on how regulations could be improved. One respondent noted that regulations need to be more prescriptive, while another noted that the regulations should only be viewed as a baseline that should have been in place anyway.

HEALTH CARE PROVIDERS

The health care industry is an extremely diverse industry, including small urgent-care facilities, family medicine practices, large hospitals and other managed health care organizations. Based on the functional differences among these organizations, cyber security is managed in a variety of ways – some operate from one central IT security office, while others have separate cyber security divisions within each business unit or regional facility. Further, their routine security procedures can differ greatly. For instance, a small clinic and a large research hospital do not view cyber security in the same way; the large hospital likely has lots of data and a valuable reputation to protect and a broad base from which to draw resources to spend on cyber security, while the small clinic has limited resources and less regulatory pressure. Therefore, we focused on larger organizations and not small offices; we analyzed small medical, dentistry and optometry practices as part of our small businesses group.

We conducted extensive interviews with large health care providers, many with multiple branch offices and hospitals, and with the North Carolina Healthcare Information and Communications Alliance, Inc. (NCHICA), a health care industry group in North Carolina.[2] We contacted 29 organizations, held informal discussions with seven organizations and conducted six formal survey interviews. The health care facilities with which we spoke described their environments as very complex – hospital staff are involved in research, clinical and administration activities. Each of these environments requires very different IT capabilities, including a variety of different and likely non-interoperable hardware and software components.

Each hospital system with which we spoke coordinated its cyber security effort and investments both at the central level and at regional and branch offices. At the central level, the Chief Information Security Officer (or his equivalent) usually tells everyone on the network what applications they can have and what user polices should be in place. However, within the branch offices doctors often have make changes in these policies to fit their stated needs. Although overall budgeting and maintenance of the network backbone and associated cyber security problems was centralized in all organizations, some gave more or less control over cyber security spending and administration to regional and branch offices.

In one instance, the branch offices under a hospital system each had security officers who made decisions about cyber security staffing, certain user policies and tracking and spending activities. Although a central budget helped to pay for some access to and maintenance of the overall network, each office had its own cyber security staff and maintained its own hardware and software, including tracking of any problems. Alternately, other organizations kept control of all staff at a central office and interacted with branch offices when necessary.

In certain circumstances, we were told that security restrictions had been reduced in clinics and hospitals to enable the use of a certain piece of software or hardware needed for a medical procedure. One hospital system with which we spoke was owned solely by the physicians, and although security is not reduced because of complaints, cyber security staff must spend a significant amount of time explaining policies and procedures that might slow productivity.

Drivers: Motivational Factors

Unlike another type of company that might lose some business if its cyber security was too weak and the IT network shut down, or if its user policies were too restrictive and users could work as efficiently, each health care organization with which we spoke noted that a patient could die if a certain IT system were to fail or if cyber security policies impeded a certain procedure. Obviously this is an extreme impact example, but it illustrates that in the medical setting both overly weak and overly strong cyber security can result in very tangible costs. As a result, several organizations stated that they have different security requirements for administrative offices, clinical settings and operating rooms. For example, password protection of systems in operating rooms has been lifted because being locked out of a computer system in this setting could restrict emergency needs.

Still, regulations seem to be the main factor accounting for approximately 45 percent of health care providers reported motivation for the level of cyber security at each health care provider with which we spoke. Most participants felt as though regulations, the Health Insurance Portability and Accountability Act (HIPAA) in particular, gave them much more flexibility in their investments, policies and procedures – several organizations noted that if they cite HIPAA compliance as the reason for a new product or service, or for a policy or procedure change, it will be approved. One organization note that the HIPAA is based largely on NIST and ISO requirements, so if an organization is in compliance with these best practice standards, then compliance with HIPAA would be easy.

Information Resources

Many health care organizations try to conduct some data tracking and analysis, but only about half indicated that they track the hours spent by staff members. They all claimed to be conducting return on investment (ROI), internal rate of return (IRR) and/or cost–benefit calculations, but rarely performed any actual quantitative analysis of their cyber security spending either ex post or ex ante. Only a small percentage of projects were justified by looking at staff time savings.

Impact and Opinion of Regulations and Standards

As mentioned above, the HIPAA has had a significant impact on the security of health care organizations. In most cases, organizations believed that the impact had been positive, though excessive monetary resources had been used. Several organizations noted that prior to the passage of HIPAA into law they had been regulated by state laws directing their treatment of personally identifiable health information for five or more years, and in all cases we heard that these organizations had to have much stronger policies and procedures in place compared to the HIPAA. If a state has stronger laws than the HIPAA, the organizations within the state must comply with the more stringent standard.

Barriers to Adoption and Potential Solutions

Hospitals mentioned a large number of barriers to adoption as compared to other organizations with which we spoke. In particular, doctors are worried about the negative effect of cyber security policies and procedures on patient care, and this has affected the level of cyber security maintained by some organizations. However, hospitals also indicated that they receive the most support of any industry for their cyber security investment needs.

MANUFACTURING COMPANIES

Manufacturing companies are actively cutting costs through supply chain integration and just-in-time supply delivery; however, according to organizations with which we spoke, increased reliance on electronic business communications and reduced inventories have increased the cost of cyber security events. The organizations included semiconductor manufacturers, conglomerates with electronics and health care products and pharmaceutical firms.

We had informal discussions with eight companies, and conducted formal survey interviews with an additional six companies. Generally, the organizations we interviewed had a similar focus and strategy related to cyber security; differences we observed seemed to be related to general organizational changes (for example, mergers and acquisitions). As compared to the other industries we interviewed, manufacturing firms viewed security as necessary for business.

Drivers: Motivational Factors

All manufacturing companies indicated that regulations, specifically the SOX, had caused their cyber security budgets to increase and, in many cases, had forced company executives to give cyber security issues more attention. Specifically, pharmaceutical firms face a large variety of regulations; in addition to SOX, they must comply with regulations from both the US Department of Agriculture (USDA) and US Food and Drug Administration (FDA) many of which have implications for their cyber security policies, procedures and solutions.

As indicated above, customer and supplier relationships are a major driver, affecting the level of cyber security maintained by many manufacturers. In several cases, companies told us that they were forced to improve security measures to conduct business with suppliers and customers.

Information Resources

Aside from small businesses, manufacturers listen to vendors more than any other industry when deciding on the hardware and software in which they should invest. Furthermore, when deciding on their cyber security staff procedures and, to a lesser extent, their user policies, manufacturers relied heavily on external public resources. Several organizations mentioned participating in various consortia, including the Federal Bureau of Investigation (FBI)'s InfraGard program and Forrester's Security Risk Management Council, and one organization noted significant information and data sharing with key clients and partners.

Interestingly, the manufacturing industry also collected less information about breaches than any other group. Although a majority of the organizations tracked the number of breaches, almost one-third did not, and only one organization tracked information on the effect specific breaches had on users and the cyber security staff. Organizations indicated that they did not see the need for tracking such information because in most instances impacts on manufacturing processes were minimal.

Impact and Opinion of Regulations and Standards

As mentioned above, the SOX has had a significant impact on the relative level of security in the manufacturing industry. In most cases, companies believe that the impact of these regulations has been positive, although several people mentioned the high compliance cost. Others indicated, however, that that SOX did not require very robust security measures and, aside from the necessary paperwork, has almost no associated compliance costs.[3]

For some organizations, additional regulations, including certain FDA and the USDA regulations and sections of the Patriot Act, have an impact on cyber security investment and implementation strategies. As in other industries, organizations dealing with multiple regulatory requirements found compliance to be very difficult.

UNIVERSITIES

Universities (and colleges) have the least-stringent cyber security user policies and overall investment strategies of any group with which we spoke. University networks are used by a variety of different types of users – university staff members, faculty performing research and students – and each group has unique needs. Universities desire open networks for researchers and students to develop new ideas and to communicate freely. State and federal regulations (for example, the Federal Information Rights and Privacy Act, or FIRPA) also restrict their ability to monitor student online activity. To employ different security guidelines effectively for different user groups, one university identified 20 different security zones on its campus, with each zone having its own set of unique security policies and procedures.

To complicate network security administration further, the user communities, particularly the student population, are a very dynamic group. Each year, approximately one-quarter of the student population leaves the network and a new group of students enter; these new students usually have a much lower level of knowledge of security than those leaving, so frequent training must occur. One university indicated that it spends a substantial amount of money on training students and faculty on security policies.

We contacted 15 universities, including a mixture of private and public institutions; had informal discussions with nine universities; and conducted seven formal survey interviews. All of the cyber security administrators with whom we spoke worked within their university's IT department, and they received a share of the IT budget. Although each organization invested in cyber security mechanisms that had relatively little effect on network performance and user convenience, the organizations had very different investment strategies.

Technically, some universities with which we spoke did not have a firewall; however, most believed the networks were still very safe. Several universities were working under an end-to-end security framework – applications had security built in and did not rely on network-level security. However, many vendors' products do not have built-in security, so organizations that followed this strategy developed more applications internally or negotiated with vendors to develop more robust internal security for their products.

Drivers: Motivational Factors

Depending on the make-up of the university, many regulations may have an impact on the level of security. Most have felt some effect from the HIPAA and the FIRPA, as well as requirements from Visa for e-commerce activities and the GLB for accounting activities. Additionally, some universities had medical schools and veterinary schools that caused them to face more stringent HIPAA requirements, as well as USDA and FDA regulations. And, if any faculty were conducting research for the Department of Homeland Security, universities faced additional regulations. The result was a multitude of different regulations affecting the way cyber security technologies, policies and procedures were maintained, as well as extensive reporting to prove compliance. In some states, additional regulations and/or state government budgeting also affects the level of security maintained by public universities.

Universities also considered current events (that is, reported breaches) to be a significant motivation for cyber security investments. More than any other group, universities indicated that security breaches in the media or reported through various government and non-profit data collection organizations caused them to react by changing their investment strategy, for example by creating different technology solutions, polices or procedures.

Information Resources

Universities are more reliant on internal private resources than any other group. In particular, they use their staff experience and internally collected data to inform their implementation strategies. In our interviews, half of the organizations commented that they believed they hired the best cyber security staff in the industry, many educated by their institutions, and that their staff were very proud of the experience and skills they maintained. Universities seemed very hesitant to talk about any need for additional information.

Furthermore, this group, on average, conducted more quantitative data analysis than the other stakeholder groups. Universities attempted to assign relative importance to attack types and security solutions and to plan their spending accordingly. However, very few tracked cyber security staff time and user time spent resolving breaches or on any proactive security activities. As such, they are likely to be underestimating costs.

Barriers to Adoption and Potential Solutions

Universities face more explicit barriers than most other groups, although on average they were more confident in the effectiveness of their cyber security activities. As discussed previously, in many cases universities are restricted by a large number of state and federal regulations and they must deal with a very diverse user community. Furthermore, because they are motivated by the idea of academic freedom, they are pushed by all groups to allow maximum network performance and minimize user inconvenience; these pressures often restrict their ability to implement robust cyber security solutions and mandate strong user policies.

SMALL BUSINESSES

We generally focused on small businesses that had a particular interest in the integrity of their data because of potential reputational (that is, potential loss of business) or legal (for example, regulatory) effects. Thus, we talked with law firms, optometry offices, pharmacies, dentist surgeries, small software companies and accounting firms. We had informal discussions with eight organizations, and conducted six formal interviews. Each organization shared a focus on the bottom line as the main driver for any internal investment decisions, particularly preventative spending, such as the costs associated with proactive cyber security activities. However, each organization approached cyber security a little differently and had a unique set of issues to address. Investment decisions are generally made by the owner(s) or senior managers within the organization. In some cases, one staff member with some interest in IT issues was designated to oversee the IT network, but the investment decisions still needed approval from senior management. Usually cyber security recommendations were made by an outside contractor who had been hired to install and maintain the IT network, including cyber security hardware and software, for the business.

The contractors were generally able to justify a basic level of cyber security measures (for example, antivirus software and firewalls); however, it seemed to be a common concern of these consultants that it was difficult to convince clients to purchase more powerful (and costly) cyber security software and hardware. Although consultants were obviously interested in encouraging organizations to spend more money to improve their profits, the organizational approval structures seemed to have some flaws.

In one law firm, for example, we were told that budget resources determined that a decision had to be made between buying more computers or and improving the network cyber security. However, we learned that money not spent on either became part of the partners' annual bonuses, so they had a personal incentive not to spend too much. The security investment was one lump sum, whereas the computers could be purchased individually; as such, the company purchased several computers and decided against additional security. We found that without quantitative measures available to justify additional spending, cyber security spending often became a lower priority in most of the small businesses with which we spoke.

One small business, a dentistry firm, had a different perspective on cyber security. The dentists owned two offices and had a network between the offices. They viewed investing in IT and the associated security as essential for the success of their business. These dentists structured patient interaction so that IT was critical to service (that is, each patient area had a computer system and monitor that displayed records, including X-rays); when the network was down, they essentially could not work. Thus, they were willing to spend extra money on cyber security to ensure network performance and data integrity.

Drivers: Motivational Factors

Of the factors affecting small businesses' level of cyber security, our interviews suggested that external management (for example, hiring a firm to install and maintain cyber security components) accounted for the majority of the basis for the cyber security measures maintained by these businesses. Despite the hierarchical restrictions that seemed to dampen spending on cyber security, when asked to rank a list of factors that influenced the decision on whether to adopt a new security measure or implement a new user policy or cyber security administrator procedure, surprisingly only the law firm ranked immediate cost and total cost of ownership first and second out of six possible choices.

In contrast, the two dentists' offices responded that the potential to improve cyber security staff productivity and the ability to improve network security were the most important factors in deciding whether to adopt a new security measure or to implement a new user policy or cyber security administrator procedure. Generally, however, cost was much more of a concern for small businesses than any other industry group we studied.

Information Resources

Small businesses paid particular attention to vendors and consultants because these were the most accessible resources. In most cases, small businesses do not hire full-time IT staff, so they must rely on contractors, other consultants and vendors' suggestions to decide what cyber security measures would be the most helpful and what vendors to select.

Contractors were the main influence on small businesses' decisions of what cyber security procedures and user policies should be in place. Contractors also used NIST best practice documents and regulatory guidelines (for example, the HIPAA). In a few cases, contractors collected data about a network, including the number of past compromises and associated costs to assess the best policies and procedures to employ. Rarely do small businesses track their resource allocation (for example, staff hours spent on specific proactive and reactive activities).

The small businesses with which we spoke were not using any quantitative techniques to justify cyber security investments. Although some were collecting data on the number of security events and incidents, the cyber security staff time needed to resolve the breaches, and the user time needed to resolve them, this information was most often used qualitatively. To justify spending, they assessed their needs based on past spending, current threats and amount of money available, the latter being the most important.

Although the US Small Business Administration, the NIST and the FBI work together in an effort to provide small businesses with resources to help them set up and maintain cyber security, it seems that few small businesses know about this information, and even fewer are able to use more than online documentation. Most of the workshops are only offered in larger cities to which many small businesses cannot travel easily, and online information is very general.

Some small businesses do use resources provided by industry associations. However, these seem largely to be in the health care industry. For example, the American Dental Association (ADA), to which four out of five dentists in the United States are members, provides cyber security information in the form of how-to CDs and booklets. Both dentists with whom we spoke indicated that they had consulted these resources.

Impact and Opinion of Regulations and Standards

Many of the small businesses with which we spoke, including an optometry office, a pharmacy and a dentist, were affected by the HIPAA because they worked with individual health care data. In general, they had to spend some money on compliance (in several cases, outsourcing the development of necessary changes), but they did not find the HIPAA to be overly burdensome. One dentists' office indicated that it would not have had any more security without the HIPAA than it did with the HIPAA, though it would have had less paperwork. Another dentists' office agreed that the HIPAA had had a positive impact on the cyber security of health information.

Most small businesses, including the law firm and software firms, are not currently affected by government regulations dictating cyber security requirements. Except for the HIPAA, no other regulation has reached into the small business arena.

Other Industry Factors

Customer and supplier relationships have an effect on the cyber security of small businesses. One dentists' office noted that vendors supplying electronic claims services required it to increase cyber security by implementing specialized equipment. Presumably, this increased the level of cyber security. Furthermore, the pharmacy with which we spoke is strengthening its cyber security in anticipation of an increase in online prescription requests and renewal services over the next several years.

As with other industries, the level of cyber security in small businesses is very dependent on the knowledge and expertise of the IT staff, or in many cases, the consultants controlling the level of cyber security. Unfortunately, businesses often do not have the resources to identify or pay highly skilled contract workers or an experienced in-house IT person. Although we did not attempt to assess the level of cyber security of each organization, it is likely that small businesses have a reduced level of expertise in cyber security when compared to larger organizations.

Barriers to Adoption and Potential Solutions

Small businesses in general do not feel as though they are in great danger from cyber security breaches; however, they also do not have the information necessary to make good investment decisions. They are budget-constrained more than any other group, and subsequently, they do not believe they have the resources necessary to invest their resources efficiently.

OTHER ORGANIZATIONS

In addition to the five specific industry groups focused on, we investigated cyber security investments within several additional industry groups that help to support the digital infrastructure of our country, namely, electric utilities and Internet service providers (ISPs). These two groups are faced with significant challenges for a variety of reasons, and currently are both under extreme pressure to increase their level of cyber security. In this section, we briefly introduce some of the problems specific to each of these two industry groups. We also surveyed and interviewed a very small number of home users; the results from this data collection are discussed below.

Electric Utilities

During the 1980s and 1990s, growth in the US transmission and distribution (T&D) system has not kept pace with the growth in electricity demand. As a result, system monitoring and real-time control have become increasingly important as capacity reserve margins have been lowered to increase system utilization. Network security is essential for the electric utility system because of the cascading nature and extremely high cost of power outages. Outage costs to utility customers can be severe, and utilities have been criticized for not making the appropriate investments to offset these costs.[4]

Based on our interviews, electric utilities have been under an extreme amount of pressure to improve their cyber security infrastructure, including the threat of government regulations. In the past, electric utilities have been able to impose their own restrictions and requirements through a self-regulatory body, the North American Electric Reliability Council (NERC). Since the passage several years ago of the NERC's Standard 1200 on cyber security, electric utilities have been 'regulated' to maintain a certain level of cyber security activity. This standard has provided a high-level and relatively non-restrictive approach to cyber security activities.

Following the major blackout in the northeastern United States in 2003 – which was liked to a software bug[5] – and possibly as a response to potential government regulation, NERC began crafting a much more restrictive set of regulations, NERC Standard CIP–002–1. According to the two electric utilities we interviewed, this new set of regulations, which has yet to be implemented, will impose a substantial cost on the industry.[6] There seemed to be significant concern about whether some electric utilities would need to request government assistance or to increase billing rates to implement the new infrastructure and procedures. Furthermore, our interviews indicated that these new regulations are causing widespread organizational restructuring; thus, cyber security investment and implementation strategies will probably look very different in the near future.

Internet Service Providers

ISPs include telecommunications companies that provide telephone service and connectivity to the Internet directly to customers. The maintenance, and hence the security, of the connections that these companies monitor and service is vital for each company to remain competitive. However, as a critical piece of the US infrastructure, this maintenance is an important issue for society as a whole. Specifically, the security of an ISP's networks can directly influence the security of its customers' networks. These companies should have significant private motivations to maintain security networks; however, they may not bear the full costs of cyber security events that also affect their customers.

We were only able to interview two ISPs, and only one participated in a formal interview; however, we also spoke with individuals at the

Information Technology Information Sharing and Analysis Center (IT-ISAC), and other experts provided information on the security investments made by ISPs. One key issue that arose was that in many cases, ISPs are required by contracts to provide substantial security measures to help their business customers comply with regulations.

More recently, there has been a push for ISPs to take a more active role in providing security to their customers. By serving as the pipeline for Internet traffic, large ISPs have the ability to detect many types of traffic that could be security attacks and to stop the more obvious traffic rather than allowing it to continue; however, this line is blurry. Several studies (for example, Evers, 2005) and well-known experts[7] have suggested that ISPs may be in the best position to cost-effectively prevent certain types of malicious behavior, such as the operation of botnets. Some have suggested using government regulations to force ISPs to take action (for example, McCullagh, 2005), others believe that the legal system should hold them accountable (Lichtman and Posner, 2004), and one recent study advocated for a certifying authority to incentivize ISPs to prevent outbound malicious traffic (Parameswaran et al., 2007). In support of these positions, models exist in the literature that attempt to address the economic incentives and disincentives for ISPs to provide increased security (Chen et al., 2004). However, these models are theoretical in nature and conclude with recommendations for further investigation of stakeholder relationships and other issues related to model specification and parameter estimation. In Chapters 7 and 12 we discuss potential recommendations for government action.

Home Users

In addition to investigating the cyber security investment decisions made by a variety of private and non-profit organizations, we conducted interviews with nine home users who subscribe to either cable modem or digital subscribe line (DSL) Internet service. In general, what we found was that the level of security maintained by users primarily depends on what the personal computer (PC) maker provides to people who purchase their computers (approximately 85 percent cited this as their top driver). Furthermore, we found that in response to a security problem, most home users (approximately 70 percent) have either purchased additional security products, downloaded free shareware security programs or hired a consultant.

To determine the implementation strategy (that is, what solutions to adopt) for cyber security, home users relied on a variety of resources, but virtually all of the respondents indicated that they did not feel comfortable with their level of understanding of security problems or potential solutions. Many initially relied on what was provided when they purchased their computers. However, over half of the individuals with whom we spoke also relied on a friend or colleague to help them decide on any additional security hardware or software to install on their computers and/or to learn about security procedures (that is, how to configure a router to be more secure) they should use.

We also asked home users to describe the amount of time and money they spend each year on cyber security products or services, excluding any products that include security components (for example, routers or operating systems). When we asked about spending habits, we found that more than 50 percent spend less than $20 per year, while the remainder spend from $21 to $80 per year. As for time spent on security issues (for example, installing patches, running debugging programs), one-third spent two hours or less per year, one-third spent between two and ten hours per year, and a full one-third spent more than ten hours per year (some up to 30 hours per year).

During our interviews, we asked whether people viewed themselves as being secure on a scale from 1 to 10, and the average response was 7.1. This indicates that home users generally feel that they are secure. However, when we discussed what information they might lose in a breach, many indicated that they do not keep personal information on their computer.

To gauge their relative willingness to pay for security, we asked participants whether they would pay their ISP to provide increased security options. More than half indicated that they would be willing to pay 10 percent more than their normal ISP monthly service rate for additional security, although only 15 percent would pay 25 percent more.

CONCLUSIONS

Financial service providers and manufacturing companies have similar outlooks on cyber security in that organizations in both industries are guided by regulations; the GLB and the SOX specifically. Drivers in other industry groups vary; HIPPA affects the health care industry, while FIRPA affects universities. No single regulation or compliance criterion influences the cyber security behavior of all organizations.

Because of the distributed nature of the Internet, no central organization or stakeholder group has the proper incentive to ensure security of the network as a whole. An increased role by Internet service providers (ISPs) has been proposed as a potential technically feasible and cost-effective means of increasing overall Internet security. In particular, ISPs could help to increase the security level of small businesses and home users, whose computers are often used by hackers to conduct illicit activities. However, given the current structure of the market, viable business models for ISP-based security solutions have not made materialized such service pervasive.

Many ISPs today offer customers 'fully external' products and services; for example, some ISPs (for instance, AOL) give users antivirus software and directions on setting up firewalls, but in most cases users are left to install and operate such mechanisms on their own.[8] In some cases, ISPs do offer 'fully internal' services to business users,[9] and several ISPs offer 'partially internal and partially external' services to home users and small business users.[10] However, small businesses are not being offered fully internal services, and partially internal/partially external services are not commonly offered.

In order to assess relevant public policy options – that is, whether government should help motivate ISPs to provide security – there is a need to investigate (1) the cost-effectiveness of potential ISP solutions, (2) the potential impact of widespread adoption of such solutions by ISPs on overall Internet security and (3) users' (large and small) willingness to pay (WTP) to improve the 'weakest link' security of home users and small businesses.

NOTES

1. See Privacy Rights Clearinghouse list of breaches at http://www.privacyrights. org/ar/ChronDataBreaches.htm.

2. The NCHICA coordinates a health care industry working group and had placed significant importance on several groups addressing security and privacy issues. One particularly important result of this work was a document that providers could give to vendors to convey their security requirements easily. See the NCHICA's website at http://www.nchica. org.

3. These companies usually had robust security programs in place prior to SOX, and thus were relatively unaffected by the regulation.

4. Significant research has analyzed the vulnerability of the electric utilities infrastructure to cyber attack, and recently the Department of Homeland Security staged a fake cyber attack that suggested major costs could result from a cyber attack (CNN, 2007).

5. A 2004 AP story distributed by CNN (http://www.cnn.com/2004/ US/Northeast/02/13/blackout.ap/) states that a software bug was likely responsible for the blackout in the Northeast.

6. NERC Standard CIP-002-1 is available at ftp://www.nerc.com/ pub/sys/all_updl/standards/rs/CIP-002-1.pdf. An analysis of the impact of the new NERC standard was published in the spring 2007 edition of *IT Compliance Magazine* (Stanton, 2007) and is available at http://www.itcompliancemagazine .com/best-practice-from-the-practitioner-8.html.

7. Bruce Schneier, a security expert and Chief Technology Officer at managed security services company BT Counterpane, has stated at several conferences and in interviews over the last couple of years months that he believes that ISPs are in the best position to make home computers more secure (FIRST, 2006). He believes that software vendors and ISPs should be the sole providers of security as part of their products and services, relieving small and large network users from having to think about security (Richards, 2007). Schneier also wrote about this on his blog in May 2007 at http://www.schneier.com/ blog/archives/2007/05/do_we_really_ne.html.

8. For the last year, AOL offered a service called Active Virus Shield, but privacy advocates criticized AOL's licensing arraignments with this program, that allowed them to send spam or install adware on users' computers. Recently, AOL stopped offering Active Virus Shield; they formed a partnership with McAfee and now offer AOL customers free McAfee software (see http://news.yahoo.com/s/infoworld/ 20070809/tc_infoworld/90879).

   Of note, in 2005 a study labelled AOL as the ISP from which the most zombie PCs cause havoc of any ISP in the world (Keizer, 2005). AOL responded by noting that as a percentage of their customers, the number of zombie computer on their network – 0.54 percent per million – was below those of Comcast (1.44 percent per million) and Verizon (1.9 percent per million).

9. Chen et al. (2004) mention that AT&T offers such services.

10. In a much less technically difficult solution, EarthLink puts the onus on their customers. They force customers to 'approve' all incoming message senders before messages can get through without filtering. This is not error proof, because a spammer could send email from a known address and it would get through.

7. Cyber Security as a Public Good: Toward Public Policy Recommendations

INTRODUCTION

Throughout the first six chapters we describe the components of cyber security that have public-goods characteristics, such as information availability and spillover benefits and costs (externalities). In this chapter we present a more formal discussion of the concept of public goods as they relate to cyber security. These concepts provide the foundation for motivating government involvement, which we describe in several forms in the four case studies presented in Chapters 8 to 11, as well as for the public policy discussions and recommendations presented in Chapter 12.

Economic theory holds than an organization will evaluate its optimal level of cyber security investment by equating the marginal benefit that it receives from an additional 'unit' of cyber security with the marginal cost of achieving that 'unit'. However, because of the public-goods nature of information per se, and of cyber security information in particular, an organization will underinvest in cyber security. This investment decision is rational from the perspective of the organization, because it can neither appropriate all of the benefits that additional investments generate, nor does it bear all of the costs associated with a computer breach that occurs in the absence of such additional investment.

We learned from our interviews, which were summarized in Chapters 5 and 6, that there are at least two barriers that lead to organizations not investing in the socially desirable level of cyber security. These barriers are also referred to as market failures and include: (1) limited reliable, cost-effective information upon which an organization can make informed cyber security investment decisions; and (2) the cost externalities that spill over to other organizations and to consumers as a result of a security breach. As a result, any cyber security investment that an organization makes, particularly of a proactive nature, will likely generate social benefits in excess of private benefits. Thus, government would like to encourage such investments by removing or lessening such barriers. For example, as suggested in Chapter 5, external public information is likely to motivate the adoption and implementation of proactive cyber security investment strategies.

GOVERNMENT'S ROLE TO ENHANCE PRIVATE INVESTMENTS IN CYBER SECURITY

Government's role to enhance private investments in cyber security is to remove or lessen the barriers that cause organizations to underinvest in cyber security from a social perspective. We illustrate this below, using two related models of the social benefits that will occur with government support, the specifics of which are discussed in the following section.

Figure 7.1 illustrates a firm's investment decision-making process. On the vertical axis is the firm's marginal rate of return on investments in cyber security, and on the horizontal axis are alternative investment levels. The organization will invest at level I_0, where the marginal private return from that investment equals the marginal private cost. However, society would like this firm to increase its investment in cyber security from I_0 to I_1 because I_1 is the investment level corresponding to marginal social benefits. The marginal social benefit is greater than the marginal private return because other firms will benefit (at no cost to themselves) from the investing firm's actions.

For the firm to do this, its marginal private cost must decrease. If the government could provide support – and we will define 'support' in the following section – to lower marginal private costs to the point where the new marginal private cost schedule intersects the marginal private return schedule, at I_1, then this socially desirable level of investment, I_1, will be undertaken by the firm.

Alternatively, consider Figure 7.2. This figure is not at odds with the implications from Figure 7.1. Rather, it illustrates the risk reduction to the firm from the government support that would lower private marginal cost in Figure 7.1.

Figure 7.2 illustrates two distributions of the rate of return from investments in cyber security.[1] The distribution on the left is the firm's existing expected distribution of return to investments in cyber security; it is

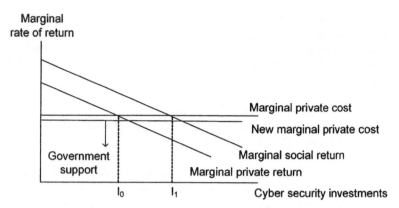

Figure 7.1 Decision model of private investment in cyber security

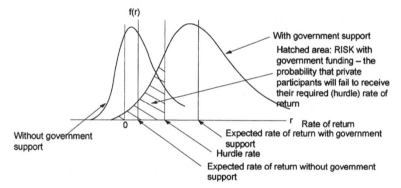

Figure 7.2 Private risk reduction from government support of cyber security

labeled 'without government support'. The distribution on the right is the one that would exist if there were government support; it is labeled 'with government support'. As drawn, with government support the expected private rate of return and the variance in the private rate of return from a cyber security investment project will increase.[2]

Consider the left distribution, the distribution labeled 'without government support'. The risk of the project equals the area under the 'without government support' distribution that is to the left of the firm's private hurdle rate.[3] As drawn, the private hurdle rate is to the right of the expected rate of return meaning that the organization will not undertake this cyber security investment project because it is not expected to realize sufficient revenue to make the investment profitable; or restated, the risk is too high.

Now, consider the right distribution – the distribution of the rate of return for the private firm with government support. With government support, the private organization's expected return is greater than its hurdle rate – the expected private rate of return with government support is the area to the right of the private hurdle rate. While government support will not increase the probability that the project will be successful, it will reduce private risk by increasing the expected private rate (due to the smaller investment needed by the firm). Hence, government support leverages the private firm's investment as illustrated by a greater expected return and a greater variance in the distribution as explained above.

The hatched area in Figure 7.2 is what is called the downside risk of an investment project. It is the probability that the project will yield a rate of return less than the private hurdle rate even with government support. Hence, the amount of downside risk with government support is visually less than the downside risk associated with the project in the case of no government support. The result is that more investment projects are undertaken by the private sector. Obviously the government needs to assess carefully the level of subsidies to provide to the private sector or it may end up incentivizing investments that are even too risky from a social perspective.

GOVERNMENTAL TOOLS TO SUPPORT PRIVATE INVESTMENTS IN CYBER SECURITY

The conceptual role of government support of private investment in cyber security for the social good was illustrated above. Here specific tools are proffered for the government to accomplish this goal.

The government could help to fund the collection, analysis and dissemination of both reliable and cost-effective information related to cyber security. Figure 4.4 illustrated how lowering the cost of information incentivized proactive measures and increased the overall social level of security. Although many trade associations and industry consortia attempt to provide such services, few do so in a product-comparative manner.[4] Furthermore, evaluating the effectiveness and efficiency of potential cyber security solutions is a complex and costly activity. In many instances, the taxonomy and metrics do not readily exist to facilitate comparisons of competing technologies. However, there is already a mechanism in place to underwrite the creation and dissemination of information; it is called the Cyber Security Research and Development Act of 2002 (Public Law 107-305).

The Act states:

Computer security technology and systems implementations lack –

(A)   sufficient long term research funding;
(B)   adequate coordination across Federal and State government agencies and among government, academia and industry; and
(C)   sufficient numbers of outstanding researchers in the field. Accordingly, Federal investment in computer and network security research and development must be significantly increased to –
(A)   improve vulnerability assessment and technological system solutions;
(B)   expand and improve the pool of information security professionals, including researchers, in the United States workforce; and
(C)   better coordinate information sharing [emphasis added] and collaboration among industry, government and academic research projects.

To operationalize this Act, funds are authorized for the National Science Foundation to meet the above goals.

Equally important as these direct funds are the indirect activities established by the Act. The Act amended the National Institute of Standards and Technology Act (15 U.S.C. 271 et seq.) 'to establish a program of assistance to institutions of higher education that enter into partnerships with for-profit entities to support research to improve the security of computer systems'. The Act also authorized the NIST 'to identify emerging issues, including research needs, related to computer security, privacy and cryptography'.

Another possibility is that the government could underwrite the research and implementation costs for organizations that are pilot-testing new innovations. This direct approach might increase private investments in innovative cyber security strategies, shifting investment toward the socially optimal proactive level (that is, toward I_1 in Figure 7.1).[5]

Related to security breach costs that spill over through the network (to other organizations and to consumers), a potential role for government is to design mechanisms that redistribute costs to provide better incentives for organizations to enhance their cyber security. Examples of this could include regulations that define activities or security thresholds that must be met, much like a uniform standard that is a common regulation to control water pollution. In particular, government could push ISPs to regulate their networks more by providing filtering and other security activities; Chapter 12 will discuss this in more detail.

The associated threat of litigation from being out of compliance or causing damage to a second party is another way to make private organizations bear the social costs of security breaches. The private sector also engages in similar activities by requiring suppliers and partners to meet cyber security requirements and conduct regular security audits. Outsourced firms often help them to help them to meet such requirements, which serve to help with regulatory compliance. Government could possibly help to support the outsourcing of security, which could lead to a higher social level of security; Chapter 12 also discusses this further.

Both new regulations and more legal pressure in the form of lawsuits by parties seeking damages from the insecurity of other firms could help to internalize cost externalities so that organizations have the proper incentives when evaluating cyber security investments.

CONCLUSIONS

While public policies have been enacted that take the form of government support needed to increase private organization's investments in cyber security, no systematic evaluation of those policies *in toto* has been conducted to the best of our knowledge. The public policies associated with the Cyber Security Research and Development Act are nonetheless precisely the types of polices that would support the conceptual models proffered in this chapter.

The following four chapters discuss four projects undertaken at the NIST that are related to cyber security, and each is evaluated from a social perspective. The NIST is an appropriate federal laboratory to implement the public policies discussed above since its mission is directly linked to the provision of technology infrastructures that have public-good characteristics.[6]

NOTES

1. This model draws directly from Link and Scott (2001).
2. It will always be the case that the expected private rate of return and the variance will increase. The expected private rate of return with government support (quantified in dollar terms) is: $r = [return - (total\ investment\ cost - government\ support)]\ /\ [total\ investment\ cost - government\ support]$. Let $Z = (total\ investment\ cost - government\ support)$. Then $r = [(return - Z)\ /\ Z] = [(return\ /\ Z) - 1]$. The variance of r is: $[(1\ /\ Z)^2 Var(return)]$, and it is a general proposition that as government support increases (and hence as Z decreases) the variance in the private return increases (since $(1\ /\ Z)$ increases). It is also a general proposition that the expected private rate of return $= E[(return)\ /\ Z - 1]$ must increase for the same reason. Further, neither the expected social rate of return nor the variance in the social rate of return change at all. The social cost and the social return are the same.
3. Some may think of the variance of the distribution as the measure of risk, thus the downside risk – the probability of a rate of return less than the hurdle rate – may seem unusual. Variance measures the possibility that the outcomes differ from the expected outcome, while the downside risk measures the probability of an outcome departing to the downside of the hurdle rate. Note that the technical risk and market risk of the project are reflected in the variance of the distribution.
4. There is indirect evidence that companies, on their own, will not cooperate in the creation and distribution of IT-related technologies, and research cooperation may be a relevant first step to collective cyber security information sharing. Here, government has a role. To illustrate the dearth of IT information sharing, consider the revealed implication of the National Cooperative Research Act (NCRA) of 1984.

    The NCRA of 1984, Public Law 98-462, was legislated, as stated in the Preamble to the Act: 'to promote research and development, encourage innovation, stimulate trade, and make necessary and appropriate modifications in the operation of the antitrust laws'.

    While the Act sets forth these objectives, it does not place them in a historical perspective. In the early 1980s there was growing concern that the US industrial sector was losing its competitive advantage in global markets. This was explicitly noted in the Research and Development Joint Venture Act of 1983, HR 4043. In the Joint Research and Development Act of 1984, HR 5041, the supposed benefits of joint research and development were first articulated from a policy perspective: 'Joint research and development, as our foreign competitors have learned, can be pro-competitive. It can reduce duplication, promote the efficient use of scarce technical personnel, and help to achieve desirable economies of scale [in R&D]'. After revisions, the NCRA of 1984 was passed.

The NCRA of 1984 created a registration process, later expanded by the National Cooperative Research and Production Act (NCRPA) of 1993 and the Standards Development Organization Advancement Act of 2004 (SDOAA), under which research joint ventures (RJVs) can voluntarily disclose their research intentions to the US Department of Justice (DoJ); all disclosures are made public in the *Federal Register*. An RJV is a collaborative research arrangement through which firms jointly acquire technical knowledge.

RJVs gains two significant benefits from filing with the Department of Justice, and these benefits are what could be referred to as a 'safer harbor' for participants in the venture. One, if the venture is subjected to criminal or civil action, the charges would be evaluated under a rule of reason that analyzes whether the venture improves social welfare. And two, if the venture is found to fail a rule-of-reason analysis, it is subject to actual damages rather than treble damages.

Since 1985, the first year of disclosures, and 2005, the last year of NSF public domain data, 950 RJVs have been filed and noticed in the *Federal Register*, but only ten RJVs have been formed related to IT – 1 of 26 RJVs in 2001, 6 of 30 RJVs in 2002, 3 of 22 RJVs in 2004, and 3 of 15 RJVs in 2005.

5. The mechanics of such a policy could be similar to that used to enact the Research and Experiment Tax Credit of 1981.

6. The Act of 3 March 1901, also known as the Organic Act, established the National Bureau of Standards within the Department of the Treasury, where the Office of Standard Weights and Measures was administratively located: 'Be it enacted by the Senate and House of Representatives of the United States of America in Congress assembled, That the Office of Standard Weights and Measures shall hereafter be known as the National Bureau of Standards ... That the functions of the bureau shall consist in the custody of the standards; the comparison of the standards used in scientific investigations, engineering, manufacturing, commerce, and educational institutions with the standards adopted or recognized by the Government; the construction, when necessary, of standards, their multiples and subdivisions; the testing and calibration of standard measuring

apparatus; the solution of problems which arise in connection with standards; the determination of physical constants and the properties of materials, when such data are of great importance to scientific or manufacturing interests and are not to be obtained of sufficient accuracy elsewhere'.

The Act of 14 February 1903 established the Department of Commerce and Labor, and in that Act it was stated that the National Bureau of Standards be moved from the Department of the Treasury to the Department of Commerce and Labor.

Then, in 1913, when the Department of Labor was established as a separate entity, the bureau was formally housed in the Department of Commerce.

In the post-First World War years, the bureau's research focused on assisting in the growth of industry. Research was conducted on ways to increase the operating efficiency of automobile and aircraft engines, electrical batteries and gas appliances. Also, work was begun on improving methods for measuring electrical losses in response to public utility needs. This latter research was not independent of international efforts to establish electrical standards similar to those established over 50 years earlier for weights and measures.

After the Second World War, significant attention and resources were given to the activities of the bureau. In particular, the Act of 21 July 1950 established standards for electrical and photometric measurements: 'Be it enacted by the Senate and House of Representatives of the United States of America in Congress assembled. That from and after the date this Act is approved, the legal units of electrical and photometric measurements in the United States of America shall be those defined and established as provided in the following sections ... The unit of electrical resistance shall be the ohm ... The unit of electrical current shall be the ampere ... The unit of electromotive force and of electrical potential shall be the volt ... The unit of electrical quantity shall be the coulomb ... The unit of electrical capacity shall be the farad ... The unit of electrical inductance shall be the henry ... The unit of power shall be the watt ... The units of energy shall be the (a) joule ... and (b) the kilowatt-hour ... The unit of intensity shall be the candle ... The unit of flux light shall be the lumen ... It shall be the duty of the Secretary of Commerce to establish the values of the primary electric and photometric units in absolute measure, and the legal values for these units shall be those represented by, or derived from, national reference standards maintained by the Department of Commerce'.

Then, as a part of the Act of 20 June 1956, the bureau moved from Washington, DC to Gaithersburg, MD. The responsibilities listed in the Act of 21 July 1950, and many others, were transferred to the National Institute of Standards and Technology (NIST) when the National Bureau of Standards was renamed under the guidelines of the Omnibus Trade and Competitiveness Act of 1988: 'The National Institute of Standards and Technology [shall] enhance the competitiveness of American industry while maintaining its traditional function as lead national laboratory for providing the measurement, calibrations, and quality assurance techniques which underpin United States commerce, technological progress, improved product reliability and manufacturing processes, and public safety ... [and it shall] advance, through cooperative efforts among industries, universities, and government laboratories, promising research and development projects, which can be optimized by the private sector for commercial and industrial applications ... [More specifically, the NIST is to] prepare, certify, and sell standard reference materials for use in ensuring the accuracy of chemical analyses and measurements of physical and other properties of materials ...'.

The NIST's mission is to promote US economic growth by working with industry to develop and apply technology, measurements, and standards. As a group, these represent infrastructure technology or infratechnologies. The NIST carries out this mission through its measurement and standards laboratories program. It provides technical leadership for vital components of the nation's technology infrastructure needed by US industry to continually improve its products and services.

PART 2

Public Policy: Case Studies and
Recommendations

8. Data Encryption Standards[1]

INTRODUCTION

The development and use of data encryption systems grew out of concerns over the security of sensitive but unclassified information within the government that was communicated through electronic channels. Information security concerns escalated as the Internet became the backbone of corporate financial transactions and was increasingly used to communicate private and personal information. It quickly became apparent that encryption standards were needed to promote the diffusion of encryption products in order to provide the information security needed for new Internet applications. This chapter provides an overview of the development of data encryption systems and discusses the economic significance of the Data Encryption Standard (DES) developed by the National Institute of Standards and Technology (NIST).

An encryption system performs two primary functions, encryption and decryption. Encryption, which has a primary purpose of ensuring primary and data integrity, involves converting data from plaintext into ciphertext so that the data are unintelligible to unauthorized parties. Decryption reverses this process. The strength of an encryption system depends upon the strength of its algorithm and on the length of the key – longer keys use more digits and that usually means greater security – used to send and receive encrypted messages.

In a symmetric cryptosystem, a single key is used for encryption and decryption. Asymmetric algorithms use different keys for encryption and decryption. Encryption algorithms differ in at least four dimensions: the mathematical sophistication and computation complexity; symmetry; the length of the keys; and the method of implementation through software and hardware.

Organizations select an encryption system based on three factors: technical issues (for example, strength and speed), infrastructure (for example, software and hardware implementation, compatibility with existing infrastructure and key requirements) and financial issues (for example, price, cost of use, licensing structure and government requirements).

The economic importance of cryptography is related to the ability of organizations to protect themselves from computer security breaches. In Chapter 2, we discussed the data and figures that support various estimates of the cost of breaches and the expenditure and investment that organizations make to prevent such breaches.

The Data Encryption Standard (DES) was developed by the NIST, then named the National Bureau of Standards (NBS), in 1977 for protecting sensitive, unclassified government information, and it became the standard for much of industry in the United States and across the world. This chapter overviews the evolution and economic significance of the DES, and we argue that the DES is representative of an important role of government in cyber security.

THE EVOLUTION OF DATA ENCRYPTION STANDARDS

The Brooks Act of 1965 (Public Law 89-306) authorized the NIST to develop standards governing the purchase and use of computers by the federal government. The Act also authorized research to support the development of these standards and for implementing them throughout the federal government. These developments were occurring in an environment of increasing concern over the security of sensitive but unclassified information within the government, and both industry and government felt the need to ensure the security of all such information that was communicated through electronic channels.

In 1968, the NIST initiated a study of government security needs, and in 1972 it made the decision to develop a government-wide standard for encrypting unclassified government information using an encryption algorithm that would eventually become a national standard. It founded a computer security program under the auspices of its Institute for Computer Science and Technology (ICIT), and charged that institute to develop a single, standard cryptographic algorithm that could be tested and certified and that would interoperate with different cryptographic equipment.

By the early 1970s, private sector research was making technological advancements toward securing personal identification numbers as they were transmitted to remote locations for verification, a key step in assuring security in a financial transaction such as a credit card charge or a withdraw from an automated teller machine (ATM). It also became clear during the early 1970s that industry as a whole was in need of cryptographic advances as Internet-based communications and electronic commerce were beginning and computer networks were in their early period of development, as overviewed in Chapter 1. Industry realized early on that no industry-wide standards existed to guide developmental efforts. As a result, incompatible products came on the market, a situation that discouraged widespread use. With multiple, non-compatible systems, the cost to potential users was high and adopters were discouraged from adoption.

It soon became apparent to all those in affected industries than an encryption standard was needed to promote the diffusion of encryption products and to stimulate new technological advancements. The early encryption industry was dominated by two alternative approaches. One was IBM's approach and the other was a key algorithm developed by Diffie and Hellman, two Massachusetts Institute of Technology (MIT) researchers.

On 15 May 1973, the NIST issued in the *Federal Register*, having coordinated with the National Security Agency (NSA), a public request for proposals for a standard cryptographic algorithm. A second request was published on 27 August 1974 because none of the respondents met the technical requirements. An algorithm based on the one originally developed by IBM several years prior emerged, and its encryption methods were called 'Lucifer'. Although patented, IBM granted in 1975 a non-exclusive, royalty-free license to anyone for its manufacture, implementation and use, and the Department of Justice (DoJ) approved its publication. The Data Encryption Standard (DES) was adopted by the Department of Commerce (DoC) on 23 November 1976, and all sensitive, unclassified government data was subsequently authorized for transfer through DES. The DES was published on 15 January 1977 as Federal Information Processing Standard Publication 46 (FIPS PUB 46). FIPS 46 was reaffirmed in 1983, 1988 and 1993. In 1997 the NIST announced its intension to select a new standard, called the Advanced Encryption Standard (AES) or also known as 'Rijndael' (a combination of the names of its inventors, Daemen and Rijmen).

The DES became the basis for numerous standards in several areas. The American National Standards Institute (ANSI) approved the DES as a voluntary standard in 1981 (ANSI X3.92), and it was widely used throughout the financial services industry. The DES was also instrumental in the e-commerce community in areas such as matching remittances to electronic invoices. As a summary, Table 8.1 lists the chronology of major DES events.

Table 8.1 Chronology of DES development efforts

Event	Date
NBS identifies need for computer security standards	August 1971
NBS initiates program in computer security	July 1972
NBS meets with NSA on encryption project	February 1973
NBS publishes request for encryption algorithms	May 1973
NSA reports no suitable algorithms submitted	December 1973
NBS publishes second request for algorithms	August 1974
NSA reports one submitted algorithm acceptable	October 1974
NSA approves publication of proposed algorithm	January 1975
DoJ approves publication of proposed algorithm	February 1975
NBS published proposed algorithm for comments	March 1975
NBS published proposed DES for comments	August 1975
NBS briefs DoJ on competition issues	February 1976
NBS holds workshop on technology concerning DES	August 1976
NBS holds workshop on mathematical foundation of DES	September 1976
DoC approves DES as a FIPS	November 1976
NBS published DES and FIPS PUB 46	January 1977

Source: OTA (1987), p. 169.

THE INDUSTRY SUPPLY CHAIN

The relationship among the NIST and the users of the DES covers three downstream tiers, and thus forms a supply chain. The first tier is composed of manufacturers of cryptographic products that incorporate the DES and the industry organizations that support them (for example, the Information Technology Industry Council). The second tier contains conformance testing services. These services were originally performed by the NIST but were transferred to private sector testing laboratories in 1995. And the third tier is the broad community of industrial users of cryptographic products employing the DES and the industry associations that support them (for example, the American Bankers Association).

The end-users with valuable proprietary information include research and development (R&D)-intensive industries (for example, pharmaceuticals, oil exploration, automotive, aerospace), financial industries (for example, bank-to-bank services, ATMs and Securities and Exchange Commission [SEC] transactions) and e-commerce (for example, networks and transportation). All commercial user segments have three objectives: preventing unauthorized disclosure of information, maintaining the integrity of electronic information and ensuring continuity of service.

There are two sources of information that document the market penetration of DES-specific products: the FIPS validation list and the US patent system. Prior to the 1970s, the market for cryptography was virtually non-existent, comprised largely of classified work for the Department of Defense, specifically for the National Security Agency. In the early 1970s, IBM and a few other firms were developing encryption technology for the banking sector.

The NIST's FIPS validation list can be used to approximate patterns of market entry over time. From 1977 to 1994, the NIST offered conformance testing services to encryption hardware manufacturers and software producers. If products were found to be in conformance with various cryptographic standards, their products were listed as 'validated'. In this way, public sector buyers, in particular, are assured that their purchases are in compliance with federal purchasing standards. Although the conformance testing services were transferred to the private sector in 1995, the NIST still maintained the validation list and it can be used to approximate the entry of firms and the entry of products into the cryptographic market.

Based on this source of information, the diffusion of the DES into the marketplace since 1977 can be roughly approximated as seen in Table 8.2. It is interesting to note that the financial sector, which was a strong advocate for the DES, entered the market in 1984. Also, 1991 was the year of the first foreign entry into this market. As seen from the table, the number of validations increased over time. It is not the case that the number of validations per year equals the number of companies entering the market with DES products because in a given year a company could obtain more than one validation.

Figure 8.1 illustrates the diffusion of DES technology over the years 1977–1998 using the number of validations per year as an index of market entry. Very roughly, the pattern described in the figure approximates exponential growth as is typical of the diffusion path of new innovations.

Table 8.2 FIPS PUB 46 validations by year, 1977–1998

Validation year	Number of validations	First validation by a company
1977	2	IBM, Collins Communication
1978	3	Borroughs Corporation, Fairchild Semiconductor, Intel
1979	3	Western Digital Corporation, GTE Sylvania
1980	3	UNIVAC, Nixdorf Computer, Racal
1981	3	Motorola, Advanced Micro Devices
1982	3	TI, Docutel/Olivetti
1983	1	ATT Bell Labs
1984	3	Chase Manhattan Bank, Lexicon
1985	1	General Electric Company
1986	3	John Hold & Associated, Frontline Software
1987	2	Cylink, Western Digital Corporation
1988	0	
1989	4	Wells Fargo, Arkansas Systems Inc., Secur-Data Systems, Inc., The Exchange
1990	4	ADT, LSI Logic, Micro Card Technologies
1991	7	Gemplus Card International, Matsushita, Newnet, Rothenbuhler, Tundra Semiconductor
1992	5	Datakey Inc., Glenco Engineering, VSLI Technology
1993	6	Global Technologies, Jones Futurex
1994	12	TASC, Cottonwood Software, GE Mobile Communications, Information Security Corporation, Logimens Inc., Northern Telecom (Entrust), Research In Motion, Secure Computing, Timestep Corporation, Transcript International, Virtual Open Network
1995	9	Motorola, Engineering Concepts, Algorithmic Research, Bolker Software Corporation, Data Critical, Logix, Vobach Systems
1996	5	Kimxhik, PenWare
1997	19	Chrysalis-ITS, Hitachi Data Systems, Digital Video Express
1998	16	Hi/fn, Chrysalis-ITS, Pitney Bowes, Certifax Corporation

Source: Leech and Chinworth (2001), p. 31.

On the basis of patent records, IBM dominated the market as would be expected because the DES was based on its technology. From 1975 to 1998, IBM was awarded 23 of the total 127 patents in the broad cryptographic class 380.29. Second was AT&T/Bell with seven patents.

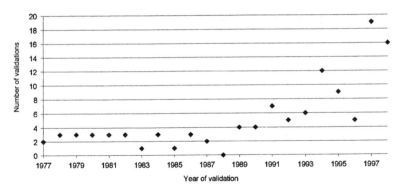

Figure 8.1 Diffusion of DES products into the market

On the basis of patent records, IBM dominated the market as would be expected because the DES was based on its technology. From 1975 to 1998, IBM was awarded 23 of the total 127 patents in the broad cryptographic class 380.29. Second was AT&T/Bell with seven patents.

AN ECONOMIC ASSESSMENT OF THE NIST'S DES

As we put forth in Chapter 7, one role of government is to overcome barriers that bring about an underinvestment in cyber security. For example, information – of which standards are an important subset – can be promulgated by the NIST and thus become a public good.

Regarding the initial publication of the DES, at least two market barriers inhibiting the development and diffusion of cryptology were overcome. The first barrier was a nascent and fragmented market for the support of encryption technology, and the second barrier was a concentrated innovation market, dominated (in retrospect) by IBM. The results of removing these barriers are five fold:

1) new market entry (that is, the expansion of the market);
2) increase in profit margins on sales of encryption products and services;
3) increase in profit margins from new online services;
4) increased operating efficiencies from new systems enabled by encryption; and

5) lower security risk to information protected by the DES and related lower insurance costs.

Beneficiaries include, respectively:

1) the buyers and sellers of cryptographic devices, equipment and systems
2) encryption device and systems manufacturers;
3) financial services providers;
4) IS managers in R&D-intensive industries and in financial services; and
5) banks, large IS managers in R&D-intensive industries.

A third barrier reduced through the NIST's activities was the high market risk associated with the introduction of new DES products over time. This barrier was overcome through the periodic reaffirmation of the DES. This reaffirmation avoided the cost of switching between products as well as transaction costs. Those benefiting included both the encryption device and systems manufacturers and the users of their products.

Counterfactual

One method to understand the economic benefits associated with the DES is to understand the historical situation that could have existed in its absence.

Few if any viable alternatives for a robust encryption standard existed in the mid-1970s when deliberations began that eventually let to the issuance of FIPS PUB 46. Although there were specific criticisms of the proposed DES, which were associated with key length, alternative algorithms offering superior benefits were not available. Alternative encryption designs were being researched at the time, but they had not progressed sufficiently to be a viable option to that of IBM.[2]

Encryption algorithms that emerged shortly after the adoption of DES were not viewed as totally acceptable alternative for a variety of reasons. In some cases, their originators would not agree to provide them on a royalty-free basis as IBM had. Foreign encryption standards also were emerging. The International Data Encryption Algorithm (IDEA) was a block cipher developed by the Swiss Federal Institute of Technology in Zurich and is used today in the application software of many e-mail systems. But the IDEA's inventors did not file for patent protection until 1992.

Next-generation approaches for verification and authorization, some of which are currently in use, include biometric technologies (for example, speech and facial pattern recognition, fingerprint imaging). Producers of these products and algorithms believe that these technologies will offer far more secure systems. However, these systems are expected to be used with the existing DES to allow for multiple fail-safe points within the total security package.

Economic Assessment

TASC, Inc. under contract to the NIST as summarized in Leech and Chinworth (2001), conducted two surveys to obtain primary data and information relevant to an economic assessment. The first survey related to the period of the mid-1970s to the mid-1980s. For this period encryption hardware manufacturers and users, active in the market at that time, were asked to estimate three things: 1) a hypothetical time interval in which industry would have established an encryption standard, in the absence of the NIST's efforts; 2) company research, development, test and evaluation costs that would have entered into the commercial market for encryption hardware and software, in the absence of the NIST's efforts; and 3) costs that would have been incurred by users (transaction costs and service process costs) in the absence of the NIST's DES program.

The second overlapping survey focused on the period from the mid-1980s to the late 1990s. This was the period of time in which the NIST evaluated and reaffirmed the DES. Manufacturers of encryption hardware and software were asked to describe the nature and the related costs of activities that their firm would have borne had the NIST not reaffirmed the DES in any of the relevant years 1983, 1988, 1993 and 1997.

Focusing primarily on the commercial banking industry because of a willingness to participate in the surveys and because of other relevant public domain data, TASC estimated benefits from the NIST's activities with the DES in terms of costs avoided by the private sector. This is a common evaluation technique. It found that tremendous social benefits were associated with the DES. In particular, the analysis concluded that the social rate of return was between 267 percent and 272 percent depending on the lag structure for benefits, and it calculated a benefit-to-cost ratio of between 58 and 145 depending on lags. Of course, these quantitative measures understate the true impact of the DES on society because they only relate to one industrial segment.

CONCLUSIONS

The development and deployment of the DES is a classic example of the role the public sector can play in supporting cyber security. The NIST's activities highlight the public-goods nature of standards and the potential for the public sector to overcome barriers to adoption of information technologies. This is also illustrated in the conformance testing services offered by the NIST to encryption hardware manufacturers and software producers. Even though the conformance testing services were transferred to the private sector in 1995, the NIST continues to oversee activities by ensuring the validation.

NOTES

1. This chapter draws directly on Leech and Chinworth (2001). Although this NIST report, prepared by TASC, is not copyrighted and is thus within the public domain, permission to drawn directly from it was obtained from Dr Gregory Tassey, senior economist within the Program Office at the NIST.
2. The RSA (Rivest–Shamir–Adelman) algorithm, for example, is a popular algorithm at the heart of many asymmetric cryptographic systems but it emerged after the DES was adopted. The algorithm was the proprietary algorithm of the RSA Public Key Cryptosystem. While used today, it does not have the social benefits that accrue with the royalty-free availability of the DES.

9. Improving Internet Standards[1]

INTRODUCTION

Internet standards, and more specifically a subset of Internet standards called communications protocols, support the most basic functionality of the Internet. This chapter focuses on one such communications protocol that lies at the heart of the Internet, Internet protocol (IP).[2] The IP enables data and other traffic to travel through the Internet and to arrive at the desired destination. It provides a standardized envelope for the information sent; specifically, the IP contains headers that provide addressing, routing and message-handling information that enables a message to be directed to its final destination over the various media that comprise the Internet.

The current generation of the IP, version 4 (IPv4), has been in use since the 1980s and has supported the Internet's worldwide growth over the last decade. With the transformation of the Internet in the 1990s from a research network to a commercialized network, concerns were raised about the ability of IPv4 to accommodate emerging demand, especially the anticipated demand for unique Internet addresses. As a result, the Internet Engineering Task Force (IETF) began work on a new generation IP, which became IP version 6 (IPv6).[3]

Technical standards can be used to help improve cyber security at the most basic level, before human actions, or lack thereof, become barriers to security. Improvements in the technology infrastructure and technical mechanisms by which people communicate on the Internet can prevent many types of attacks from occurring.

Industry stakeholders and Internet experts generally agree that IPv6-based networks in many ways would be technically superior to IPv4-based networks.[4] Specific to the themes of this book, the redesigned header structure in IPv6, including new flow labels, and the enhanced capabilities of the new protocol could provide significant security benefits to Internet users, network administrators and software applications developers. Further, some experts believe that widespread IPv6 adoption could spur increased research and development of and interest in transitioning to a new network security model, in which techniques such as Internet protocol security (IPsec) could be more commonly and effectively used.

Based largely on these perceived security benefits, in June 2003 the US Department of Defense (DoD) announced that all hardware and software being developed, procured or acquired for its Global Information Grid (GIG) would have to be IPv6-capable by 1 October 2003.[5] In August 2005 the US Office of Management and Budget (OMB) issued a memorandum stating that by June 2008 all federal government agencies' infrastructure must be using IPv6 and agency networks must interface with this infrastructure. This decision of the OMB was based not only on the perceived security and efficiency benefits to the government, but also on the idea that government could help by spurring the demand for new IPv6-enabled products and services, thereby jump-starting the market and providing incentives for start-up companies to develop new enhanced products and services that would be supported by a more advanced IP structure.

This chapter leverages the results of a study conducted for the National Institute of Standards and Technology (NIST) referred to as the NIST study (Gallaher and Rowe, 2005) to investigate the costs and benefits of IPv6 adoption and government's potential role. We focus on the security implications that are expanded in Rowe and Gallaher (2006).

OVERVIEW OF IPv6

Designed in the mid-1990s, IPv6 has slowly been integrated into most major networking hardware and software sold today. Cameras, cell phones and refrigerators are beginning to be equipped with IPv6 addresses in an effort by vendors to use the characteristics of IP to enhance product features and provide new services. As of 2005, the majority of routers sold are IPv6-capable[6], and by 2008, most operating systems and application software on the market will be IPv6-capable. As an example, in 2004, Sony successfully integrated IPv6 addresses into all of its Internet-capable products. Assuming demand for IPv6-based applications increases and users begin to 'enable' IPv6 in consumer products and corporate networks, this chapter investigates whether networking security could be improved and, if so, at what cost.

IPv6-based networks would be technically superior to IPv4-based networks in many ways. The increased address space available under IPv6 could stimulate development and deployment of new communications devices and new applications. IPv6 also could enable network restructuring to a more hierarchical structure, possibly without network address translation (NAT) devices, to occur more easily.[7] The redesigned header structure in IPv6 (which includes new flow labels) and the enhanced capabilities of the new protocol could provide significant security benefits.

However, the timing of significant US IPv6 adoption is uncertain. Currently, the installed base of network-based vendor and propriety products (hardware and software), as well as networking IT staff skills and organizational procedures and policies, are all rooted in IPv4 characteristics and capabilities. As such, many sources suggest that IPv4 will continue to be used for many years. Further, some security experts and researchers propose that an entirely new communications infrastructure should be developed, possibly without the use of the Internet protocol (IP). The National Science Foundation (NSF) is sponsoring an initiative called the Global Environment for Networking Investigations (GENI) aimed at researching such possibilities, and could spend as much as $300 million over the next several years.[8] Some suggest that organizations should not incur costs to move to IPv6 but, rather, should wait to transition to an entirely new communications infrastructure.

As organizations weigh these broad considerations, it is important to note that there is disagreement among security experts about the characteristics and timing of security benefits associated with IPv6. Some experts believe that IPv6 could spur increased research and development (R&D) of and interest in transitioning to a new network security model, in which techniques such as Internet Protocol Security (IPsec) could be more commonly and effectively used.[9] However, many of IPv6's enhanced capabilities have also been made available in IPv4, albeit with varying levels of performance. As a result, vendors and consumers may continue to use IPv4 for a significant period of time (perhaps with further augmentation) to avoid or to defer the costs of upgrading to IPv6. Many of the prospective benefits of IPv6, moreover, appear to be predicated on the removal or modification of 'middleboxes', such as NAT devices and firewalls, that affect direct communications between end-user devices via the Internet. It remains to be seen whether or when such devices will be either phased out or made transparent to end-to-end (E2E) Internet communications and applications.

Further, widespread adoption of IPv6 will likely entail substantial transition costs because today's Internet comprises almost entirely IPv4-based hardware and software. We estimate the cost for all major US stakeholders to transition to IPv6 during the period 1997–2025 to be approximately $25 billion, approximately $20 billion between 2008 and

2017. In addition to the explicit cost to transition, many experts have noted that using IPv6 networking could result in decreased network security for a certain period during which network operators become more familiar with the new protocol and hackers identify flaws in initial IPv6 implementations.

The following section provides a discussion of the potential security costs and benefits of IPv6 and the likely timing and magnitude of such. The information therein comes from our interviews with industry experts and stakeholders, mainly in 2004 and 2005, as well as from responses to a Request for Comments issued by the US Department of Commerce on January 21, 2004 (US Department of Commerce, 2004).

Security Implications of IPv6

Although the general consensus is that widespread IPv6 adoption could result in significant benefits in IT security, among other network performance improvements, significant disagreement exists concerning the size of these benefits and whether adopters could recover the incremental costs of an accelerated transition from IPv4 to IPv6.[10]

Many experts and industry representatives contend that IPv6 would provide a greater level of security than is available under IPv4. NTT/Verio, a US Internet service provider,[11] stated that because IPv6 was designed with security in mind; it is inherently more secure than IPv4, which does not have integrated security fields (DoC, 2004).[12] Other industry representatives note that support for IPsec is mandatory in IPv6, but only optional in IPv4, which should lead to more extensive use of IPsec in IPv6 networks and applications (DoC, 2004).[13]

BellSouth suggested that incorporating IPsec into the IPv6 protocol stack may reduce incompatibility between different vendors' implementations of IPsec (DoC, 2004).[14] Further, the massive increase in addresses made possible via IPv6 may enhance security by making it difficult for hackers to identify and attack IP addresses by performing exhaustive address and port sweeps (DoC, 2004).[15]

Widespread deployment of IPv6 may indeed produce security benefits in the long term; however, the near-term benefits are much less clear. Although IPsec support is mandatory in IPv6, IPsec use is not. In fact, many current IPv6 implementations do not include IPsec (DoC, 2004).[16]

Although most parties believe that increased use of IPsec would improve security, others are less certain. Motorola asserts that IPsec, in its current form, cannot defend against denial-of-service attacks (DoC, 2004). [17] BellSouth questions whether IPsec can strictly eliminate spoofing (DoC,

2004).[18] More broadly, VeriSign suggests that IPsec may have been rendered irrelevant by the rise of attacks and security threats for which IPsec-based solutions are either unhelpful or counterproductive (DoC, 2004).[19] Others note that IPsec provides only network-level security and, as a result, may need to be supplemented by other measures (DoC, 2004).[20]

Although optional, IPsec is being widely deployed in IPv4 (DoC, 2004).[21] Several stakeholders have stated that there are no significant functional differences in the performance of IPsec in IPv6 and IPv4 networks (DoC, 2004).[22] Any differences in performance are attributable to the presence of NATs in most IPv4 networks, which interfere with E2E communications using IPsec (DoC, 2004).[23] Thus, to the extent that NAT persists in IPv6 networks, it may reduce the security benefits available via the new protocol.[24]

Furthermore, experts generally agree that implementing any new protocol, such as IPv6, would be followed by an initial period of increased security vulnerability,[25] and that additional network staff will be necessary to address new threats posed by a dual network environment (DoC, 2004).[26] Current IPv4 users benefit from 20 years of effort spent identifying and addressing security issues. As IPv6 becomes more prevalent, many security issues will likely arise in new IPv6 networks and applications as attackers give it more attention. On the other hand, the experience gained from running IPv4 networks should help bring security levels in IPv6 networks up to the level of current IPv4 networks fairly rapidly (DoC, 2004).[27]

Re-evaluating the Security Model

To use fully the capabilities of IPv6 and IPsec to provide security on an E2E basis, enterprises would likely need to re-examine their existing security models (DoC, 2004).[28] Most enterprises currently implement security measures at the perimeter of their corporate networks (for example, firewalls). By so doing, they can monitor and control outside access to hosts within the corporate network at a limited number of points, much as the rulers of a medieval city could control the flow of people in and out at a few gates cut into the city's walls. In that way, the enterprises can provide a desired level of security for their networks and their users at a reasonable cost in terms of equipment and personnel.

If an enterprise allows its employees to establish communications with non-enterprise users on an E2E basis, the enterprise is forced to use other security techniques. For example, the entire organization could adopt an E2E security approach instead of the traditional perimeter security model.

Alternatively, the enterprise could retain its perimeter approach but open holes in that perimeter for certain communications (for example, teleconferencing) or for certain employees. In either event, the enterprise would need to plan carefully to ensure that the new security model does not expose the enterprise to new external threats. Many enterprises may be reluctant to assume that risk, particularly when the benefits cannot be guaranteed.[29]

Implementation of E2E security might require developing new tools and policies. The principal impediment to widespread use of IPsec, for example, appears to be the absence of a public key infrastructure (PKI) and associated trust models, which are both necessary to effectively manage widespread IPsec operations (DoC 2004; Gallaher and Rowe, 2005).[30] Extensive research must be conducted, and an organizational authority (trusted by all users) will need to be set up to manage the PKI system. Until the required security infrastructure is created and all privacy concerns and legal considerations are resolved (DoC, 2004),[31] a process that could take several years, IPv6 is not likely to stimulate any more use of IPsec than IPv4 does today (DoC, 2004).[32]

Thus, it is likely that in the first three to five years of significant IPv6 use the user community will, at best, see no better security than what can be realized in IPv4-only networks today. During this short-term period, more security holes would probably be found in IPv6 than in IPv4, and IPv4 networks would continue to have, at a maximum, the same level of security issues as they do currently. In the longer term (that is, 15 to 20 years), however, security may improve if organizations are motivated to restructure their networks and use E2E security mechanisms, such as IPsec.[33]

IPv6 TRANSITION COSTS

The incremental costs associated with IPv6 deployment between 1997 and 2025 are estimated to have a present value of approximately $25 billion, primarily reflecting the increased labor costs associated with the transition.[34] Although these cost estimates seem large in an absolute sense, they are actually quite small relative to the overall expected expenditures on IT hardware and software.[35] They are even smaller relative to the expected value of potential market applications that could result from IPv6 use and significant network improvements, including enhanced security.

Figure 9.1 provides the general framework used to investigate the four stakeholder groups that will incur the costs and realize the benefits associated with the transition from IPv4 to IPv6: infrastructure vendors, application vendors, Internet service providers (ISPs) and Internet users.

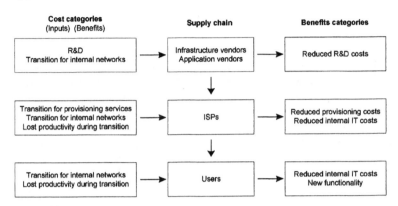

Figure 9.1 Supply chain stakeholders, costs and benefits

Infrastructure vendors include manufacturers of computer networking hardware (for example, routers, firewalls and servers) and systems software (for example, operating systems) that supply the components of computer networks. Major companies in this category include Microsoft, IBM, Juniper, Cisco and Hewlett-Packard.

Application vendors include suppliers of e-mail, file transfer protocol (FTP) and Web server software and database software, such as enterprise resource planning (ERP) and product data management (PDM) software. SAP and Oracle (which recently merged with PeopleSoft) are some of the largest companies in this group.

Internet service providers (ISPs) are companies that provide Internet connectivity to customers. National backbone ISPs (for example, MCI, AT&T and Sprint) provide connectivity to larger companies, some institutional users and national and regional ISPs (for example, AOL and Earthlink) that provide Internet connectivity to home and small business users.

Internet users represent a large, diverse group of entities ranging from corporate, institutional and government organizations to independent users, including small businesses and residential households. A subset of this stakeholder group is infrastructure users, companies that use the Internet to provide products and services to customers. Mobile telephone service providers and services such as OnStar are examples of these companies.

General Cost Categories

Labor resources will account for the bulk of the transition costs associated with IPv6. Although some additional physical resources may be needed, such as increased memory capacity for routers and other message-forwarding hardware,[36] these costs are anticipated to be negligible. Labor resources needed to transition to IPv6 are linked to three general business activities within the Internet supply chain: product development, Internet provisioning services and internal network operations. Product development activities are conducted by infrastructure and application vendors; service provisioning activities are conducted by ISPs; and internal network operations are conducted by all vendors, ISPs and users.

Table 9.1 shows the underlying transition cost categories included in each of the business activities. As is apparent, ISPs and users would incur costs in the same categories. Additionally, several other cost categories, such as network testing and standards and protocol development, span multiple business activities and, thus, several stakeholder groups.

Penetration Metrics

The penetration of IPv6 into the market is likely to be a gradual process and will probably never reach 100 percent of applications or users. Figure 9.2 illustrates the structure by which the cost analysis uses the timing associated with the development and availability of IPv6 infrastructure products (for example, hardware and software) and applications, as well as the enabling of these products and applications by ISPs and users.[37] Events are generally sequential in that ISPs enabling their network is conditional on the availability of IPv6-capable hardware and software. These four curves are the key penetration metrics for the cost analysis because they capture the timing of expenditure.

For infrastructure and applications vendors, R&D development expenditures (labor) to integrate IPv6 into their products are the primary expenditure category associated with the transition from IPv4 to IPv6. The primary expenditures for ISPs and users are labor costs associated with enabling IPv6 capabilities. The four penetration curves in Figure 9.2

Table 9.1 Cost categories by business activity

Business activity	Product develop-ment	Pro-visioning services	Internal network operations	Brief description
Affected stakeholders	Vendors	ISPs	Vendors, ISPs and users	
Cost categories				
R&D	●			Labor allocated to basic product design and development (e.g., coding or prototyping)
Product testing	●	●		Labor allocated to testing product interoperability, debugging, etc.
R&D staff training	●			Labor and training class expenses for R&D staff
Standards and protocol activities	●	●	●	Labor allocated to developing internal standards for company products
Network management software (upgrade)*		●	●	Labor allocated to network-specific management and monitoring software
Network testing		●	●	Labor allocated to testing interoperability between network components with IP capabilities
Installation effort		●	●	Labor allocated to installing IPv6 transition mechanisms
Maintaining network performance		●	●	Labor allocated to maintaining transition mechanisms, such as dual stack, and ensuring high network performance
Training (sales, marketing, and technical staff)	●	●	●	Labor and training class expenses for sales, marketing

Note: *This category is intended to include the costs of upgrades to any network management tools, assuming that these costs result from the need to transition to IPv6 network management tools.

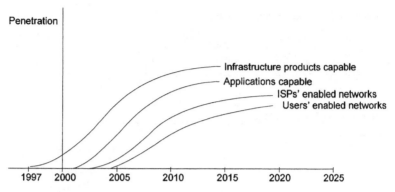

Figure 9.2 Example of penetration curves used for cost analysis

represent the likely timing of development and deployment of IPv6 capabilities and enablement, and thus the likely timing when costs have been and will be incurred.

Note that the penetration of IPv6 capabilities (that is, when ISPs and users have IPv6-capable infrastructure components and applications in place, but they are not enabled) is not a key component in determining the timing of costs for these two groups. This is because the incremental variable cost of IPv6 products is negligible compared to IPv4 products – almost all the costs are associated with applications' R&D and enabling IPv6 functionality.[38] As a result, the penetration of capabilities is not a factor in determining baseline transition costs for users, but this timing does affect infrastructure and applications vendors' development costs. However, the penetration of capabilities is important in assessing the alternative deployment scenarios presented below. The penetration of capabilities provides an upper bound on how much the enabling of IPv6 can be accelerated without adding the additional costs of early retirement of hardware and software.

Quantitative Cost Estimation Methodology

The penetration curves illustrated in Figure 9.2, representing the estimated share of infrastructure products and applications that are IPv6-capable and the share of networks that are IPv6-enabled at a given point in time, imply that the costs will be distributed over time as stakeholders gradually engage in transition activities. These curves represent the point in time when products and applications become available to customers and networks become enabled. However, activities leading to and supporting these achievements or milestones are distributed before and after the point of product roll-out or system enabling.

Figure 9.3 provides an example of the potential time distribution of labor expenditure surrounding the enablement of a network system.[39] To be clear, this figure represents the likely cost distribution for one user, not all US users. In the figure, $t = 0$ represents the date when a network is IPv6-enabled. However, the majority of the costs are borne prior to $t = 0$ as networking staff are trained and the system is reconfigured. Lower costs associated with testing and monitoring are then experienced after the enabling date.

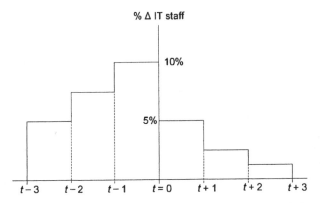

Figure 9.3 Example of the distribution of IT staff resources needed to enable IPv6 in a user network

Costs are expressed as the percentage of IT staff time devoted to IPv6 transition activities. Thus, in this illustrative example, 10 percent of a company's IT staff in the year prior to becoming enabled $(t - 1)$ will be devoted to the IPv6 transition. In the year after enabling $(t + 1)$, the share of resources decreases to 5 percent of IT staff time. This number is multiplied by the average IT staff wage rate to obtain the cost per IT staff member associated with the IPv6 transition for each year before and after enabling IPv6 systems.

Figure 9.4 shows the penetration of IPv6-enabled user systems and determines the timing of the costs. For example, in this hypothetical figure, 2 percent of systems are enabled in the year 2015 $(t = 0)$.[40] This implies that

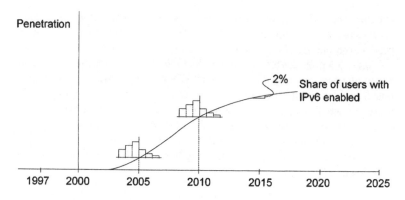

Figure 9.4 Example of US users' enablement over time

2 percent of affected US IT staff[41] in 2014 ($t - 1$) are devoting 10 percent of their time to IPv6 transition activities, and 2 percent of affected US IT staff in 2015 ($t = 0$) are devoting 5 percent of their time to IPv6 transition in 2015 ($t = 0$) are devoting 5 percent of their time to IPv6 transition activities.

Combining the distribution of costs surrounding enabling (Figure 9.3) and the timing of system enabling (Figure 9.4) yields the cumulative cost curve shown in Figure 9.5.[42] As shown below for user costs, this cost distribution–timing approach is used to calculate the time series of transition costs for infrastructure vendors' product development, application vendors' product development, ISPs' provisioning service enabling, and users' system enabling.

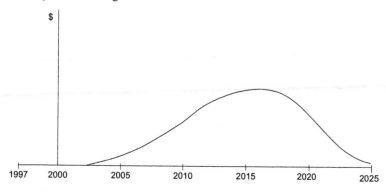

Figure 9.5 Example of US users' transition costs over time

Stakeholder Penetration Curves

The penetration curves presented in Figure 9.6 reflect cumulative IPv6 transition activities over time. The curves are dependent on each other in that hardware and software must be available prior to ISPs' transitioning networks to support IPv6 users. The four curves in Figure 9.6 also represent different adoption activities for each of the four major industry stakeholder groups. The first two curves represent when IPv6 products and services will be capable, and the final two curves represent when components of the system will be enabled. More specifically, the four curves can be interpreted as follows:[43]

- By 2003, the average infrastructure (Inf) vendor will have integrated IPv6 capabilities into 30 percent of the routers and network products it offers.
- By 2008, the average application (App) vendor will have integrated IPv6 capabilities into 30 percent of the software it offers that uses network features.
- By 2010, the average ISP will have enabled 30 percent of its network to manage IPv6 transmissions.
- By 2012, the average user will have enabled 30 percent of its local network to handle IPv6 communications.

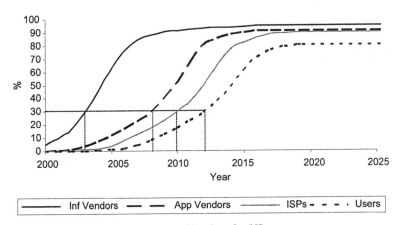

Figure 9.6 Penetration estimates of IPv6 in the US

IPv6 adoption rates will differ significantly across and within individual companies. For example, users in the financial, telecommunications and defense sectors will likely be more aggressive in transitioning to IPv6 compared to other sectors that manage less-sensitive information. Also, within a company, certain divisions or business operations will transition before others.

The average penetration estimates presented in the curves in Figure 9.6 capture both differences in adoption rates across companies and the gradual adoption process within companies.[44]

Users' Capabilities and Enabling Curves

Figure 9.7 presents users' capable and enabled penetration curves and illustrates the lag between when users obtain IPv6 capabilities through product replacement or upgrades and the time at which they decide to enable these products. The enabled curve in Figure 9.7 is the same as the users' enabled curve in Figure 9.6, and both were derived from the NIST study.

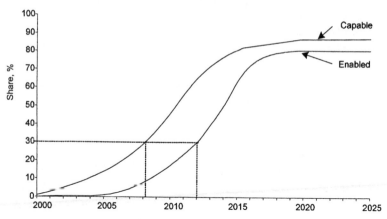

Figure 9.7 IPv6-capable and IPv6-enabled US user networks

Users will acquire IPv6 capabilities primarily as part of routine hardware and software upgrades. For example, we project that 30 percent of users' systems will be IPv6 compatible by 2008. Nearly all edge routers[45] being sold today are IPv6-capable, either in hardware or software, according to participating stakeholders. Large organizations, which routinely upgrade their networking components, should have IPv6 capabilities in the next five to seven years. However, medium-sized and small businesses and independent users will likely not upgrade in significant numbers for several more years.

On average, IPv6 hardware and software will be enabled approximately five years after users receive IPv6 capabilities. For example, we project that users will have enabled 30 percent of their systems by 2012. As initial operating systems and routers become enabled and early adopters provide lessons learned, IPv6 adoption activities will likely accelerate as users begin to transition a significant share of their applications.[46]

Breakdown of Costs

Based on the penetration projections and methodology described above, we estimate that expenditure for US stakeholder groups to transition to IPv6 will be approximately $73 billion over the period 1997 to 2025.[47] These transition costs equate to a present value (PV), discounted (at 7 percent annually) to 1997, of $25 billion ($2003). The year 1997 is used as the base year because it is the year in which IPv6 costs were first incurred. From this point forward, all costs are in $2003 and are discussed in PV terms, referenced to 1997.

Table 9.2 provides estimated annual transition costs broken down by stakeholder group. Government and non-government users account for approximately $23 billion of total US IPv6 development and deployment costs (about 91 percent) with non-government users representing the large majority, $22 billion of the US total (85 percent).[48] The remaining costs are associated with total vendors, $2 billion (7 percent), and total ISPs, $136 million (0.5 percent).

For infrastructure and application vendors, Table 9.2 breaks down costs into additional R&D costs necessary to integrate IPv6 into products ($1855 million in PV 2003 dollars) and additional IT costs to transition internal company networks to IPv6 ($121 million). For ISPs, costs are broken down into additional IT costs to transition service provisioning networks[49] to IPv6 ($121 million) and additional IT costs to transition internal company networks to IPv6 ($15 million).

Table 9.2 Estimated US IPv6 adoption cost totals, broken down by stakeholder group ($ millions)

	Infrastructure vendors		Application vendors		Total vendors	ISPs		Total ISPs	Government users	Non-government users*	Grand total
	R&D	Internal	R&D	Internal		Provision	Internal				
1997	17.7	0.0	0.0	0.0	17.7	0.0	0.0	0.0	0.0	0.0	17.7
1998	47.3	0.0	0.5	0.0	47.8	0.0	0.0	0.0	0.0	0.0	47.8
1999	88.6	0.0	2.1	0.0	90.7	0.1	0.0	0.1	0.0	0.0	90.8
2000	160.9	0.0	9.1	0.0	170.1	0.6	0.0	0.6	0.3	3.7	174.7
2001	234.8	0.2	21.9	0.0	256.9	1.5	0.0	1.5	3.5	45.5	307.5
2002	302.7	0.7	35.3	0.2	338.9	2.4	0.1	2.5	12.6	162.3	516.4
2003	329.3	1.5	49.1	0.3	380.2	4.7	0.2	5.0	25.7	330.5	741.4
2004	295.3	2.8	58.4	0.6	357.2	8.3	0.4	8.7	47.6	610.9	1 024.3
2005	223.0	5.5	71.3	1.2	301.0	12.5	0.8	13.3	92.6	1 189.4	1 596.2
2006	143.2	8.8	87.4	1.9	241.3	14.9	1.3	16.2	148.3	1 905.2	2 311.0
2007	79.7	11.7	100.4	2.6	194.5	17.5	1.7	19.2	198.9	2 554.6	2 967.1
2008	44.3	14.4	142.6	3.2	204.6	20.3	2.1	22.4	244.8	3 145.1	3 616.9
2009	25.8	16.8	169.6	3.7	216.0	25.1	2.5	27.6	284.8	3 659.7	4 188.1
2010	19.2	19.9	203.1	4.4	246.6	31.8	3.0	34.7	337.6	4 338.2	4 957.1
2011	16.2	25.0	171.2	5.5	218.0	40.7	3.8	44.4	423.8	5 446.4	6 132.6
2012	14.0	31.1	86.3	6.9	138.3	43.0	4.7	47.7	527.9	6 783.9	7 497.8
2013	10.3	35.1	48.0	7.8	101.2	34.1	5.3	39.4	595.4	7 651.2	8 387.3

168

Year											
2014	5.2	34.5	23.1	7.6	70.3	22.1	5.3	27.3	584.5	7 512.0	8 194.2
2015	2.2	27.8	4.5	6.1	40.6	15.1	4.4	19.5	471.6	6 063.1	6 594.9
2016	0.0	20.0	1.0	4.4	25.4	9.3	3.3	12.6	339.6	4 367.8	4 745.4
2017	0.0	14.1	0.0	3.1	17.2	5.1	2.5	7.6	239.3	3 081.1	3 345.2
2018	0.0	9.5	0.0	2.1	11.6	2.6	1.8	4.4	162.4	2 092.3	2 270.7
2019	0.0	5.9	0.0	1.3	7.2	0.9	1.2	2.2	100.4	1 294.7	1 404.4
2020	0.0	3.6	0.0	0.8	4.4	0.4	0.8	1.2	61.6	795.6	862.8
2021	0.0	2.0	0.0	0.4	2.5	0.1	0.5	0.6	34.5	446.3	483.9
2022	0.0	0.9	0.0	0.2	1.1	0.0	0.2	0.3	15.8	204.1	221.3
2023	0.0	0.4	0.0	0.1	0.5	0.0	0.1	0.1	6.7	86.5	93.7
2024	0.0	0.2	0.0	0.0	0.2	0.0	0.0	0.0	2.9	37.0	40.1
2025	0.0	0.0	0.0	0.0	0.0	0.0	0.0	0.0	0.7	8.8	9.5
Total	2 059.8	292.6	1284.8	64.7	3701.9	313.0	46.1	359.1	4963.8	6 3816.0	7 2840.7
Present Value ($2003)	1 284.8	99.3	571.0	21.9	1977.0	120.7	15.3	136.0	1 683.4	2 1637.9	2 5434.3

Note: Infrastructure vendors and applications vendors incur both R&D costs of integrating IPv6 into their products and services, as well as internal user transition costs. ISPs incur both the cost of integrating IPv6 into their customer (provisioning) network and their internal user network.

* This does not include vendors' and ISPs' internal network transition costs. See separate columns.

Cost Categories and Supplemental Data

This cost analysis focuses on valuing the labor activities associated with the transition from IPv4 to IPv6. By 2008, the vast majority of network hardware, operating systems and network-enabled software packages (for example, databases, e-mail) are likely to be sold with IPv6 capabilities. Based on information provided by participating stakeholders in the NIST study, we predict that IPv6 capabilities will penetrate the hardware and systems software markets and become integrated into ISP and user networks in an additional two to three years as part of routine upgrade cycles with little to no increase in product price (marginal cost) to ISPs and users.[50] Thus, our analysis assumes that hardware and software costs to upgrade to IPv6 will be negligible for most Internet users (that is, the upgrade costs will be no different from routine annual upgrade costs without IPv6) and that labor costs will constitute the majority of the cost of upgrading to IPv6 for users.

Labor costs for ISPs and users were estimated by determining the share of IT staff resources needed to facilitate the transition to IPv6 and applying this share to the total population of IT staff involved in Internet activities. Wage data for each occupational category were also obtained from the Bureau of Labor Statistics (BLS). A single aggregate IT staff wage rate was calculated by weighting the category wage by the number of employees in each category. The average IT staff wage ($2003) is estimated to be approximately $68 per hour.

Bureau of Labor Statistics occupational categories are not available for infrastructure and application vendors staff engaged in product R&D, even though R&D expenditures are predominantly labor costs. Thus, for infrastructure and application vendors, IPv6 transition costs were calculated as a share of R&D expenditures. The share and timing of R&D expenditures were estimated based on the interviews. Annual R&D expenditures for Internet infrastructure and application vendors were obtained from NSF (2002).

Internet Users' Costs

To transition to IPv6, we estimated that users will spend approximately $23.3 billion between 1997 and 2025 (see Table 9.2 for annual breakdowns). This number includes both government and non-government costs totaling $1.7 billion and $21.6 billion, respectively.[51]

Figures 9.8 and 9.9 were used to develop the time series of costs shown in Figure 9.10 for Internet users. As shown in Figure 9.8, most user costs occur in the two-year period prior to enabling IPv6 capabilities, with follow-up transition activities ongoing for an additional five years. Combining data provided by interview participants with the penetration curve in Figure 9.9 results in the time-series cost curve in Figure 9.10. Annual costs for users are projected to peak around 2013.

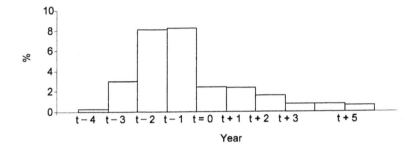

Figure 9.8 Percentage of IT staff dedicated to IPv6 transition for Internet users

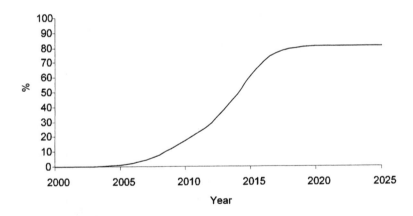

Figure 9.9 Percentage of US user networks IPv6-enabled

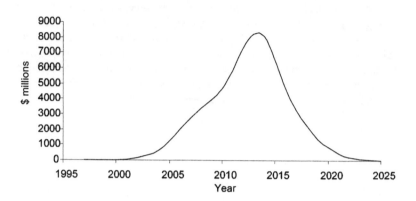

Figure 9.10 Annual spending by US users to become IPv6-enabled

Assumptions and Underlying Data: User Estimates

Internet users form the largest stakeholder group with approximately
2 200 000 IT staff directly affected by the transition to IPv6.[52] In Table 9.3,
the relative cost distribution is broken down for users into activity
categories. However, the costs will likely vary widely for individual
organizations within each user group – corporate, institutional, government
and independent users. For example, based on information provided by
stakeholders, we believe that independent users, comprised of home users
and small businesses, will incur virtually no cost to move to IPv6 because
they would gain IPv6 enablement over time without additional testing and
installation costs.[53]

Medium-sized businesses, on the other hand, will likely incur the largest
relative increase in IT spending to transition to IPv6. The majority of these
costs will be related to core networking operations and staff training, the
size of which does not increase proportionally to the size of an organization.
As a result, the cost per member of IT staff for medium-sized businesses
will be larger than for larger businesses.

Regardless of cost differences, which are non-linear in relation to
organizational size, users' costs in general will depend heavily on several
common factors: existing organizational network infrastructure, including
servers, routers, firewalls, billing systems and standard and customized

Table 9.3 Distribution of IPv6-related transition costs for users

Category	Distribution of total transition costs
	Internal network costs (%)
Network management software (upgrade)	18
Network testing	18
Installation effort	24
Maintaining network performance	16
Training (sales, marketing, and tech staff)	24

software programs; the type of organization (that is, some types of services could be interrupted or damaged during a transition); the future needs and desires of the organizational network; and the level of security required during the transition.[54]

As an example, in 2004 the Defense Research and Engineering Network (DREN), the Department of Defense's recognized research and engineering network, completed an IPv6 pilot project in which IPv6 was deployed in infrastructure components in the core network and at twelve High Performance Computer Centers (HPCs). This process included the upgrading of networks, DNS software, other IP infrastructure, computer server operating systems and desktop operating systems at each HPC.

Costs for transitioning each site included hardware – between $500 and $2000 per router to expand the memory;[55] training – between $30 and $2500 per person at each site, plus their time;[56] and installation labor – approximately 400 hours of labor to transition numerous high-capacity networking components.[57] This process took approximately six to nine months to complete. The DREN had previous experience in both testing IPv6 and working with operational IPv6 networks; therefore, their transition costs are likely to be low compared to many other organizations (Baird, 2004).

Alternate IPv6 Deployment Scenarios

Although our base case estimates are based on a wide breadth of information from stakeholders and experts who participated in the NIST study, we concede that they could be either too aggressive or not aggressive enough. To address such concerns, we asked interview participants to speculate about the possibility of alternate scenarios. When asked about the possibility that the transition could take longer to occur, all respondents indicated that the total costs would be the same as the estimated 'base case' costs. However, stakeholders indicated that IPv6 penetration could occur much more quickly than the base case scenario if, for example, some new application was developed that was highly demanded and required IPv6. In this case, the costs would be much higher. Figure 9.11 presents the most likely transition timelines for IPv6 costs (to be borne by all stakeholders) based on the interviews we conducted. In general, this 'base case' reflects the penetration of IPv6 capabilities as part of normal hardware and software upgrades and the enabling (turning on) of IPv6 capabilities at a later time as applications become available and demand for IPv6 functionality grows.

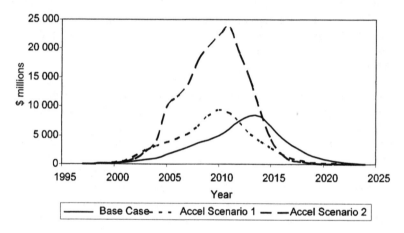

Figure 9.11 Timeline of costs for base case and accelerated deployment scenarios

Participating stakeholders indicated that there is significant uncertainty about the projected timeline for IPv6 deployment. As a result, interview participants were asked to estimate differences in costs under two alternative accelerated deployment scenarios:

- Scenario 1: IPv6 capabilities are enabled at the same time as capabilities are acquired (that is, during routine upgrades of hardware and software).

- Scenario 2: The penetration of IPv6 capabilities is accelerated as well, leading to the early replacement of some hardware and software. Enabling is therefore further accelerated to match the earlier acquisition of capabilities compared to Scenario 1.

Figure 9.11 illustrates the time series of costs under the base case and two accelerated deployment scenarios in $2003. In Scenario 1, participating stakeholders indicated that the level of effort (labor hours) associated with the transition to IPv6 will increase by approximately 5 percent as activities are compressed as a result of accelerating enablement by three years. This 5 percent increase in effort, along with accelerating the time series of costs by three years, leads to a 25 percent increase in the PV of US deployment costs or an additional $975 million.

In Scenario 2, participating stakeholders indicated that accelerating the replacement of hardware and software by one year, in addition to a four-year acceleration of enablement, would significantly increase the cost of IPv6 deployment. Scenario 2 represents approximately a 285 percent increase in the PV of US deployment costs, or an additional $15.2 billion. In other words, the degree of acceleration significantly affects the PV of the costs incurred.

Of note, these estimates do not try to estimate additional indirect costs associated with increased problems, such as new security breaches and/or interoperability problems, if a decrease in testing time results in less secure or more inefficient organizational networks for a certain period. However, industry and expert interviews indicate, empirically, that these costs would likely be incurred during an accelerated transition.

CONCLUSIONS

IPv6 adoption could contribute to the improvement of network security for all users and subsequently reduce limitations for vendors developing products that require E2E security. By stimulating the development of new security models and motivating organizations to consider restructuring their network architecture, IPv6 could have a significant positive effect on security. However, IPv6 adoption will cause new security holes to develop.

In general, significant IPv6 adoption is not certain – some stakeholders may prove resistant to incurring any transition costs due to difficultly in predicting significant near-term benefits, and the fact that research on alternate Internet redesign ideas continues (for example, the development of a non-IP-based communications infrastructure). Although many user applications and organizational network components are currently IPv6-capable (or will be very soon) and US government agencies are planning to enable IPv6 by 2008 (or shortly thereafter), widespread adoption of IPv6 (requiring enablement of related infrastructure and applications) is likely several years away for most organizations. Any transition will result in costs to all stakeholders, particularly if users decide to upgrade network equipment to gain IPv6 capabilities prior to routine upgrade cycles. Given the qualitative nature possible in any analysis of the benefits of IPv6, no general conclusions can be drawn concerning the net effects of a transition to IPv6; however, it appears that significant benefits from IPv6 adoption are likely to result in the long term.

Stakeholders considering when (or whether) to transition to IPv6 will have to make their decisions individually, based on what they observe as their costs and potential benefits. However, since this calculation will not include any concern for the spillovers benefits (positive externalities) that may flow to other Internet users when they move to IPv6, they will likely take longer to switch than is socially optimal, creating a role for government involvement. To this end, government has already helped with the development of IPv6 and accelerated its adoption through several mechanisms: the NIST helped with the development of the IPv6 standard and has tested IPv6 and documented advice on the adoption and use of such, and the DoD and OMB adoption mandates have significantly accelerated the market for IPv6 products and services, likely decreasing the costs and increasing the quality and variety of products for later adopters.

NOTES

1. The focus of and much of the data referred to in this chapter come from a report for NIST by Gallaher and Rowe (2005).
2. The Internet Protocol (IP) is a type of communications protocol. A communications protocol is a set of rules and conventions that control the format and relative timing of message transmission between two points within a computer network.
3. Technical information on IPv6 can be found within the Internet Engineering Task Force (IETF) Requests for Comments (RFCs) documents that contain the relevant standards.

4. For a brief discussion of the reasons for developing a next-generation IP and the IETF's activities in that area, see Huston (2003).

5. See Stenbit (2003).

6. Hardware and software become capable when the IPv6 functionality is integrated into products and purchased by organizations. According to Nortel Networks, IPv6-capable products were sold as early as 1997 (Shaikh, 2005). However, even after the necessary networking components are IPv6-capable, they will need to be enabled (turned on) to support IPv6 communications.

7. Network address translation (NAT) devices are used to 'enable multiple hosts on a private network to access the Internet using a single public IP address' (Wikipedia, 2007). Many potential benefits hinge on removing and/or changing the management of 'middleboxes', such as NAT devices and firewalls, because they currently disrupt certain types of host-to-host connections. Improved security and new quality of service (QoS) capabilities, which could result from IPv6 adoption, will likely not be seen without the removal of NATs, major changes to Internet security models being used today, and considerable research and testing in other areas.

8. Currently, the GENI initiative is in the early stages, but it is anticipated that it will include both a research grant program and an experimentation facility designed for exploratory research and testing. NSF managers and others note that open-ended research aimed at identifying a completely new, more secure and useable networking infrastructure is ongoing currently, but the NSF initiative, which seeks to involve other government agencies as well as the private sector and other countries, will greatly increase the funding available for and interest in such research (Markoff, 2005).

9. IPsec is a set of protocols developed by the Internet Engineering Task Force (IETF) to support the secure exchange of packets at the IP layer. IPsec has been deployed widely to implement virtual private networks (VPNs). IPsec consists of two optional security headers: Encapsulating Security Payload (ESP), which can provide both encryption and integrity protection, and Authentication Header (AH), which provides only integrity protection. The ESP header is more widely used. Both headers support two modes: transport and tunnel. In transport mode using ESP, IPsec protects only the data portion (payload) of each packet but leaves the header untouched. In tunnel mode with ESP, IPsec protects both the payload and the inner header (that of the ultimate recipient), but leaves the outer header untouched. On the receiving side, an IPsec-compliant device decrypts and authenticates each packet. For IPsec to work, the sending and receiving devices must agree on secret (symmetric) keys that are used to provide encryption and integrity protection. This is accomplished

through a protocol known as Internet key exchange (IKE), which also allows hosts to authenticate mutually using digital certificates or other methods and negotiates the IPsec protections to be provided and the cryptographic algorithms to be used.

10. The timing of the transition from IPv4 to IPv6 for any particular adopter, as well as the existing network infrastructure, could dramatically affect the costs incurred and the benefits realized.

11. NTT/Verio was the first US ISP to offer IPv6 service (Marsan, 2004).

12. See NTT/Verio comments at 13. Microsoft commenters also stated that IPv6 is a 'new, more secure protocol' that could help make North America a 'Safe Cyber Zone' (DoC, 2004). See Microsoft comments at 11.

13. See, for example, Cisco comments at 3; GSA comments at 6; MCI comments at 4.

14. BellSouth comments at 3.

15. See Cisco comments at 3.

16. See, for example, Alcatel comments at 4; BellSouth comments at 3; Cisco comments at 3, 17; Internet2 comments at 3; VeriSign comments at 9.

17. Motorola comments at 4.

18. BellSouth comments at 4.

19. VeriSign comments at 2.

20. See Alcatel comments at 3 (need to secure critical subsystems such as neighbor discovery and routing); Electronic Privacy Information Center (EPIC) comments at 2 (need to secure applications).

21. See Qwest Communications International Inc. (Qwest) comments at 4; VeriSign comments at 2.

22. See BellSouth comments at 3; Cisco comments at 3; Internet2 comments at 3.

23. See Internet2 comments at 3; MCI comments at 5. Cisco asserts that work-arounds are becoming available that will permit E2E IPsec even across NAT. Cisco comments at 3.

24. Some commenters suggested that removing NAT to implement IPsec fully may reduce security for some users (DoC, 2004). Other commenters suggested that deploying IPv6 may be hindered by the absence of IPv6-compatible security 'tools' (for example, firewalls, intrusion detection systems). Development and deployment of such tools, like the continued use of NAT, may interfere with E2E communications using IPsec (DoC, 2004). Some commenters suggest that the removal of NAT to implement IPsec fully may reduce security for some users. See, for example, Motorola comments at 3.

25. Tassey et al. (forthcoming) provide a discussion of the public-good nature of complex standards such as IPv6 and the myriad of substandards that must be in

place (and agreed on) to support a standard such as IPv6. The public-goods nature of standards is related to the issue of decreased short-term security because without enough investment to ensure a certain minimum level of security risk associated with the move to IPv6, many organizations will wait to transition indefinitely. Private firms individually are not motivated to incur substantial costs for such infrastructure development and testing; therefore, they must rely on organizations such as the IETF and government agencies such as the NIST.

26. See Cisco comments at 14; Network Conceptions comments at 9.
27. See Internet Security Alliance (ISA) comments at 2.
28. See, for example, Public Hearing Transcript, supra note 41, at 59 (remarks of Latif Ladid, NAV6TF), 149–151 (remarks of Preston Marshall, DARPA).
29. It is difficult to implement a perimeter security model for a network with mobile users because, in a mobile environment, there may be no 'perimeter' to defend. Thus, as more employees use mobile communications devices (for example, phones, laptops and personal digital assistants or PDAs), more enterprises will be compelled to develop alternatives to perimeter security, including E2E approaches (DoC, 2004). See Public Hearing Transcript, supra note 41, at 156–157 (remarks of Preston Marshall, DARPA).
30. See BellSouth comments at 3; Cisco comments at 3; Hain comments at 4; NAv6TF comments at 9; NTT/Verio comments at 15.
31. See BellSouth comments at 4.
32. See BellSouth Comments at 3–4.
33. According to Gallaher and Rowe (2006), approximately three-quarters of organizations (ISPs, users and vendors) participating in interviews indicated that they believe the government should have some role in the transition to IPv6 for both government and non-government organizations. See Gallaher and Rowe (2006) for a more detailed discussion of the potential roles that government could play and the views of industry.
34. All cost and benefit estimates are presented in 2003 dollars (hereinafter $2003).
35. Based on estimates provided in the 'Gartner 2004 IT Spending and Staffing Survey Results' report and Census data, annual expenditures on Internet hardware and software in the United States in 2003 totalled approximately $123 billion.
36. Motorola notes that routers would need at least four times their current content addressable memory to operate as efficiently as they do today when accessing both IPv4 and IPv6 addresses in a dual-stake environment. Further expanded buffers and routing tables would need more memory (DoC, 2004). See Motorola comments at 6. Motorola notes that routers would need at least four

times their current content addressable memory to operate as efficiently as they do today when accessing both IPv4 and IPv6 addresses in a dual-stake environment. Further expanded buffers and routing tables would need more memory. Also see Alcatel comments at 4.

37. Figures 9.2 to 9.5 should be interpreted only as examples used to help explain the methodology we used to estimate the costs of transitioning to IPv6.

38. We generally assumed, based on information provided by participating stakeholders in the NIST study, that routine upgrades will provide hardware and software upgrades necessary prior to IPv6 enablement for almost all ISPs and user networks and that all interoperability problems have been solved (otherwise, purchasers could incur these latter costs).

39. Figure 9.3 is one example distribution based on our research and interview activities.

40. This means that in the year 2015, 2 percent of users have enabled or 'turned on' IPv6 capabilities. This does not mean that only 2 percent of all users are enabled by this point.

41. IT staffing figures, including wage rates, were determined using data from the US Department of Labor, Bureau of Labor Statistics.

42. The main curve in Figure 9.4 is the same as the 'Users enabled networks' curve in Figure 9.2.

43. The penetration curves were developed based on interviews to reflect the likely distribution of IPv6 transition activity and hence provide the basis for estimating the time line of costs. Vendors were asked when they would have IPv6 products available, which provided information on the timing of their R&D activities. ISPs were asked when they expected to offer IPv6 services, indicating the timing of their enabling activities. Similarly, users were asked when they would enable parts of their system, also indicating enabling activities.

44. The penetration curves should neither be interpreted as the percentage of companies that have transitioned to IPv6 nor as the volume of IPv6 traffic. For example, we project, based on information from participating stakeholders, that most ISPs will be offering some level of IPv6 service in the near future by enabling a limited portion of their network; however, it could take several more years for all internal or provisioning networks to be completely IPv6-enabled.

45. By edge routers, we mean the majority of routers used by enterprise users. This does not include larger backbone routers used by ISPs and large enterprises.

46. It is important to note, as mentioned previously, that many assumptions had to be made to perform this analysis (for example, IPv6 demand will increase and IP will remain the communications medium of choice). We relied on interviews with industry experts and a variety of stakeholders representing all affected groups, so our transition timing and cost projections are intended to provide informed estimates to assist network operators and policy-makers considering the impact of IPv6 adoption and its likely timing.

47. These years were selected because our analyses used 'adoption' rates beginning with some infrastructure vendors in 2000, continuing until 2020. Thus, we estimated costs both before and after enablement or integration of IPv6.

48. We calculated all stakeholder cost estimates based on aggregated data provided by stakeholders in the interview phase. As such, we estimate government user costs will be approximately $1.7 billion, and non-government user costs will be approximately $21.6 billion. The sum is $23.2 billion. This amount is 92 percent of the estimated total cost to all stakeholders.

49. 'Provisioning networks', as discussed in this chapter, are defined as ISP subnetworks responsible for providing connectivity to the Internet to customers. These networks are always separate from internal networks used by employees.

50. The exception is that for ISPs and large enterprises the transition of some networking pieces to IPv6 may require additional hardware and software costs. For example, additional memory will be needed in forwarding hardware pieces to continue current network performance given the larger size (128 bits vs. 32 bits in IPv4) of IPv6 addresses. Additionally, mainframes and billing systems might need hardware or software upgrades ahead of routine upgrades, which occur very infrequently for these devices, depending on the specific needs of a network (DoC, 2004). See Motorola comments at 6; Alcatel comments at 4.

51. These figures are based on information provided by stakeholders participating in the NIST study.

52. This figure represents our estimate based on BLS (2003) data and stakeholder interviews from the NIST study.

53. These users do not have network management software or major networking hardware that would need to be enabled. Routing upgrades would provide equipment and software that would be IPv6-enabled several years into the future, but no additional cost should be seen.

54. For example, an e-business would be much more reliant on the security of its network than a lumber manufacturer. Although the lumber manufacturer may experience problems related to a breach in security, it can continue to operate

the plant. The e-business could be affected much more significantly by one-off or more frequent security problems during a transition to IPv6.

55. We received this information during a phone interview on 17 September 2004 with John M. Baird, IPv6 pilot implementation manager with the DoD High Performance Computing Modernization Program (HPCMP). According to Baird, assuming a router runs at 40 percent of capacity regularly, if IPv6 addresses are used, the same routers would regularly be running at 80 percent of capacity. Therefore, routers will need approximately double the memory to ensure spikes do not crash the systems.

56. Several sites purchased commercial training at a cost of between $600 and $2250 per person; the Defence Research and Engineering Network (DREN) provided a half-day on-site orientation, training and planning seminar, and staff used numerous books, CDs and videos to help them understand the implications of IPv6.

57. Each site had several computers, massive file servers, a few high-speed networks and an average of approximately 45 desktop and laptop computers and visualization workstations.

10. Infrastructure for Software Testing[1]

INTRODUCTION

Cyber security is directly linked to the quality of software used on a computer or network. Software applications help to control both the flow and the security of information on the Internet. Software errors can have significant impacts on Internet operations and thus organizational efficiency. In addition, hackers spend significant amounts of time identifying and exploiting errors and weaknesses in operating systems and other network-connected software, including security software.

Industry and consumer watchdog groups have long questioned the level of effort software vendors invest in software testing prior to releasing their products. It is common practice for the software industry to release beta versions and even final versions anticipating errors will be found and patches will be distributed. Arora et al. (2007, p. 3) state:

> Many members of the security community have recommended regulations aimed at providing incentives for software vendors to minimize the time window of exposure to end users.

This approach to software development may have been acceptable when errors simply led to an individual system failure and user inconvenience. However, with today's interconnected networks and heightening cyber security concerns, errors or weaknesses in software can be quickly exploited and impact millions of users almost instantly.

Software has become an intrinsic part of business since the 1990s. Virtually every business in every sector of the United States depends on software to aid in the development, production, marketing and support of its products and services. Advances in computers and related technology have provided the building blocks upon which new industries have evolved. Innovations in the fields of robotic manufacturing, nanotechnology and human genetics research all have been enabled by low-cost computational and control capabilities supplied by computers and software.

With this growth, software quality has become an increasing important issue as programs become more complicated and different vintages of software are integrated. According to Frye (2007, p. 45):

> ... software has not been measuring up, and problems with poor quality have plagued the [software] industry. Many experts say things haven't improved much over the last several years, despite the increased recognition and attention paid to quality issues.

Reducing the cost for developing improved software quality is an important objective of the US software industry. However, the complexity of the underlying software needed to support the US's computerized economy is increasing at an alarming rate, and that rate of increase is a contributing factor to increases in the cost of cyber security. The size of software products is no longer measured in terms of thousands of lines of code, but in millions of lines of code. This increasing complexity along with a decreasing average market life expectancy for many software products has heightened concerns over software quality and related cyber security issues.

In actuality many factors contribute to the quality issues facing the software industry. These include marketing strategies, limited liability by software vendors, and decreasing returns to testing and debugging. At the core of these issues is the difficulty in defining and measuring software quality. Common attributes include functionality, reliability, usability, efficiency, maintainability and portability. But these quality metrics are largely subjective and do not support rigorous quantification that could be used to design testing methods for software developers or support information dissemination to consumers. Information problems are further complicated by the fact that even with substantial testing, neither consumers nor software users reliably evaluate the quality of products until after purchase and installation. This leads to the following questions:

- Are software vendors providing the socially optimal level of software quality to support cyber security?
- If not, what market failures are leading to an underinvestment in software testing?
- Is there a role for government involvement is ensuring software quality in order to promote cyber security?

This chapter overviews the determinants of software quality, evaluating the factors that influence the level of effort software developers invest in software testing. We investigate whether the socially optimal level of software testing may deviate from the private sector investment due to market failures and if so, what role the public sector may play in narrowing this gap.

Our analysis is informed by information collected during a study for the National Institute of Standards and Technology (Gallaher and Kropp, 2002). Surveys were conducted with both software developers and industry users of software. Data were collected to develop quantitative estimates of the economic impact of inadequate software testing methods and tools. Two groups were selected for this type of detailed analysis: automotive and aerospace equipment manufacturers, and financial services providers and electronic communications equipment manufacturers who interact with financial services providers. The findings from these two industry groups were then used as the basis for estimating the total economic impact for the US manufacturing and services sectors.

OVERVIEW OF SOFTWARE TESTING AND QUALITY

Issues of Software Testing

The historic approach to the software development process, which focused on system specification and construction, is often based on the waterfall model (Andersson and Bergstrand, 1995). Figure 10.1 shows how this process separates software development into several distinct phases with minimal feedback loops. The requirements are first defined, then systems are developed to correspond to the design. Testing occurs in two stages: the program itself is tested first, followed by a test of how the program works with other programs. Finally, normal system operation and maintenance take place. The waterfall model can be used in a component-based world for describing the separate activities needed in software development. For example, the requirements and design phase can include identifying available reusable software.

Feedback loops throughout the entire development process increase the ability to reuse components. Reuse is the key attribute in component-based software development (CBSD). When building a component-based program, developers need to examine the available products and how they will be integrated not only into the system they are developing, but also into all other potential systems. Feedback loops exist throughout the process, and each step is no longer an isolated event.

Cyber Security

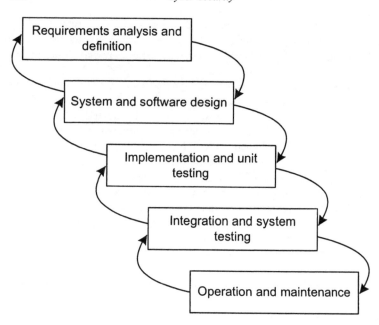

Figure 10.1 Waterfall model of software development

Figure 10.2 illustrates the hierarchical structure of software testing stages, software testing tools and standardized software testing technologies. Standardized software testing technologies such as standard reference data, reference implementations, test procedures and test cases (both manual and automated) provide the scientific foundation for commercial testing tools. The hierarchical structure of commercial software testing technologies illustrates the foundational role that *standardized* software testing technologies play.

Software testing activities and goals are generally classified into three types: (1) conformance testing activities assess the conformance of a software product to a set of industry-wide standards or customer specifications; (2) interoperability testing activities assess the ability of a software product to interoperate with other software; and (3) performance testing activities assess the performance of a software product with respect to specified metrics, and the target values of those metrics are typically determined internally by the software developer.

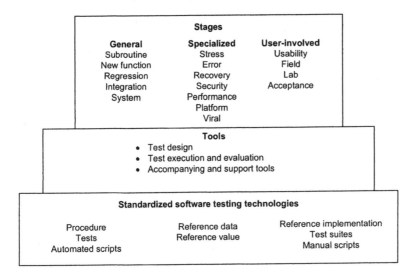

Figure 10.2 Commercial software testing infrastructure hierarchy

Conformance testing, interoperability testing and performance testing provide categories of metrics by which software quality is measured. However, developing a common set of underlying metrics by which software can be evaluated has proven to be extremely difficult and standards are not commonly accepted throughout the industry.

Issues of Software Quality

Quality is defined as the bundle of attributes present in a commodity and, where appropriate, the level of the attribute for which the consumers hold a positive value. Defining the attributes of software quality and determining the metrics to assess the relative value of each attribute are not formalized processes. Compounding the problem is that numerous metrics exist to test each quality attribute.

Because users place different values on each attribute depending on the product's use, it is important that quality attributes be observable to consumers. However, with software there exist not only asymmetric information problems (where a developer has more information about quality than the consumer), but also instances where the developer truly does not know the quality of his own product. It is not unusual for software to become technically obsolete before its performance attributes have been fully demonstrated under real-world operational conditions.

As software has evolved over time, so has the definition of software quality attributes. McCall et al. (1977) first attempted to assess quality attributes for software. Their software quality model characterizes attributes in terms of three categories: product operation, product revision and product transition.

In 1991, the International Organization for Standardization (ISO) adopted ISO 9126 as the standard for software quality (ISO, 1991). It is structured around six main attributes listed below (sub-characteristics are listed in parenthesis):

- functionality (suitability, accurateness, interoperability, compliance, security)
- reliability (maturity, fault tolerance, recoverability)
- usability (understandability, learnability, operability)
- efficiency (time behavior, resource behavior)
- maintainability (analyzability, changeability, stability, testability)
- portability (adaptability, installability, conformance, replaceability).

Although a general set of standards has been agreed on, the appropriate metrics to test how well software meets those standards are still poorly defined. Publications by the Institute for Electrical and Electronics Engineers (IEEE, 1988, 1996) have presented numerous potential metrics that can be used to test each attribute. These metrics include: fault density, requirements compliance, test coverage and mean time to failure.

The problem is that no one metric is able to measure unambiguously a particular quality attribute. Different metrics may give different rank orderings of the same attribute, making comparisons across products difficult and uncertain.

Software Testing Inadequacies

Software testing is the action of carrying out one or more tests, where a test is a technical operation that determines one or more characteristics of a given software element or system, according to a specified procedure. The tools of software testing are hardware and/or software, the procedures for its use and the executable test suite used to carry out the testing (NIST, 1997).

Historically, software development focused on writing code and testing specific lines of that code. Very little effort was spent on determining its fit within a larger system. Testing was seen as a necessary evil to prove to the final consumer that the product worked. As shown in Table 10.1, Andersson and Bergstrand (1995) estimated that 80 percent of the effort put into early software development was devoted to coding and unit testing. This percentage has changed over time. Starting in the 1970s, software developers began to increase their efforts on requirements analysis and preliminary design, spending 20 percent of their effort in these phases.

Table 10.1 Allocation of effort in software development

	Require-ments analysis	Preliminary design	Detailed design	Coding and unit testing	Integra-tion and test	System test
1960s–70s	10%			80%	10%	
1980s	20%		60%		20%	
1990s–2005	40%	30%		30%		

Source: Andersson and Bergstrand (1995) and Gallaher and Kropp (2002).

In the 1990s, software developers started to invest more time and resources in integrating the different pieces of software and testing the software as a unit rather than as independent entities. The amount of effort spent on determining the developmental requirements of a particular software solution has increased in importance. Forty percent of the software developer effort is now spent in the requirements analysis phase.

Testing activities are conducted throughout all the development phases shown in Table 10.1. Formal testing conducted by independent test groups accounts for about 20 percent of labor costs. However, estimates of total labor resources spent testing by all parties range from 30 percent to 90 percent (Beizer, 1990).

Numerous issues affect the software testing infrastructure and may lead to inadequacies. For example, competitive market pressures may encourage the use of a less than optimal amount of time, resources and training for the testing function (Rivers and Vouk, 1998). Further, with current software testing tools, developers have to determine whether applications and systems will interoperate.

In addition, the need for certified standardized test technology is increasing. The development of these tools and the accompanying testing suites often lag behind the development of new software applications (ITToolbox, 1999). Standardized testing tools, suites, scripts, reference data, reference implementations and metrics that have undergone a rigorous certification process would have a large impact on the inadequacies listed above. For example, the availability of standardized test data, metrics and automated test suites for performance testing would make benchmarking tests less costly to perform. Standardized automated testing scripts along with standard metrics would also provide a more consistent method for determining when to stop testing.

In some instances, developing conformance testing code can be more time consuming and expensive than developing the software product being tested. Addressing the high testing costs is currently the focus of several research initiatives in industry and academia. Many of these initiatives are based on modeling finite state machines, combinatorial logic or other formal languages (Tai and Carver, 1995; Cohen et al., 1996; Apfelbaum and Doyle, 1997; NIST, 1997).

A MODEL OF SOFTWARE TESTING INFRASTRUCTURE

In actuality many factors contribute to the quality issues facing the software industry. These include marketing strategies, limited liability by software vendors and decreasing returns to testing and debugging. However, underlying these issues is a group of core market failures which suggest a role for public sector involvement.

Market failures leading to a suboptimal level of software quality can be generally grouped into three broad categories:

- information problems where consumers cannot assess the quality of software (no certification process, the life of software is too short for reputation to be known and so on);
- imperfect contracts where vendors do not bear the costs associated with poor-quality software; and
- difficulty for developers to appropriate returns to research and development in software testing methods and tools.

The cost of an inadequate infrastructure for software testing can also be expressed as the benefit of an improved infrastructure for software testing.

These values (cost and benefit) are symmetrical. They are properly measured as either the minimum amount of money all members of society would collectively require to forego the improved infrastructure or as the maximum amount of money all members of society would collectively pay for the improved infrastructure.

An improved testing infrastructure could have several potential impacts on software developers and end-users. Understanding the mechanism through which costs are incurred (or benefits foregone) is an important first step in developing a cost taxonomy for estimating the economic impact of the failure to achieve these improvements. In this case, an appropriate measure of the economic impact of an inadequate infrastructure for software testing is the difference in the profits of developers and users given the current testing infrastructure as compared with the counterfactual infrastructure (discussed below).

More specifically, for developers the appropriate measure of the value that would be placed on an improved infrastructure for software testing is the profit difference between conditions with the current testing infrastructure and conditions with the counterfactual infrastructure. If π represents the profit the developer receives over the entire product lifecycle, and if π' represents the profit the developer receivers over the entire life cycle under the counterfactual conditions (for example, hypothetical improvements in testing infrastructure), then the benefit of an improved software testing infrastructure to a developer is the developer's difference in profit: $(\pi' - \pi)$. Alternatively, this profit difference can be viewed as the cost to the developer of failing to provide the improved infrastructure. The industry-level values are the sum of the company-level profit differences for all companies in the software industry.

Consider a software developer that is maximizing profit, π, with respect to the level of research and development (R&D) expenditure it will devote to product quality. The level of quality of the developer's software can be thought of as the inverse in the number of bugs remaining in the product including its level of interoperability with complementary products or legacy systems. The greater the number of bugs, the greater the likelihood of a security breach, although that relationship is certainly not one-to-one and perhaps not even linear.

The profit-maximizing software developer will continue to invest in software testing as long as the marginal cost of obtaining an additional unit of quality is less than the marginal benefit of the additional unit of quality.[2] As shown in Figure 10.3, the marginal cost of pre-sales quality increases

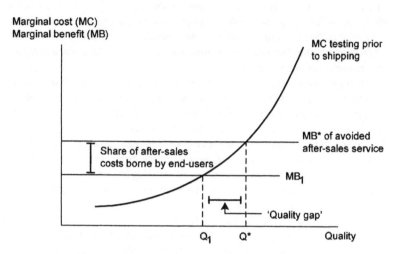

*Figure 10.3 Minimize joint costs of pre-sales testing and after-sales service
(holding price and quantity constant)*

exponentially and the marginal benefit of avoided after-sales service is
represented as being constant. The constant marginal benefits curve reflects
a fixed avoided after-sales service cost per unit of quality.[3]

If the developer bears all the after-sales service costs (or if the developer
and end-user are the same entity, such as with in-house software
development), as shown by MB*, the optimal level of quality is Q^*. Q^* also
reflects the optimal social level of software quality. However, if the
developer only bears part of the after-sales costs, the marginal benefit (MB)
of quality to the developer is less, as represented by MB_1. As a result, the
developer will select a quality level of less than Q^*, represented by Q_1 in
Figure 10.3. The result is a quality gap of $(Q^* - Q_1)$.

ESTIMATING THE COST OF INADEQUATE SOFTWARE TESTING

To estimate the social costs attributed to an inadequate infrastructure for
software testing, a precise definition of the counterfactual environment is

needed. Clearly defining what is meant by an inadequate infrastructure is essential for eliciting consistent information from industry respondents.

In the counterfactual scenario we keep the intended functionality of the software products released by developers constant. In other words, the fundamental product design and intended product characteristics will not change. However, the realized level of functionality may be affected as the number of bugs (also referred to as defects or errors) present in released versions of the software decreases in the counterfactual scenario.

The driving technical factors that do change in the counterfactual scenario are the timing of bug discovery in the software development process and the cost of fixing them. An improved infrastructure for software testing has the potential to affect software developers and users by (1) removing more bugs before the software product is released for sale, (2) detecting bugs earlier in the software development process and (3) locating the source of bugs faster and with more precision.

A key assumption is that the number of bugs introduced into software code is constant regardless of the types of tools available for software testing. Bugs are errors entered by the software designer or programmer, and the initial number of errors depends on the skill of and techniques employed by the programmer.[4]

The development of software involves three main processes: system software design; implementation and unit testing; and integration testing, as the subcomponents of the software product are assembled and then the product is released. Errors are generated or introduced at each stage of the software development process, beginning with system software design, moving to implementation and unit testing, and then ending with integration testing. An improved infrastructure would find the bugs within or closer to the stage in which they were introduced rather than bugs being found later in the production process or by the end-user of the software product. The later in the production process that a software error is discovered, the more costly it is to repair.

Developers' Costs of Identifying and Correcting Errors

Table 10.2 illustrates this increasing cost of repairing a bug with a hypothetical example showing the relative differences in the cost of repairing bugs that are introduced in the requirements gathering, analysis and architectural design stage as a function of when they are detected. For example, errors introduced during this stage and found in the same stage

Table 10.2 Relative cost to repair defects when found at different stages of
*   software development (example only)*

Requirements gathering and analysis/ architectural design	Coding/ unit test	Integration and component/ system test	Early customer feedback/beta test programs	Post-product release
1X	5X	10X	15X	30X

Note: X is a normalized unit of cost that can be expressed in terms of person-hours, dollars, etc.

cost 1X to fix, where X is a normalized unit of cost that can be expresses in terms of person hours, dollars and so on. But if the same error is not found until the integration and component/system test stage, it costs ten times more to fix. This is due to the re-engineering process that needs to happen because the software developed to date has to be unraveled and rewritten to fix the error that was introduced earlier in the production process. However, bugs are also introduced in the coding and integration stages of software design.

A complete set of relative cost factors is shown in Table 10.3 and shows that regardless of when an error is introduced it is always more costly to fix it downstream in the development process.

Conceptually there is no need to restrict the diagonal elements in Table 10.3 to equal 1. Each column has its own unique base multiplier, and this could capture, for example, that errors introduced during integration are harder to find and correct than coding or design errors.

The relative cost factors for developers shown in Table 10.3 also illustrate that errors are found by users in the beta testing and post-product release stages because typically not all of the errors are caught before the software is distributed to customers. When users identify an error, developers bear costs related to locating and correcting the error, developing and distributing patches and providing other support services. Users bear costs in the form of lost data, foregone or delayed transactions and product failures; however, users' costs are not included in developers' relative cost factors and were estimated separately.

The total cost of errors can be calculated by combining the relative cost factors with the number and distribution of errors. Table 10.4 shows an example of the frequency distribution of where errors may be found, in relationship to where they may be introduced.

Table 10.3 Relative cost factors of correcting errors as a function of where errors are introduced and found (example only)

	Where errors are found				
Where errors are introduced	Requirements gathering and analysis/ architectural design	Coding/ unit test	Integration and component/ system test	Early customer feedback/ beta test programs	Post-product release
Requirements gathering and analysis/ architectural design	1.0	5.0	10.0	15.0	30.0
Coding/unit test		1.0	10.0	20.0	30.0
Integration and component/ system test			1.0	10.0	20.0

Table 10.4 Example of the frequency (%) of where errors are found, in relationship to where they were introduced

	Where errors are found					
Where errors are introduced (%)	Require-ments gathering and analysis/ architec-tural design	Coding/ unit test	Integration and component/ system test	Early customer feedback/ beta test programs	Post-product release	Total
Requirements gathering and analysis/ architectural design	3.5	10.5	35	6	15	70
Coding/unit test		6	9	2	3	20
Integration and component/ system test			6.5	1	2.5	10
Total	3.5	16.5	50.5	9	20.5	100

The smoothed cumulative distribution of error detection is depicted in Figure 10.4. The data in this figure exhibit the classic S-shape of the cumulative distribution of the discovery of errors with respect to life-cycle stages as published by several researchers (Vouk, 1992; Beizer, 1984). The distribution in Figure 10.4 along with the values in Table 10.4 are important because they illustrate the main problem plaguing the software development industry for years: most software errors are found during the middle to later stages of development, namely integration through primary release, which happen to be the most expensive stages to fix errors (Rivers and Vouk, 1998).

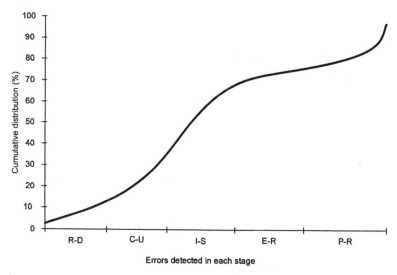

Notes:

R-D: Requirements gathering and analysis/architectural design
C-U: Coding/unit test
I-S: Integration and component/system test
E-R: Early customer feedback/beta test programs
P-R: Post-product release

Figure 10.4 Typical cumulative distribution of error detection

Combining the distribution of where errors are found (Figure 10.4) with the relational cost factors to correct the errors (Table 10.3) provides a step-wise depiction of developers' costs. In Figure 10.5, the area below the graph represents the costs associated with errors detected in the various stages of the software life cycle. Thus, if the total amount that software developers spend on testing and correction activities were known, the average cost per bug and the individual step-wise areas could be determined.

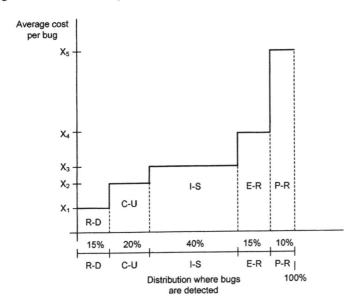

Notes:

R-D: Requirements gathering and analysis/architectural design
C-U: Coding/unit test
I-S: Integration and component/system test
E-R: Early customer feedback/beta test programs
P-R: Post-product release
The area under the step-wise curve represents the total cost of fixing bugs.

Figure 10.5 Software testing costs shown by where bugs are detected (example only)

The cost to developers of an inadequate software testing infrastructure relative to the counterfactual scenario (of an improved software testing infrastructure) is shown in Figure 10.6. The impact of an inadequate infrastructure for software testing on fixing errors can be calculated from the impact that an improved software infrastructure would have on two metric categories: the relative cost to fix errors based on when they are introduced and when they are found (Table 10.2) and the distribution of where errors are detected (Table 10.4).

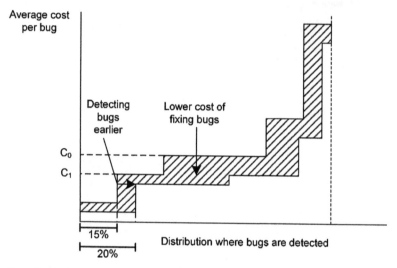

Note: Hatched area represents the developers' costs due to an inadequate infrastructure for software testing.

Figure 10.6 Cost reductions of detecting bugs and fixing them faster (example only)

For example, the cost to fix a bug that occurred during the coding stage that is not discovered until the integration phase may decrease from C_0 to C_1 if enhanced software testing tools decrease the time needed to locate the error's source. Additionally, with better testing tools, more bugs introduced in the requirements stage might be found during that stage, increasing the percentage of bugs found in this stage from 15 to 20 percent.[5]

An inadequate infrastructure for software testing will lead to errors being identified later in the development process and more resources being needed to locate and correct the source of the error. These consequences affect developer costs throughout the software's life cycle through changes in the following:

- labor costs – additional employee and contract labor expenditure for pre-purchase testing and error correction, installation and post-purchase repair;
- software costs – additional or redundant testing software purchases;
- hardware costs – additional expenditure on equipment, computers and other physical technologies used in the testing process;
- after-sales service costs – additional nontesting and debugging activities such as fielding an increased number of service calls and the distribution of patches;
- delay costs – discounted value of lost profits due to time delays in product releases and delayed adoption by users due to large numbers of bugs in early software versions; and
- reputation costs – lost sales or market share due to highly publicized product failures.

To quantify developer costs, our survey analysis asked for the software development companies' total pre-release testing costs and post-release (after-sales) service costs. We asked them to divide the pre-release testing costs into total labor costs, software expenditure, hardware expenditure and external testing services. The remaining developer interview questions addressed the incremental impact of an inadequate software infrastructure. We developed metrics first for current development practices, referred to as the baseline scenario, and second for the counterfactual scenario of improved testing capabilities.

During the case studies, we asked developers to describe changes in labor costs in terms of changes in relative cost factors. Labor costs account for most of the impact of an inadequate software testing infrastructure on software developers. However, we also asked developers to estimate the impact of improved testing capabilities on hardware and software expenditures.

Users' Costs of Identifying and Correcting Errors

The primary impact for users associated with the counterfactual of an improved infrastructure for software testing is that fewer bugs would make it to the software operations stage. This would lead to lower user maintenance costs and lower software failure costs.

A key assumption in the counterfactual scenario is a reduction in the number of bugs encountered by users during business operations. In some instances it may be unrealistic to assume that an improved infrastructure will lead to the detection of all bugs during software testing. As part of the developers' surveys, we asked developers to estimate what they consider to be a feasible percentage reduction in error (passes on to users) with an improved software testing infrastructure. This percentage reduction is used in the following analysis to estimate user cost reductions from a feasible infrastructure improvement.

Inadequate software testing affects users through uncertainty concerning the number of bugs remaining in software that is released, as well as the actual number of bugs remaining. Users are at the end of the supply chain and are the source of benefits and costs realized from software quality. For example, if there is a software failure that prevents a transaction from occurring or delays the release of a new product, these costs affect the users.

User costs associated with software errors begin with the software purchase decision. Users evaluate the set of potential software products that are available to them, and compare price and quality. This search process is costly and requires time because users do not have complete information about the quality of all of the software products that they could purchase. This lack of ability to compare across products based on price and quality is magnified by an inadequate software testing infrastructure, because uncertainty about bugs and interoperability increases. As a result, users must spend additional time and resources to determine which product to buy, and in some instances may delay purchasing new software products until more information about software quality is revealed by early adopters. Delays in adoption reduce the benefits from the new software and in turn lead to reductions in economic welfare.

Once users have decided to purchase a product, they must install and incorporate it into their business operations. If the software is a custom product, implementation can be very costly and may involve significant effort by both users and developers. Custom products must frequently be integrated with legacy systems, and errors leading to interoperability problems may exist in both the new software and the legacy software. Bugs encountered while implementing a custom product can lead to delays in bringing the system online and the need for special patches and interface programs. The potential for excess costs due to an inadequate software testing infrastructure may be great at this point. To a lesser extent, these problems also potentially exist when implementing commercial software products. However, typically implementation problems such as errors leading to improper or incomplete installation are minimal with commercial software.

The final stage of the process for users occurs after the product has been implemented and business operations begin. At this point, additional bugs that cause the system to fail may emerge that were not captured during development and implementation. Costs associated with bugs in this stage can be catastrophic and include loss of production data and customer information, lost sales, production delays and lost reputation and market share.

The general cost categories for software users are described below:

- labor costs – additional employee and contract labor (third-party integrators) expenditures for testing, installation and repair of new software due to an inadequate infrastructure for testing the software before it is purchased.
- failure costs – costs associated with catastrophic failure of software products.
- performance costs – impact on users' operating costs when software does not perform as expected; these include the cost of 'work-arounds' and loss of productivity when purchased software does not perform as anticipated.
- redundant systems – additional hardware or software systems that users maintain to support operations and back up data in case of a software failure attributable to an inadequate infrastructure for software testing.
- delayed profits – discounted value of time delays in production and transactions attributable to an inadequate software product.
- sales forfeited – discounted value of foregone transactions due to an inadequate software product.

Redundant systems resulting from inadequate software testing represent a significant, but less publicized, economic impact. Companies commonly maintain parallel systems for up to a year or more as a security measure against catastrophic failures. If an improved software testing infrastructure could reduce the probability and severity of bugs remaining in products after purchase, the time window for redundant systems could be greatly reduced.

The number of bugs still remaining in software products with an improved software testing infrastructure is a key assumption that we clearly addressed in the counterfactual scenario and related data collection efforts. Because assuming that all bugs can be removed is not realistic, users were asked how different cost categories will be affected by a partial reduction in bugs (25, 50 or 75 percent reduction). Our approach to quantifying the impact of removing most but not all of the bugs users encounter is to:

- estimate the total cost of bugs to users; and
- determine which costs are linearly related to the number of bugs encountered and which costs are non-linearly related.

Users were asked to estimate the total cost of bugs in each cost category. We found that it was simpler for software users to provide information on their total costs associated with bugs as opposed to marginal changes in costs associated with an incremental decrease in bugs. Users were then asked to assess general trends in how the total costs they provide would change as the number of bugs is reduced. For example, how would each cost category change if bugs were cut in half or reduced by 75 percent? For product failure or installation, the cost of bugs may be linearly related to the number of bugs (that is, if product failures are reduced by 75 percent, then repair and lost sales would be reduced by 75 percent). However, for other cost categories, such as redundant system costs, a 75 percent reduction in the probability of bugs may not significantly reduce the need for back-up systems.

Figure 10.7 illustrates the relationship between user costs and the percentage reduction in bugs. The case studies investigated the shape of these curves for each cost category listed in Table 10.5. These relationships are useful for conducting sensitivity tests. The relationships in Figure 10.7 also allow us to estimate the upper and lower bounds for economic impacts associated with ranges, such as 50 to 100 percent, of reductions in the number of bugs.

CASE STUDIES OF THE ECONOMIC COST OF INADEQUATE SOFTWARE TESTING

This section investigates the excess costs resulting from an inadequate infrastructure for software testing incurred by software developers and users in the automotive and aerospace industries and in the financial services

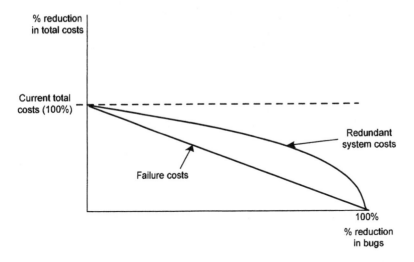

Figure 10.7   Relationship between users' costs and percentage reduction in bugs

sector. The impact estimates are based on interviews with software developers and users in the supply chains of these sectors.

Impact estimates were developed relative to two counterfactual scenarios. The first scenario investigates the cost reductions if all bugs and errors could be found in the same development stage in which they are introduced. This is referred to as the total cost of an inadequate software testing infrastructure. The second scenario investigates the cost reductions associated with finding an increased percentage (but not 100 percent) of bugs and errors closer to the development stages where they are introduced. The second scenario is referred to as the cost reduction from feasible infrastructure improvements.

Economic Impact in the Automotive and Aerospace Industries

We conducted a case study with software developers and users in the transportation equipment manufacturing sector to estimate the economic impact of an inadequate infrastructure for software testing. This case study focused on the use of computer-aided design, computer-aided manufacturing and computer-aided engineering (CAD/CAM/CAE) and product data management (PDM) software. We conducted interviews with ten software developers (vendors) and 179 users of these products.

Developers of CAD/CAM/CAE and PDM software indicated that in the current environment, software testing is still more of an art than a science, and testing methods and resources are selected based on the expert judgment of senior staff. Respondents agreed that finding the errors early in the development process greatly lowered the average cost of bugs and errors. Most also indicated that the lack of historic tracking data and inadequate tools and testing methods – such as standard protocols approved by management, available test cases and conformance specification – limited their ability to obtain sufficient testing resources (from management) and to leverage these resources effectively.

Users of CAD/CAM/CAE and PDM software indicated that they spend significant resources responding to software errors (mitigation costs) and lowering the probability and potential impact of software errors (avoidance costs). Approximately 60 percent of the automotive and aerospace manufacturers surveyed indicated that they had experienced significant software errors in the previous year. For those respondents who experienced errors, they reported an average of 40 major and 70 minor software bugs per year in their CAD/CAM/CAE or PDM software systems.

Table 10.5 presents the economic impact estimates for the development and use of CAD/CAM/CAE and PDM software in the US automotive and aerospace industries. The total annual cost impact on these manufacturing sectors from an inadequate software testing infrastructure is estimated to be $1.8 billion and the potential cost reduction from feasible infrastructure improvements is $0.6 billion per year. Users of CAD/CAM/CAE and PDM software account for approximately three-quarters of the total impact, with users in the automotive industry representing about 65 percent and users in the aerospace industry representing 10 percent. Developers account for the remaining one-quarter of the costs.

Economic Impact in the Financial Services Sector

We conducted a second case study with four software developers and 98 software users in the financial services sector to estimate the economic impact of an inadequate infrastructure for software testing. The case study focused on the development and use of Financial Electronic Data Interchange (FEDI) and clearinghouse software, as well as the software embedded in routers and switches that support electronic data exchange.

*Table 10.5   Cost impacts on US software developers and users in the
transportation manufacturing sector due to an inadequate
testing infrastructure ($2000)*

	The cost of inadequate software testing infrastructure ($ billions)	Potential cost reduction from feasible infrastructure improvements ($ billions)
Software developers		
CAD/CAM/CAE and PDM	$373.1	$157.7
Software users		
Automotive	$1229.7	$377.0
Aerospace	$237.4	$54.5
Total	$1840.2	$589.2

All developers of financial services software agreed that an improved system for testing was needed. They said that an improved system would be able to track a bug back to the point where it was introduced, and then determine how that bug influenced the rest of the production process. Their ideal testing infrastructure would consist of close to real-time testing where testers could remedy problems that emerge right away rather than waiting until a product is fully assembled. The major benefits developers cited from an improved infrastructure were direct cost reduction in the development process and a decrease in post-purchase customer support. An additional benefit that respondents thought would emerge from an improved testing infrastructure is increased confidence in the quality of the product they produce and ship. The major selling characteristic of the products they create is the certainty that each product will accomplish a particular task. Because of the real-time nature of their products, the reputation loss can be great.

Approximately two-thirds of the users of financial services software surveyed (that is, primarily banks and credit unions) indicated that they had experienced major software errors in the previous year. For the respondents that did have major errors, they reported an average of 40 major and 49 minor software bugs per year in their FEDI or clearinghouse software systems. Approximately 16 percent of those bugs were attributed to router and switch problems, and 48 percent were attributed to transaction software problems. The source of the remaining 36 percent of errors was unknown.

Typical problems encountered due to bugs included increased person-hours needed to correct posting errors, temporary shut-down of software systems leading to lost transactions, and delay of transaction processing.

Table 10.6 presents the empirical findings. The total cost impact on the financial services sector from an inadequate software testing infrastructure is estimated to be $3.3 billion. Potential cost reduction from feasible infrastructure improvements is $1.5 billion.

Table 10.6   Cost impacts on US software developers and users in the financial services sector due to an inadequate testing infrastructure ($2000)

	The cost of inadequate software testing infrastructure ($ millions)	Potential cost reduction from feasible infra-structure improvements ($ millions)
Software developers		
Router and switch	$1897.9	$975.0
FEDI and clearinghouse	$438.8	$225.4
Software users		
Banks and savings institutions	$789.3	$244.0
Credit unions	$216.5	$68.1
Total financial services sector	$3342.5	$1512.6

Software developers account for about 75 percent of the economic impacts. Users represented the remaining 25 percent of costs, with banks accounting for the majority of user costs.

National Impact Estimates

The two case studies generated estimates of the costs of an inadequate software testing infrastructure for software developers and users in the transportation equipment manufacturing and financial services sectors. The per-employee impacts for these sectors were extrapolated to other manufacturing and service industries to develop an approximate estimate of the economic impact of an inadequate infrastructure for software testing for the total US economy.

Table 10.7 shows national annual cost estimates of an inadequate infrastructure for software testing are estimated to be $59.5 billion. The potential cost reduction from feasible infrastructure improvements is $22.2 billion. This represents about 0.6 and 0.2 percent of the US's $10 trillion dollar gross domestic product (GDP), respectively. Software developers accounted for about 40 percent of the total impact, and software users accounted for the about 60 percent.

Table 10.7 Costs of inadequate software testing infrastructure on the national economy ($2000)

	The cost of inadequate software testing infrastructure ($ billions)	Potential cost reduction from feasible infrastructure improvements ($ billions)
Software developers	$21.2	$10.6
Software users	$38.3	$11.7
Total	$59.5	$22.2

CONCLUSIONS

The public sector has a significant role to play in assuring software quality, which in turn is a key determinant of cyber security and consequently, the efficient user of IT systems. For a range of reasons, the private sector has difficulties appropriating the return to investments in software quality. The result is an underinvestment in research and development and software testing activities targeted at enhancing software quality.

The problem is primarily informational in nature in that there is a lack of operational metrics to measure and certify software quality and thus a dearth of useful, reusable software assurance tools. Quality is not observable to consumers and is difficult for vendors or third parties to document and verify. As a result, when consumers can not distinguish between high- and low-quality software, research has shown that market forces tend to drive quality to the lowest common denominator.[6] Reputation effects from highly publicized software defects and security events provide some incentives for vendors to minimize software vulnerabilities. However, many experts feel that there exists a significant gap between the level of software quality being provided by the private sector and what would be socially optimal (that is, the level that would minimize the total cost of errors to society).

Viewed from a simple supply and demand framework, the public sector can influence the level of software quality provided by the private sector through two general approaches:

- increasing the 'demand for quality' by making software quality more observable to consumers at the time of purchase; and/or
- increasing the 'supply of quality' by lowering the cost of software testing activities.

Both of these relate to improvements in the technology infrastructure supporting software development and have public-goods characteristics which support a need for government involvement. Over the past several years, NIST has been working with DHS on a project called SAMATE that has three main goals: 'assess Software Assurance (SwA) methods and tools to identify what can prevent failure and vulnerabilities, develop metrics for their effectiveness, and identify gaps in SwA methods and tools' (Black, 2007). DHS also has a Software Assurance Program that 'seeks to reduce software vulnerabilities, minimize exploitation, and address ways to improve the routine development and deployment of trustworthy software products' (DHS, 2007). However, thus far these programs have not resulted in significant improvements in software testing standards or tools.

At the core of the information problem is the difficulty in defining and measuring software quality. Quality metrics are largely subjective and do not support rigorous quantification that could be used to design testing methods for software developers or support information dissemination to consumers. This lack of observable quality not only impacts upon consumers' purchase decisions, but also prevents the functioning of the insurance market that could be use to hedge against the risk of security events or catastrophic failure.

The availability of standardized testing tools, suites, scripts, reference data, reference implementations and metrics that have undergone a rigorous certification process would have a significant impact on the inadequacies listed above. For example, the availability of standardized test data, metrics and automated test suites for performance testing would make benchmarking tests less costly to perform. Standardized automated testing scripts along with standard metrics would also provide a more consistent method for determining when to stop testing.

Coordinating and supporting the development of standard metrics and test methods is a classic area for public sector involvement. Third-party certification systems and information dissemination across vendors and to consumers are also important roles government agencies could support.

In some instances, developing conformance testing code can be more time-consuming and expensive than developing the software product being tested. The development of these tools and the accompanying testing suites often lag behind the development of new software applications. Addressing the high testing costs is currently the focus of several research initiatives in industry and academia. However, additional work and resources are needed.

By supporting research to develop the infrastructure for software testing, the public sector could incentivize vendors to increase testing activities without the heavy-handed approach of regulation or litigation. If well-established and proven testing tools were available and cost-effective, vendors indicated during our interviews that they would be quickly adopted.

In addition, even more important than lowering costs (labor hours) is the need to shorten testing time. The competitive market pressure of being first to market with a new product type or feature encourages the release of software with only the basic levels of quality assurance. Perfect software is worthless if it misses its window of opportunity, and every day a product release is delayed shortens its already short life expectancy.

In general, software testing tools, methods and standards need to be widely available and accepted by the industry. They function best as public goods and do not fit the profit model of patenting or licensing. As a result, organizations such as the National Science Foundation, the NIST and the ISO have important roles to play in coordinating and funding research into the underlying infrastructure technologies supporting software testing.

NOTES

1. Our analysis is informed by information collected during a study for the National Institute of Standards and Technology (Gallaher and Kropp, 2002).
2. The MC curve represents the distribution of costs for a given level of testing technology. Additional testing resources move a developer along the curve. An improved testing infrastructure will shift the MC curve down.
3. It is unclear whether bugs found after a large amount of testing has already been conducted are more costly or less costly to fix. Thus, we assume a flat MB curve, implying that the average cost per after-sales bug is constant with

respect to the level of quality. We do, however, recognize that they are more costly to find.

4.   There is a distinction between inadequate software testing and inadequate programming skills or techniques. For example, Carnegie Mellon Software Engineering Institute has developed the Personal Software Process (PSP) and the Team Software Process (TSP) that are designed to reduce the number of errors in the program when it is first compiled. In general, the PSP and TSP involve individual programmers tracking their errors to improve their programming skills, and team members thoroughly reviewing code to identify errors prior to compiling and run-time testing. For this study, we define these programming activities as upstream and not part of the software testing process. Thus, the number of errors generated as part of initial software coding does not change in the counterfactual scenario. It is the process of identifying and correcting these exogenous errors that changes.

5.   Note that the total number of errors introduced into the software is assumed to be unchanged in the counterfactual. These bugs are a normal and expected part of the software production process. The distribution of the bug's location and the cost of fixing the errors change. Although improved software development tools could result in fewer errors being introduced – a proactive improvement – we focus on improvements in software testing – a reactive improvement.

6.   Information asymmetries have been widely discussed in the economic literature using examples such as the used-car market for lemons and moral hazard in insurance markets.

11. Insider Threats and the Case for Role-Based Access Control[1]

INTRODUCTION

As organizations increase the functionality and information offered on internal networks, controlling internal staff (that is, 'insiders') access to information and other resources becomes more important and complex. Organizations must develop and enforce access policies that protect sensitive and confidential information; prevent conflicts of interest; and protect the system and its contents from intentional and unintentional damage, theft and unauthorized disclosure. As documented in Chapter 2, internal security failures can disrupt an organization's operations and can have financial, legal, human safety, personal privacy and public confidence impacts (Ferraiolo et al., 1992).

Access control systems are generally used to determine what operations (for example, save, edit, copy, paste) users and groups of users can perform on what resources. The fundamental problem is that many systems and applications for which access control is enforced are based on proprietary methods for creating and managing users and groups. Further, system-specific terms and definitions are developed for operations and objects. For many organizations, the number of such systems can be in the hundreds or even thousands, the number of users can range from the hundreds to the hundreds of thousands and the number of resources that must be protected can easily exceed a million.

This chapter investigates insider threats and access control, and presents a case study analysis of role-based access control (RBAC). RBAC is a system designed to centrally manage privileges by providing layers of abstractions (that is, identities or job categories) that are mapped one-to-many to real users, real operations and real resources. Managing permissions in terms of the abstractions reduces complexity and provides visualization and context for implementing complex access control policies.

Our analysis is informed by information collected during a study for the National Institute of Standards and Technology (Gallaher, O'Connor and Kropp, 2002). Since our analysis, RBAC adoption has increased significantly (Stallings, 2008).

THE INSIDER THREAT AND ROLE-BASED ACCESS CONTROL

Insiders, typically organizational employees, have significant advantages over external hackers. Being behind the firewall they can by-pass physical and technical security measures designed to deter unauthorized access. In addition, they frequently have special knowledge of security practices and systems. Insiders may be aware of technical weaknesses or flaws, or they may be able to take advantage of certain security practices that are not always fully implemented. In many cases the simple implementation of existing policies can deter insider breaches; however, loosely enforced policies and procedures create opportunities.

Inherently, there is a trade-off between access control security and organizational efficiency. For example, simple, broad access procedures are less costly to implement and manage. In addition, granting blanket access permissions may reduce downtime and increase the flexibility and/or productivity of staff. However, these benefits come at the cost of increased vulnerability to insider breaches. It is not always possible to be aware of which employees may be experiencing financial problems or may be motivated by greed.

Insider threats are fundamentally different from external threats and generally are not detected by standard intrusion detection systems (IDSs). In assessing these threats, it is important not only to understand the security relationships and interactions of computers and network systems, but also to know how individuals interact and support these systems. A study conducted by the CERT Program at Carnegie Mellon University identified the following characteristics of insider threats: insiders were typically disgruntled employees, motivated by revenge for a negative work-related experience; insiders exhibited concerning behavior prior to the breach; insiders who committed IT sabotage held technical positions; and the majority of the insider attacks followed termination from their place of employment.

RBAC offers greater administrative efficiency as well as the ability to intuitively administer and enforce a wide range of access control policies. In RBAC dictates that permissions are associated with roles and users are made 'members' of roles, thereby acquiring the role's permissions. The implementation of this basic concept has been shown to simplify access control management greatly. Roles are centrally created for the various job functions in an organization, and users are assigned roles based on their responsibilities and qualifications. As such, users can be easily reassigned from one role to another.

Users can be granted new permissions as new applications and systems are incorporated, and permissions can be revoked from roles as needed. For example, if a user moves to a new function within the organization, the user can simply be assigned to the new role and removed from the old one, whereas in the absence of RBAC, the user's old privileges would have to be individually located, revoked and new privileges would have to be granted.

To provide further administrative efficiency, RBAC allows roles to inherit other roles, and as such form role hierarchies with 'higher' roles having all rights of 'lower' hierarchical roles.[2] RBAC provides the capability to visualize and manage user privileges across heterogonous platforms and applications. By centrally storing and managing roles as both collections of users and collections of privileges, RBAC is able to define, constrain, review and enforce access control policies as user/role, role/role or role/privilege relationships. RBAC is considered to be policy-neutral in that through the use of role hierarchies and constraints, a wide range of security policies can be expressed that include traditional discretionary access control (DAC) as well as a variety of nondiscretionary separation-of-duty policies.

Although role-based security models have existed for more than two decades, their application has until recently been limited. To date, most systems have based access control on the discretion of the owner or administrator of the data as opposed to basing access on organizational or policy needs, as is done with RBAC. These owner-controlled systems worked adequately for small local area networks (LANs) but have become cumbersome to manage and prone to error as networking capabilities and types of usage have increased.

Alternative Access Control Technologies

Several competing technologies are used to address access control. Whereas RBAC determines access to data based on organizational policy or needs, alternative models base access control on the discretion of the owner or administrator of the data. Under many alternate models, an end-user's identity determines which access permissions are needed. This section describes three such access control models: access control lists (ACLs), DAC and mandatory access control (MAC). Figure 11.1 compares RBAC to the latter two access control technologies. RBAC offers a more efficient method for assigning users access permission than these more traditional access control models.

Access control lists

One of the most common access control models is the use of ACLs. When using ACLs, every piece of data, database or application has a list of users associated with it who are allowed access. In this system, it is very easy for the security administrator to see which users have access to which data and applications. Changing access to the piece of information is straightforward; an administrator simply adds or deletes a user from the ACL.

Each set of data or application has its own ACL, but there may or may not be a corresponding list that gives the network administrator information on all of the pieces of information to which a particular user has access. Only by examining each piece of data individually and checking for access can the security administrator find any potential security violations. If all accesses by a particular user need to be revoked, the administrator must examine each ACL, one by one, and remove the user from each list. When a user takes on different responsibilities within the organization, the problem gets worse. Rather than simply eliminating the user from every ACL, the network administrator must determine which permissions need to be eliminated, left in place or altered.

Network administrators have made several attempts to improve ACLs. In some cases, users can be put into groups, making it easier to change the ACL. In other cases, elaborate rules can be applied to ACLs to limit access to particular pieces of data.

Discretionary access control

The main concept of DAC is that the individual who owns the data is able to control access to the data. ACLs are regarded as one implementation of DAC. DAC governs access to information based on the user's identity and rules that specify which users have access to which pieces of information. Whereas ACLs are lists that specify which users can access a particular piece of data, DAC consists of a set of rules that specify which users are

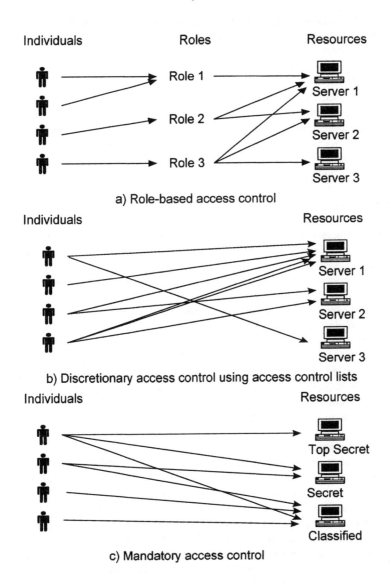

Figure 11.1 Alternative access control technologies

allowed to access the data. When a user requests access to a particular piece of data, the server searches for a rule that specifies which users are allowed to access the information. If the rule is found, the user is given access; if not, the user is denied. For example, a rule may state that users from a certain group are not allowed to read a particular data file.

Rule-based DAC is an advancement over ACLs, but it is still susceptible to human error and therefore suffers from potential security violations. DAC does not impose any restrictions on data access for a particular user. Once users can access data, they can change or pass that information onto any other user without the security administrator's knowledge (Sandhu and Samarati, 1994).

Mandatory access control

MAC is a departure from other access control mechanisms because it is based on hierarchical security labels and assigns each user and each piece of information or application a particular security level (for example, classified, secret, top secret). Two common principles are then applied to determine if a user has access to a particular piece of information: read down access and write up access.

Read down access gives a user the ability to access any piece of information that is at or below their own security level. If a user has a secret security level, he or she is able to access secret and classified material but not top secret material. Write up access states that a subject's clearance must be dominated by the security level of the data or information generated. For example, someone with a secret clearance can only write things that are secret or top secret. With these two access control principles, information can only flow across security levels or up security levels.

RBAC Technical Characteristics

RBAC offers an alternative to traditional DAC and MAC policies. RBAC allows organizations to specify and enforce security policies that map naturally to their structure. That is, the natural method for assigning access to information in an organization is based on the individual's need for the information, which is a function of their job or role within the organization. RBAC allows a security administrator to use the natural structure of the organization to implement and enforce security policy. This technology decreases the cost of network administration while improving the enforcement of network security policies.

Access control is generally concerned with determining what users and groups of users can perform, using what resources. The fundamental problem is that each system and application for which access control is enforced has a proprietary method for creating and managing users and groups, and a system-specific meaning of operations and objects.

RBAC is designed to manage privileges centrally by providing layers of abstractions that are mapped one-to-many to real users and real operations and real resources. Managing permissions in terms of the abstractions reduces complexity and provides visualization and a context for implementing complex access control policies. Abstractions can be centrally managed, resulting in real permissions on real systems.

In taking advantage of these abstractions, RBAC offers greater administrative efficiency as well as the ability to intuitively administer and enforce a wide range of access control policies. In RBAC, permissions are associated with roles, and users are made members of roles, thereby acquiring the role's permissions. The implementation of this basic concept has been shown to simplify access control management greatly. Roles are centrally created for the various job functions in an organization, and users are assigned roles based on their responsibilities and qualifications. As such, users can be easily reassigned from one role to another. Users can be granted new permissions as new applications and systems are incorporated, and permissions can be revoked from roles as needed. For example, if a user moves to a new function within an organization, the user can simply be assigned to the new role and removed from the old one, whereas in the absence of RBAC, the user's old privileges would have to be individually located and revoked, and new privileges would have to be granted.

The remainder of this section provides more details on the interaction among roles, users and permissions. It also discusses the RBAC models that have been developed and compares them to alternative access control models, such as access control lists and MAC.

RBAC users, roles and permissions

Traditionally, the prevalent approach to granting access to information within a particular database or access to a particular application is to establish specific permissions for each user within an organization. If the user requires access to multiple applications and databases, the user must be assigned permissions for each resource. This approach is problematic for several reasons. When users enter, leave or change responsibilities within an organization, updating the permissions of each user is difficult, time-consuming and possibly error-prone (Barkley et al., 1997). In addition, this approach leads to potential violations of information and system security. RBAC avoids these problems because it uses the user's role as the key to access rather than the user's identification, as shown in Figure 11.1.

In a role-based model, each user may be assigned to multiple roles, and each role may have multiple users. The roles that users are assigned depend on their job responsibilities, and each role is assigned permissions. Permissions determine the data and applications that may be accessed, and each role is assigned the set of permissions that are necessary for the user to perform their required tasks. Users' roles can pertain to specific jobs (for example, bank teller, bank manager), geographic locations (for example, New York, Chicago) or individual descriptors (for example, trainee, shift supervisor). In most situations, users within the organization change more frequently than the roles or job functions within the organization. By associating roles with permissions and changing the users within the roles, administrative expenses decrease. If an organization experiences a significant amount of worker turnover relative to role turnover, RBAC can provide significant cost savings (Ferraiolo and Kuhn, 1992).

Least privilege
Roles improve security within a network by using the principle of least privilege. When a role is created within an organization, the user's level of access to information needs to be determined. Least privilege means that once access requirements are determined, that role should only be given permissions to accomplish the required tasks; no additional permissions should be given. In networks without role-based policies, users often have access permissions exceeding what is necessary. Where job responsibilities overlap job categories, administrators may be unable to limit access to sensitive information. RBAC improves security within the network because it prevents users from having access to information outside of their roles. This denial of access prevents users from circumventing the security policy within the network.

Separation of duties
Within a larger task that the organization must accomplish, several subtasks may need to be performed. Because the subtasks may be separated into different roles, it is extremely difficult for a single individual to engage in fraud against the organization. The most common example of separation of duties is the separate subtasks involved in authorizing a payment for a particular transaction. By separating submission for payment and authorization for payment into separate roles, no individual can accomplish both tasks. This mutually exclusive separation reduces the possibility of

fraud within the organization. The specific separation of duties depends on the nature of the tasks and subtasks that the firm must accomplish. In some cases, the complete separation of tasks (submission and authorization) may be too difficult. Thus, the security advantage is outweighed by the additional transactions cost of accomplishing the task. In these cases, a more dynamic separation of duties could occur where the permissions within the role allow for submission and authorization. However, the same user cannot submit and authorize the same payment. A cross-check of user and role within the same task could be added to the system to accomplish the desired task (Ferraiolo and Kuhn, 1992).

THE BENEFITS OF RBAC

Several organizations, including the National Institute of Standards and Technology (NIST), have been working since the early 1990s to define a common standard for RBAC and to spur its implementation by providing research and development support to this emerging technology.[3] Currently, RBAC and RBAC-enabled products are growing in popularity and commercial use, and the market for these products is expected to continue to grow rapidly in the near future.

Using roles to determine and manage access, permissions allow system administrators to incorporate least privilege and separation of duties better into administrative policies. As discussed, RBAC exists in many forms, but even its simplest form is an improvement over alternative methods. Joshi et al. (2001, p. 71–72) state:

> RBAC features such as policy neutrality, principle of least privilege, and ease of management make [RBAC models] especially suitable candidates ...
> Such models can express both DAC and MAC policies, as well as user-specific policies. In essence, RBAC models can provide a generic framework for expressing diverse security requirements.

Several key advantages of RBAC are described below, along with the factors that influence the magnitude of possible benefits.

Simplified Systems Administration

Once an RBAC system is established, the costs associated with administering and monitoring the network are lower than those associated with many other access control models. Several factors influence the magnitude of the cost decrease. First, the greater employee turnover and the number of people changing roles, the greater the cost savings of RBAC relative to other access control systems. Second, some firms or organizations are very dynamic, and user roles and permissions change quickly. In these environments, RBAC is more efficient in moving users in and out of given roles and changing the permissions of given roles than competing access control systems. This improved efficiency is observable in the decrease in labor hours that the computer network support team spends on administrative tasks.

In addition to reducing system administration costs, the automated access control systems supported by RBAC reduce the burden on upper management. In alternative access control systems, upper management is integrally involved in determining individual privileges and authorizing access for each new employee. RBAC's organizational structure supports the automation of this process.[4]

Several issues must be weighed when granting access permissions. Security administrators need to balance the complexity of the position being assigned privileges, the complexity of the organization, the security level required, the data and application needs of the position, and the organizational issues. By assigning a predetermined role to the user, the labor expense of assigning permissions is significantly reduced, thus freeing labor resources for other tasks.

RBAC is a scalable model, meaning that the model can work as well in large environments covering several offices and classes of users as it can in one-office environments. Roles matching job positions may be determined in a central office, but the actual assigning of roles to or changing of roles for new employees can be done at each branch office by an administrator. This concept, frequently referred to as delegated administration, can be of particular benefit to organizations with several branch, subsidiary or contractor locations, such as health care plans, insurance companies, banks and similar organizations.

Enhanced Organizational Productivity

RBAC also has the potential to enhance the system by which firms and organizations structure their information systems. Because of the greater flexibility and breadth of network design associated with RBAC, the model can be adapted to mirror the organizational structure. This creates the potential for new and innovative ways of structuring the organization, altering the routing of information or changing the organization's production processes. Organizations can benefit from the consistency in infrastructure across divisions or units within the same entity. Additionally, improved business standards may result in cost savings. The synergistic improvements that may occur within a company could have potentially large impacts on employee productivity.

Reduction in New Employee Downtime

RBAC accelerates bringing new employees to full productivity. New employees are employees who are new to the organization, or existing employees who are placed in a new position within the company. During an initial period of establishing and verifying access, new employees may only be marginally or partially productive. The RBAC structure enables the automation of and reduces the time required for this process.

Enhanced Systems Security and Integrity

Role-based access models offer improved security and audit trails over alternative methods. RBAC is able to reduce the impact from security violations in two ways. First, RBAC can decrease the likelihood that a security violation occurs. Second, if a security violation occurs, RBAC can limit the damage from the violation. Roles limit the possibility of internal security breaches from individuals who should not have access to the data and applications associated with each function. Furthermore, because privileges are not assigned manually, it is less likely that the security administrator will make an error and inadvertently grant a user access to information or applications to which he or she would otherwise be prohibited.

Additionally, productivity may increase from RBAC's improved security of network resources and increased information access. As a result, organizations may increase their confidence in their computer systems and be able to increase the sharing of resources, being less concerned about potential security violations.

Simplified Regulatory Compliance

In an age of increasing electronic integration, data security and integrity have become political and economic issues. Incidences of breaches in data security are well documented,[5] as is the sharing of personal information among companies trying to find a stronger foothold in today's highly competitive markets.

To protect the confidentiality of both individuals and their personally identifiable information, recent federal laws have included provisions that dictate the type of and the extent to which individuals' information can be shared both within and external to an organization. These laws, as discussed in previous chapters, including the Health Insurance Portability and Accountability Act (HIPAA) and the Gramm–Leach–Bliley Act (GLBA) of 1999, require data managers to maintain securely and limit the distribution of data. To comply, companies are required to use access control policies that will safeguard data. RBAC is one such policy that may be well suited (and cost effective) for this purpose.

Although HIPAA does not explicitly mention any given access control model in the final rule, its implementer, the Department of Health and Human Services (DHHS), specifically espouses RBAC as a good security model to help safeguard health data. Figure 11.2 is a simplified example of how RBAC can be used to comply with HIPPA from the perspective of a health care organization (HCO). Using an RBAC system, an HCO can limit which users can access which types of data. For example, a billing clerk at a doctor's office may access a patient's contact and billing information but not their medical history. A doctor, on the other hand, has full access to the patient's medical history.[6]

BARRIERS TO THE ADOPTION OF RBAC

Two general categories of market failure affect RBAC: barriers to the technological development and integration of RBAC into software products, and barriers to the adoption and implementation of RBAC-enabled products by end-users. The first set of barriers primarily affects software developers (and in-house developers) of RBAC-enabled products and are in large part due to RBAC's generic technology attributes. The second set of barriers is related to RBAC's infratechnology characteristics and primarily affect adoption and implementation by end-users.

NIST has helped to reduce both of these types of costs; however, here we describe the barriers to adoption prior to NIST's involvement.

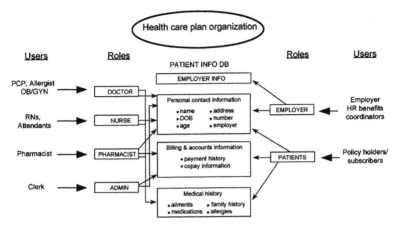

Figure 11.2 Heath care industry example of using RBAC to control access to sensitive information

Barriers to Technology Development and Integration of RBAC Models into Software Products

The barriers to private sector development and integration of RBAC into software products stem from the uncertainty about the success and costs of the applied research and product development needed for RBAC adoption and the difficulties in appropriating returns to private sector investments. These barriers are rooted in the concept of generic technologies, which have many of the characteristics of public goods. 'Generic' implies that once a base model has been developed, it may be easily applied in numerous other commercial settings, including other companies appropriating the model for use in competing products.[7] RBAC is a generic technology for this very reason. The development of generic technologies is generally slow because once the knowledge is generated and the standardization of a technique occurs, appropriating the benefits to the innovating entity is difficult.

Generic technologies are similar to public goods in that they have the characteristics of non-rivalry and non-excludability.[8] RBAC is non-rival because one firm's use of RBAC does not affect another firm's use. RBAC is also non-excludable because one firm cannot prevent another firm from using the fundamental concepts of roles as the basic technology is advanced and becomes public knowledge.[9] Public goods are typically underprovided by private markets as compared to their socially optimal levels of provision (Stiglitz, 1988).

This section discusses the barriers to developing and integrating RBAC models in commercial software products that result from RBAC's generic technology characteristics. These barriers include the need for technical expertise outside the software industry's domain, the lack of a consistent definition for RBAC, and the difficulty in appropriating returns to investment.

The first two factors lead to uncertainty in the success and costs of RBAC R&D. The third factor leads to uncertainty in the organization's ability to appropriate returns from its RBAC investments. All of these factors can delay the availability of RBAC-enabled products.

Technical expertise outside the software industry's domain

Although the fundamental concepts of roles are common knowledge, the capability to formalize model specifications needed to implement RBAC models is beyond the knowledge base of existing staff in many software companies. The lack of understanding of the programming requirements or a lack of awareness of RBAC models makes software companies hesitant to commit to RBAC development.

The lack of knowledge and staff expertise in the area of RBAC increases the uncertainty of both the technical feasibility of developing successful RBAC-enabled products and the development costs and time frame. These uncertainties increase the project risk and create significant barriers to investment in new RBAC-enabled software products. The risk impacts are further magnified by the fact that most business managers (decision-makers) are risk-averse, weighing potential downsides greater than equivalent potential upsides in the probability distribution of returns.

The NIST's RBAC project addresses these market failures by demonstrating the technical feasibility of RBAC products through its programs. In addition, the NIST's patents, papers, and the conferences it sponsors disseminate the basic RBAC generic technology from which private companies can develop market applications.

Lack of consistent definition

RBAC is a broad open-ended technology that ranges from very simple role structures to complicated hierarchies and constraints. As a result, the development of a single model is not appropriate. However, the lack of agreement on a set of fundamental concepts and underlying terminologies created a barrier to the development of RBAC-enabled products in the

1990s. As with the development of many new technologies, evolving RBAC models have typically used different terminology to describe similar concepts and functionalities. The fact that RBAC has simultaneously emerged from many different commercial and academic backgrounds has also contributed to the lack of consistent definitions and has increased confusion.

The lack of consistent definitions has slowed the implementation of RBAC. As a result, software developers have difficulty leveraging publicly available information and consumers of RBAC products have difficulty evaluating and comparing different products. The development of the NIST model was one of the first attempts at presenting industry with a set of consensus RBAC concepts and terminology. The NIST has followed this model development with a proposed standard for RBAC, which was developed in collaboration with industry and academics.

Difficulty of appropriating returns to investment
RBAC models are generic technologies that can benefit a wide range of industries. It is technology that will be integrated into a variety of products targeted at different market segments. As a result, it is difficult for individual companies in the private sector to appropriate fully the returns from their investments in RBAC because technology spillovers and imitation are likely to be high. For organizations to engage in R&D to develop a new technology, several conditions need to be in place. One of these is the ability to appropriate the market returns that are generated when a new technology is introduced into the marketplace.

Market returns to R&D can take two separate forms: private and social. Private returns can be thought of as the profits that individual organizations receive from selling the new technology – the price per good minus the R&D and production costs. Social returns are the benefits that accrue to all of the other participants in the market in which the technology was implemented by one firm or other markets that may benefit from using that technology. Jaffe (1998) describes these benefits as spillovers. For example, when an organization engages in R&D, other organizations learn what has worked and what has not worked. They can then reverse-engineer the process or otherwise gain 'knowledge' from the activities of the first organization. Because organizations cannot fully appropriate the spillovers, firms underinvest relative to the socially optimal rate.

However, the existence of market spillovers does not constitute a need for government action; other conditions must also be met. If the private return is large, there may be enough of a market incentive for the innovating company still to engage in research and development (R&D). Jaffe emphasizes that knowledge spillovers are a market failure when the private returns fail to reach a specific societal hurdle rate when the social returns do exceed the hurdle rate. In these cases, suboptimal private investment is likely to occur.

Because of the appropriability issues discussed above, it is generally accepted that government needs to fund research in generic technologies to the point where market applications become profitable for the private sector (that is, where the risk-adjusted expected rate of return to investment in RBAC products exceeds the companies' internal rate of return criteria) (Scott, 1999). The NIST's involvement mitigates market appropriation issues by providing the research foundation to which all have access. Firms are then able to produce and market products that build on the NIST's research and therefore incur only the incremental R&D costs for orienting the RBAC applications needs of their current and prospective products towards their customer base. This makes investment in RBAC-enabled products more attractive for the private sector and accelerates the availability of commercial RBAC-enabled products.

A second advantage of this approach by the NIST is the limitation of users being locked into a specific product or firm. When the generic technology is publicly available, software products from competing companies are more likely to be interoperable and to work together in integrated systems. This increases competition and lowers barriers to entry in the access control market.

Barriers to Implementation of RBAC-Enabled Products

The second category of barriers to developing and adopting RBAC is implementation barriers that affect end-user investment decisions. These barriers can affect an end-user organization's decision of whether to implement a role-based access policy and hence RBAC-enabled products. Many of the tools needed to support end-users' adoption of RBAC fall into the category of infratechnologies.

In an ideal scenario, an organization will establish and design operations processes and then create an infrastructure that will execute those processes, providing to each member only the tools needed to perform one's function (Byrnes, 1997).

Information systems are designed and built to support the roles that correspond to these processes. Each role is assigned a series of permissions defined by their position and function within the organization. Ideally, the system is clearly defined and agile, making the addition of new applications, roles and employees as efficient as possible.

According to software developers and end-users, however, the ideal scenario rarely occurs. Business processes and employee positions, both formal and informal, are pre-existing and entrenched, impeding turnkey implementation of new systems and management philosophies. Because RBAC requires roles to be established within the workplace, organizations implementing a role-based system may need to complement their information access policies with their general administration policies. Subsequent realigning of workflow and positions, to whatever extent necessary, may be very expensive, difficult and time-consuming.

The remainder of this section discusses the impediments for current and potential end-users; beyond the direct cost of purchasing the software, we discuss the cost of testing and installing RBAC. These impediments are not insurmountable, but they do factor into organizations' business decisions concerning adoption. Herein we depart from analyzing RBAC as a software component and take the position of a potential end-user, focusing on the issues that arise during RBAC adoption. Interviews with software developers, end-users and technical specialists, as well as articles in the popular press inform our discussion of implementation barriers. These impediments are divided into three general categories: role engineering costs, migration costs and systems structure costs.

Role engineering costs
The process of defining and implementing roles is known as 'role definition' or 'role engineering'. According to the software developers interviewed, role engineering can be a contentious and time-consuming process, but it is integral to RBAC's success. Role engineering entails defining the roles that will determine which employees have access to which data and to which applications. Also determined are roles' relationships to one another, role hierarchy and role constraints. As this process progresses, implementers may see benefits in rethinking how work is allocated and completed within the organization. Role engineering may be the costliest component of implementation because, even for an RBAC system, defining roles may take three to four months according to developers.

Workflow processes may be realigned as informal access rights are formalized and roles defined. Transitioning to a role-based system formalizes many relationships within an organization (Byrnes, 1997). This process may have the added benefit of introducing organizational clarity into the workplace. Many organizations grant ad hoc access control as new applications are installed or job definitions change. The changeover to a centralized system may bring many of those types of issues to bear.

It is expected that role-engineering expenses will decrease over time because of the development of new software tools and increased familiarity with the process of defining and assigning roles. Several companies have developed or are in the process of developing software tools that help to define roles automatically using existing patterns of access permissions gleaned from user databases. These tools should reduce the labor expense of manually defining and creating all roles. Furthermore, as companies and consultants become familiar with the implementation process, a learning curve effect should emerge. What is not clear, however, is what the total impact on role engineering these two developments will have. The relative ease or difficulty of the role definition process will depend on an entity's organizational and administrative structure, an attribute that varies widely among firms.

The NIST has developed specific tools to assist end-users in role engineering. The tools include RGP-Admin, a tool for managing role and permission relationships, and AccesMgr, a graphical user interface for managing access control lists for Windows NT files. Through the development of these tools, the NIST has lowered the cost, and hence lessened the barrier, to adopting and implementing RBAC-based systems.

Migration costs

Any time a new information system is installed, an organization will accrue costs. This is especially true if the decision is to implement a new access control system. The costs of migrating to a role-based system are fourfold: salaries and consultants' fees; software purchases and licensing agreements; computing resources and infrastructure; and customization costs. These costs may differ depending on the scope of the package being installed, the size of the firm or the number of licenses, and the migration complexity.

One of the largest cost components of installing an RBAC system is the salaries and benefits of the team tasked with its implementation. Tasks include not only the implementation and migration of the software system purchased, but also staff training, software package selection and the customization process. In addition to staff labor expenses, consultants may be hired either to implement the systems migration completely or to offer their expertise on some component of it. Outside consultants may also be hired to customize a prepackaged system or help with role definition.

In addition to purchasing the software itself, an organization may invest in software support services and new systems infrastructure. The software agreement may involve a sliding fee scale based on the number of licenses purchased and a software maintenance agreement. Depending on the package's system requirements, buyers may need to build or enhance their systems' infrastructure. The expense of buying, installing and maintaining computing resources can be high. Costs may rise further if network resources must be maintained solely or partly to help migrate from one system to another. The migration and transaction costs from migration to RBAC have certainly slowed its adoption, but thus far, the NIST has not specifically focused its efforts on how firms can migrate from one access control system to RBAC. Future work by the NIST in supporting migration from other access control systems to RBAC may be valuable.

Systems structure and interoperability costs

If a large firm with access control concerns could choose to adopt an access control system, interviews suggest that today most would choose RBAC. However, most firms made the decision on how to control access to information before RBAC was a candidate at the time. The choice set included ACLs, DAC and MAC. Once the access control system decision was made and implemented, networks evolved through time and became firm-specific. User definitions and permissions were created based on the potentially thousands of employees that work for a particular firm. Lock-in of the access control system has occurred in many firms (Hilchenbach, 1997). The market failure associated with this inability to break out of this problem has slowed the adoption of RBAC by users. However, adoption has increased, as discussed previously.

As new systems are installed, administrators may have to rectify years of inefficiencies, such as informal access rights, disorganized systems and different organization structures among divisions. The move towards disciplined centralized systems often means realigning the organizational aspects of affected systems and creating a more cohesive, formal structure.

Because of the time and cost involved, it is likely that a large organization will adopt RBAC at an incremental pace. By spreading out implementation over a long period of time or waiting until new applications or systems come online, companies avoid a costly, risk-prone full roll-out.

An additional barrier to developing commercial RBAC products is the wide range of operating systems that users employ. Even within one firm or organization, multiple operating systems are often needed. As firm size increases, so does the number of operating systems (Ferraiolo et al., 1992). At the same time as firm size increases, the importance of access control also grows (*Infosecurity Magazine*, 1999). Thus, larger firms need an access control system that is able to operate across multiple operating systems.

In addition, security features need to be effective across sectors of the firm or organization without being overly intrusive to the user. This trait is referred to as interoperability. Interoperability is the ability to communicate and transfer data or information across different activities and platforms. For example, an access control system that displays perfect interoperability would be able to communicate with the security and administrative network across an entire firm without any disruptions or complications.

The NIST's activities have been influential in helping develop a framework for addressing interoperability problems, a major barrier to adoption of RBAC. Hilchenbach (1997) agrees: 'NIST is a driving force behind the move to standardize RBAC.' By developing common standards, firms in different industries are now able to implement RBAC across the multiple platforms within their organization, and lessen the lock-in effect. In addition, the development of common standards lays the groundwork for future positive network externalities across companies. Once a common playing field is established, software developers and network administrators are able to engage in activities that will offer future improvements to RBAC.

Product acceptance and comparison

When making purchasing decisions, buyers of software products gather information about the various potential products and then make a decision based on the comparison of characteristics across products. These comparisons could include cost, quality, reliability and capacity. For this process to be effective, consumers must have an understanding of what they are getting from a product and producers must be able to prove that they are delivering what the consumer wants.

Prior to the NIST's involvement, no commonly agreed upon definition of RBAC existed. Without a definition, firms that were interested in either upgrading their existing access control system or purchasing new access control systems may have been unable to compare attributes across commercial RBAC products.

Without a set of metrics that consumers are willing to accept as standards for a particular piece of technology, software firms are unable to prove that their product is reliable in addressing security issues and effective at reducing administrative costs. The entire industry was lacking a yardstick or common definition. If producers and consumers cannot agree on the product they are selling, market transactions are unlikely to happen. A study by the NIST (Ferraiolo et al., 1992) found that part of the reason why RBAC had not been implemented was the lack of a 'stamp of approval' from a third party. Ferraiolo et al. (1995) make this clear by stating: 'The lack of definition makes it difficult for consumers to compare products and for vendors to get credit for the effectiveness of their products in addressing known security problems.'

The NIST's work at defining RBAC has addressed this failure by engaging in efforts that generate a common yardstick that all software developers can use. Specific projects have included surveys of security needs and the development of a formal RBAC model to demonstrate its effectiveness and reliability. Developing a formal RBAC model is a strategy that has proven successful in other markets.

MODELING THE BENEFITS OF RBAC-ENABLED PRODUCTS

The impact of RBAC-enabled products and services are modeled as an annualized flow of benefits and costs. Figure 11.3 illustrates the flow from the perspective of an individual company associated with installing an RBAC system. These benefits and costs are measured relative to the counterfactual of an alternative access control system such as an ACL, DAC or MAC that is already in place. Traditional investment theory states that if the net present value (NPV) of the flow of benefits is greater than zero, then a company should undertake the investment project subject to its financing constraints.

As shown in Figure 11.3, the life cycle of an RBAC system for users can generally be segmented into three phases: system customization, system implementation and system operations. System customization includes determining which system is best for the individual firm, purchasing the system, planning the migration and defining preliminary roles. During this phase an organization produces a comprehensive business plan and prepares to roll out RBAC in its organization. This phase of the project can involve six months of planning, on average, during which several tasks must be accomplished. These tasks include: customizing software; performing additional programming; developing request and approval processes for changes in user assignments; and developing a set of roles, role hierarchies and role restriction and interactions that clearly capture the company's business activities. The organization determines what roles need to be

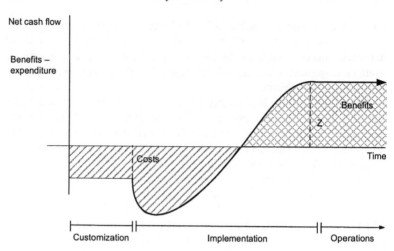

Figure 11.3 Flow of end-user costs and benefits of RBAC

created and what information needs to be associated with which role. Although role definition begins during this phase, it is an iterative process, and roles will evolve and be redefined over time.

System implementation is typically a two-phase process that involves rolling out the new systems to end-users and re-establishing user privileges via roles. First, information administrators must determine the privileges that each user needs based on their job function. Second, they must determine and define the role that corresponds to each employee's particular job function. Implementation can be the most costly part of the project and typically occurs over six months. Some benefits of RBAC will be realized soon after implementation begins, as employees are gradually converted to the RBAC system and as new employees are processed using the new system.

Once fully implemented, the organization using RBAC is said to be in the operations phase. At this point, the benefits (relative to alternative access control systems) include reduced administrative costs, decreased worker downtime as they are assigned new privileges, and fewer and less severe security violations. Access activities in this phase include moving users in and out of roles and defining new roles as needed. Figure 11.3 shows these benefits, Z, as a steady flow over time.

COLLECTION OF BENEFIT AND COST DATA

To collect information on the benefits and costs of RBAC, we conducted an in-depth case-study with a multi-line insurance company (hereafter, referred to as the Company), and we conducted an Internet survey of security administrators sent to subscribers of *Information Security Magazine,* a leading trade publication for information and systems security administrators. Ninety-two administrators responded to the survey. In addition, we conducted telephone interviews with major telecommunications firms and commercial banks.

Case Study Results

The Company's primary line of business is the provision of an array of insurance products, including home, auto, business and life insurance. Like many multi-line insurers, the Company does not sell directly to policyholders, but it instead teams with locally operated independent insurance agents. These local insurance agents market and sell products within their area, contracting with the Company upon selling a policy. The Company's annual revenues are measured in the billions, it has several thousand employees, and it works with hundreds of agencies located across the United States.

At the time of the case-study, the Company was in the middle of rolling out RBAC to its internal and external user population; the roll-out occurred in two stages. First, the Company provided electronic services to its customer base, the local insurance agencies, via the Internet. The system uses RBAC to provide systems security and to relieve maintenance and administrative pressures by delegating administration. As this process nears completion, the Company is devoting more resources to its internal migration from identity-based ACLs to RBAC.

The Company expects that using RBAC will increase productivity and increase its amount of new business annually. RBAC will also provide the level of security required by an institution with a large number of users and a wide variety of user types, including potentially competing insurance agents. The Company was not able to provide any quantitative information concerning security benefits; however, it openly discussed the other benefits it expected to accrue and costs it expected to incur.

Benefits of using RBAC to manage extranet users

The Company's client base consists of hundreds of independent insurance agencies located across the United States, each employing approximately three agents and their support personnel. Traditionally, insurance agents interacted with the Company through telephone calls and written communication. Agents contact the Company directly to determine rates, receive quotes and obtain other information. After receiving information from the Company, agents then recontact prospective policyholders to inform them of the results. The process of contacting the Company directly to determine rates and to gather other information translated into a significant amount of time between a customer's inquiry and the sale of the policy. If the customer should choose to purchase the policy, the agent must then initiate a process whereby the policy is enacted and the appropriate forms are filed at the agency and mailed to the Company. The Company would supplement its records with information obtained from agents in the additional mailings and other communications. The process of completely selling a policy, including mailing and final data entry, could take as long as four to six weeks.

RBAC is the technology enabling the Company's strategic e-business initiative. The RBAC software will grant or deny user access to data and applications as users' roles dictate. In essence, the software is the platform to which data and applications will be linked. Agents will interact with the Company over the Internet. Agents will be assigned roles that allow them to enter policyholder information, examine rates and sell products instantly to customers. The goal is to allow agents to maintain, access, determine and interact with policy information and details electronically. The Company also estimates that the ability to instantly register and sell products to prospective policyholders will increase its amount of new business by 10 to 20 percent annually.

The Company could have selected an alternative access control model, but it would have been more costly, although the extent of the additional cost is unknown. What is known, however, is that a non-RBAC solution would have entailed a larger programming component, which would have increased installation and customization costs. The system would also have been far more costly to operate and less secure for several reasons related to systems administration and maintenance, such as user directory maintenance and user account maintenance (that is, no delegated administration).

Figure 11.4 illustrates the net benefits to the Company on a quarterly basis. Although the software and hardware costs were incurred solely during

Net cash flow

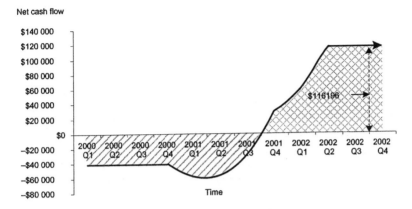

Figure 11.4 Company's quarterly flow of net benefits

the fourth quarter of 2000, Figure 11.4 conceptualizes these particular costs over the entire 2000 calendar year. This adjustment was made because the labor costs were distributed evenly over time, when in reality some months may have seen more labor activity than others. With this minor smoothing, costs and benefits closely mirror the theoretical next cash flow over time hypothesized in Figure 11.3.

Internet Survey Results

Based on the survey results, RBAC is found to reduce the amount of time needed to perform several administrative activities, relative to alternative access control models. In addition, significant benefits are estimated for reduced employee downtime due to the use of RBAC. RBAC was also cited as reducing the severity and frequency of security violation, but survey respondents were unable (or unwilling) to quantity these benefits.

RBAC reduces administrative processing time

Table 11.1 presents the amount of time required to perform four common activities using RBAC and non-RBAC models: assigning existing privileges to new users, changing existing users' privileges, establishing new privileges for existing users and terminating privileges.

RBAC reduces the amount of time needed to assign privileges to new users by 5.5 minutes. RBAC reduces the time required to terminate a user's

Table 11.1 Average task time (minutes) by access control system

	Assigning existing privileges to new users	Changing existing users' privileges	Establishing new privileges for existing users	Terminating privileges
RBAC systems	6.9	6.6	8.0	4.7
Non-RBAC systems	12.4	7.8	9.2	7.6
Difference	5.5	1.2	1.2	2.9

privileges by nearly 3 minutes. The time needed to alter a user's privileges or establish new privileges is reduced by slightly more than 1 minute with RBAC.

These four basic tasks are performed repeatedly every year and encompass a high percentage of an organization's total annual number of hours spent on systems administration. Table 11.2 presents the average number of times survey respondents conduct each of the four activities on an annual basis, both in absolute terms and per employee. The Internet survey respondents were with little exception large firms, each employing thousands of workers and maintaining vast information resources and networks. Consequently, it was common for one respondent to provide activities and time estimates for several different access control technologies.

It is important to distinguish between new users and new employees. New users may be new employees as well as current employees that are granted new permissions. Because many firms also maintain multiple access control systems and have many users with multiple user identifications (IDs), the number of new users may significantly exceed the number of new employees hired annually. As such, the per-employee estimate included in Table 11.2 should not be used to approximate employee turnover.

The per-employee average number of tasks performed allows us to estimate the administrative benefits a firm may accrue using RBAC when it is coupled with RBAC time-savings estimates and the average wage of employees performing the tasks. Using wage estimates provided by the Bureau of Labor Statistics, we estimated the loaded wage for systems administrators in 2000 to be $51.62 per hour.[10]

The averages in Tables 11.1 and 11.2 underlie the benefits calculation portion of the economic model used to estimate the economic impact of RBAC. Based on this information, as shown in Table 11.3, an average firm

Table 11.2 Number of times administrative tasks are performed

Administrative task	Average number of times per year	Per year, per employee
Assigning existing privileges to new users	1802	1.30
Changing existing users' privileges	1975	1.50
Establishing new privileges for existing users	1000	1.06
Terminating privileges	452	0.22

Table 11.3 Systems administration benefit for a typical company with 100 000 employees

Administrative task	RBAC time savings per task (minutes)	Average number of tasks per year	Annual total benefit ($2000)
Assigning existing privileges to new users	5.5	130 000	$615 138
Changing existing users' privileges	1.2	150 000	$154 860
Establishing new privileges for existing users	1.2	106 000	$109 434
Terminating privileges	2.9	22 000	$54 889
Total			$934 321

with 100 000 employees could expect to save approximately $934 000 a year on systems administration using RBAC. Assigning existing privileges to new users accounts for over two-thirds of the administrative benefits.

RBAC increases productivity

Information to estimate the reduction in new employee downtime was provided by telephone and Internet survey respondents, and this benefit component is included in the quantitative impact estimates. The length of downtime reported by survey respondents for new employees or current employees changing positions varied. Estimates ranged from one to 24 work hours, with most falling between four and eight work hours. For current RBAC users and those in the process of implementing RBAC, the average employee downtime was 4.3 hours. Non-RBAC users experienced an average of 8.8 hours in downtime (see Table 11.4). Thus, RBAC yields an average benefit of 4.5 fewer hours of new employee downtime.[11]

Table 11.4 Reduction in new employee downtime (hours)

Metric	Non-RBAC system	RBAC system
Maximum downtime value	24.0	8.0
Minimum downtime value	0.5	0.5
Average downtime value	8.8	4.3

However, the term 'downtime' is somewhat misleading. Conversations with IT professionals and managers revealed that employees are not totally unproductive when they do not have their permissions – they are simply less productive. Other activities, such as reading printed materials, attending meetings, attending orientation, introducing themselves to clients and coworkers, can be accomplished without access privileges. Some firms have temporary user IDs that new employees are assigned until the permanent ID is received. Knowledgeable professionals suggest that employees are about 80 to 90 percent productive during this downtime. Therefore, we assume that new employees are about 85 percent as productive as they could otherwise be, given that they are new to the position.

Table 11.5 shows the downtime reduction benefits of RBAC compared to non-RBAC systems. The difference of 4.5 hours, with a productivity loss of 15 percent yields a productivity loss of 0.67 hours. Using the average number of new employees per user in Table 11.2, a typical company with 100 000 employees would benefit approximately $3.4 million per year.

Table 11.5 Benefits from reduced downtime for a typical firm with 100 000 employees

Metric	Non-RBAC system
Change in average employee downtime (RBAC vs. non-RBAC)	4.5 hrs
Productivity loss (15%)	0.67 hrs
Hourly rate	$39.46
New users per employee	1.3
Annual benefits (100,000 employees)	$3,436,966

Notes: According to the 2000 *National Occupational Employment and Wage Estimates* published by the Bureau of Labor Statistics, the mean hourly wage rate for civilian white-collar workers is $19.73 per hour, or $41 038 annually. This estimate was multiplied by 2 to estimate the additional cost to the employer for employee benefits, such as employer-sponsored health and dental insurance and 401(k) contributions, as well as administrative and overhead costs.

RBAC reduces the severity and frequency of security violations

When a security violation occurs, firms and organizations experience direct and indirect costs. RBAC systems are designed to mitigate the possibility of these violations occurring, although we were unable to quantify the extent to which they will do so. Respondents were less willing to reveal information on security violations and were unable to quantify the potential benefit of RBAC. Thus, benefits from reduced security violations are not included in the quantitative impact estimates. However, depending on the industry and the nature of the security violation, the impacts of RBAC are potentially large.

In a 2000 *Infosecurity Magazine* survey, nearly 2000 information security managers were asked if they had experienced a security violation within the past year from employee access abuse, unauthorized access by outsiders, access abuse from non-employee authorized users or the leakage of proprietary information. According to Information Security, 58 percent of the respondents reported violations due to employee access abuse, 42 percent due to unauthorized access by outsiders, 14 percent due to access abuse by non-employee authorized users, and 24 percent due to the leakage of proprietary information (Briney, 2000).

Not only are security violations occurring with frequency, but they are also costly. Table 11.6 presents average cost per violation from the Computer Security Institute (2001). Updated data are presented in Chapter 2, but these data correspond to the year in which this case study was conducted. Theft of proprietary information and financial fraud are typically the most costly forms of security violation.

Software development and installation costs

However, the benefit of RBAC will not be realized without costs. Software developers indicated that on average they incurred $550 000 in R&D expenditure to develop RBAC-enabled products. In addition, based on our in-depth case-study with a multiproduct financial services firm, the average end-user customization and implementation costs are estimated to be $78.36 per employee. These costs are incurred once per employee.

Customization and installation costs of RBAC are based on the case study findings and on information gathered from respondents that had implemented or were implementing RBAC at the time of the surveys. Table 11.7 shows per-user customization and implementation costs broken down by software expenditure, hardware expenditure, consulting fees and in-house labor expenditure. These one-off costs are estimated to be approximately $78 per user.

Cyber Security

Table 11.6 Average cost per security violation, 1999–2001 ($ thousands)

Type of violation	1999	2000	2001
Theft of proprietary information	1848	3033	4448
Sabotage	164	970	199
Telecom	77	66	55
System penetration	103	245	454
Insider abuse of net access	94	307	357
Financial fraud	1471	1647	4421
Denial of service	116	109	122
Virus contamination	45	180	244
Unauthorized access to information by insider	143	1125	276
Telecom fraud	27	212	502
Active wiretapping	20	5000	0
Laptop theft	87	59	62

Source: Computer Security Institute (2001).

Most of the survey respondents stated that the process of rolling out RBAC took or would take about one year, and that the process of bringing users online in the RBAC system takes approximately six months. They also indicated that hardware purchases were made to facilitate migration and implementation, and that they hired consultants, either the software vendor or a third-party organization, to assist in implementation. However, internal labor expenses accounted for nearly 80 percent of total customization and implementation costs.

Per employee impact estimates

Table 11.7 also shows a summary of the annual per-user benefits from adopting RBAC. Annual benefits are the sum of administrative benefits (assigning and terminating privileges) and reduced employee downtime (productivity) costs. As shown in Table 11.7, productivity costs account for about 78 percent of the $43.71 benefits per user. However, this is likely to be a lower-bounds estimate because the benefits from reduced security violations are not included.

Table 11.7 Summary of a user company's costs and estimated benefits

Variable	Dollar value	Economic metric
BENEFITS		
Improved management of employees' permissions using RBAC	$9.34	The cost difference between RBAC and non-RBAC policies to manage employees' user accounts
Reduction in new employee downtime	$34.37	Reduction in the amount of time an employee is without access permissions
Reduced severity and frequency of security violations	Not quantified	Security violations from employee access abuse, unauthorized access by outsiders, access abuse from non-employee authorized users or the leakage of proprietary information
Total annual benefits	$43.71	
COSTS		
Software expenses	$12.00	Software purchases, including maintenance and support agreements
Hardware expenses	$2.00	Hardware purchases to support systems migration and e-business strategy
Consulting fees	$2.40	Fees paid to consultants to assist in the implementation process
Labor expenses	$60.81	Labor expenses of employees tasked with implementing RBAC systems and e-business strategy
Role engineering expenses	$1.15	Labor expenses related to determining the characteristics of roles to be used
Total one-time costs	$78.36	

National impact estimates

The growth of employees managed using RBAC systems was projected to the year 2006. It was estimated that by 2006, between 30 and 50 percent of employees in the service sector and between 10 and 25 percent of employees in non-service sectors would be managed by RBAC systems. Because of the uncertainty surrounding the penetration estimates, high, medium and low penetration scenarios were estimated.

Given the final penetration rate with a particular scenario, we fitted a logistic S-shaped curve to the data for each industry and then aggregated the curves with respect to time. Figure 11.5 shows the aggregate curves for the three penetration rate scenarios, where each curve is an employee-weighted penetration curve that aggregates industry penetration.

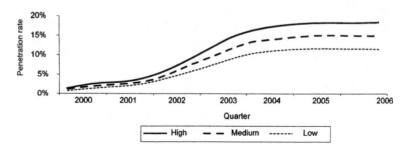

Figure 11.5 Aggregate penetration rates for low, medium and high rate scenarios

Table 11.8 summarizes the benefits and costs associated with RBAC. In the medium penetration rate scenario, the estimated NPV of net benefits (benefits less costs) from 2000 to 2006 are $671.1 million. Costs are expressed as negative benefits.

CONCLUSIONS

RBAC is a technology that offers an alternative to traditional discretionary access control (DAC) and mandatory access control (MAC) policies. RBAC has the potential to increase cyber security by allowing companies to specify and enforce security policies that map naturally to the organization's structure. Based on interviews with software developers and companies using RBAC-enabled products, we projected that the net present value of the benefits of RBAC (to 2006) for the US economy have the potential to be approximately $670 million. However, to realize these benefits, government must continue to play a role in promoting the underlying generic technologies and infratechnologies needed for RBAC development and deployment.

RBAC highlights a common theme with the adoption of many cyber security technologies. Because security benefits are difficult to quantify, the most frequently adopted technologies are those with ancillary (non-security)

Table 11.8 NPV of benefits and costs of RBAC, 2000–2006

	2000–2006 (year 2000 dollars)		
	Low penetration scenario (millions)	Medium penetration scenario (millions)	High penetration scenario (millions)
R&D expenditure: software developers and in-house development	−53.2	−53.2	−53.2
End-users' customization and implementation costs	−85.1	−161.7	−260.2
End-users' operation benefits	466.2	886.0	1426.2
NPV benefits of RBAC	327.9	671.1	1112.8

benefits, such as reduced employee downtime or increased IT staff efficiency. However, basing security related investments on their ancillary benefits may not lead to an optimal (security included) investment strategy.

NOTES

1. Our analysis is informed by information collected during a study for the National Institute of Standards and Technology (Gallaher, O'Connor, and Kropp, 2002).
2. For example, the role of doctor is hierarchically superior to the role of nurse, if the doctor has (inherits) all of the privileges of the nurse and the users authorized for the doctor role are also authorized for the nurse role.
3. For a detailed description of RBAC model definitions and the specific functionality included in the different RBAC models, see Sandhu et al. (1997).
4. Industry experts indicated that automation was possible with alternative access control methods; however, the concept of roles greatly enhanced the benefits associated with automation.
5. See Privacy Rights Clearinghouse list of breaches at http://www.privacyrights. org/ar/ChronDataBreaches.htm.
6. Health care systems in some cases are well ahead of other industries in their use of IT and integration of records (see discussion of VA electronic health records system at http://en.wikipedia.org/wiki/ Electronic_health_record), but mostly the health care system of the US is far behind other industries in digitizing

records and developing access systems. In particular, the prospect of patients having access to their records via the Internet is likely to be several years into the future.

7. Although RBAC is an important concept for developing access control systems, it should not be considered an infratechnology. Infratechnologies are technical tools, including scientific and engineering data, measurement and test methods, and practices and techniques, that are widely used in industry (Tassey, 1997). RBAC is not an infratechnology because its main effect is to provide a technology platform (that is, a generic technology) rather than leverage the efficiency of R&D, production or market transactions.

8. Public goods, unlike private goods, are characterized by consumption non-rivalry and by high costs of exclusion. Rationing of such goods is undesirable because the consumption of a public good does not impose costs on society as it does not reduce the amount of the good available to others. Further, the costs of excluding those who do not pay for the infratechnologies (for example, through patenting) are likely to be high because they are typically embodied in products and processes (that is, techniques), rather than in products that can be sold.

9. One way for a company to appropriate the returns from R&D is to limit the spread or use of its technical innovations through secrecy, patents or licenses. However, in the case of RBAC, because it is embodied as a software product, it is difficult to prevent imitation through reverse engineering. Similarly, patents and licenses provide less protection for software products compared to other areas of technology innovation because competing firms are frequently able to invent around the existing patent, effectively preventing the innovating firm from appropriating all of the returns associated with an innovation.

10. According to the 2000 National Occupational Employment and Wage Estimates published by the Bureau of Labor Statistics, the mean wage for network and computer systems administrators is $25.81 per hour, or $53 685 annually. This estimate was multiplied by 2 to estimate the additional cost to the employer for employee benefits, such as employer-sponsored health and dental insurance and 401(k) contributions, as well as administrative and overhead costs.

11. The downtime savings estimate is not directly comparable to the RBAC systems administration benefits because the downtime estimate represents elapsed business hours from the time the new employee starts to the time they receive access. Changes in administrative time include paperwork and processing time needed to complete the task of actually assigning the

permissions within the system. The difference between the two is the time the new employee's request sits in the queue waiting to be processed.

12. Public Policy Alternatives

INTRODUCTION

Typically, when the private sector thinks of government involvement in market activity it envisions regulation, command-and-control policies, excessive paperwork and overall inefficiency. The alternative is simply to leave markets alone and let the invisible hand solve all the allocation problems. This philosophy seems to have worked well over the last few centuries, with exceptions of course, as evidenced by unprecedented growth in wealth and technology innovation in our nation of the USA and in other market-oriented economies. However the Internet has many invisible hands, not all of which are capable of working together much less working tougher constructively.

Historically, the US public sector has been involved in ensuring the security and safety of our nation's food chain, drug supply and work place. We have come to expect security in most aspects of our daily lives. Thus, individuals are surprised and even shocked at how pervasive identity theft has become. With personal information and intellectual property becoming society's most valuable commodities, the issue is: How can we protect information without hindering its desired flow?

In reality, without public sector involvement to provide infrastructure and enforce laws, efficient markets as economists envision them would collapse. The challenge with regard to privacy is then to determine how best the private sector and public sector should interact so as to create orderly and functioning markets without stifling drivers of economic growth including efficiency, creatively and innovation. Restated the problem is, how can the public sector leverage the power of market incentives and free enterprise to optimize social welfare?

The distributed, yet interconnected nature of the Internet magnifies the need to understand what motivates the behavior of individual organizations. The security of our nation's information systems depends on the actions of multitudes of users, who themselves represent a wide range of stakeholder groups. As a result, the proper alignment of incentives across these diverse stakeholders is an important function that, we contend, the public sector is uniquely qualified to provide. As such, the public sector has an important, and perhaps even vital, role to play in the cyber security imperative.

As we have emphasized throughout the earlier chapters, little is known about how organizations evaluate their cyber security investments, where organizations obtain relevant information and how organizations assess the benefits and costs of such investments. Our interview-based survey findings and case-study analysis represent an important step toward understanding these complex issues and identifying the means by which the public sector could influence the type and level of cyber security investments. Still more information is needed before definitive public policies can be evaluated and recommended.

Two facts are clear: different industries are motivated by different cyber security drivers and concerns, and different industries rely on alternative sources of information to support their cyber security investment and implementation strategies. However, our interviews and case studies point to some common issues related to the public-goods nature of cyber security that could help inform government's role in enhancing the imperative.

IMPLICATIONS OF THE PUBLIC-GOODS NATURE OF CYBER SECURITY

The public-goods nature of information per se and information networks in particular provides insight into the barriers affecting the development and adoption of cyber security solutions. Economic theory holds that an organization should evaluate its optimal level of cyber security investment by equating the marginal benefit that it receives from an additional unit of security with the marginal cost of achieving that additional unit. However, because of the public-goods nature of cyber security, it is likely that the optimal level of investment from a private perspective will be less than the optimal level of investment from a social perspective – a point we emphasized in Chapter 7. Furthermore, the optimal investment from a private perspective could be improved with the use of additional resources to enable more robust, quantitative investment analysis.

Typically, public goods are thought of as being used by all, but that no one entity is sufficiently incentivized to provide the public good optimally. The interesting fact about information infrastructure is that every element is owned by a for-profit entity, which has an incentive to assure that its part of the information infrastructure is functioning well. That said, there are likely parts where such incentives become perverse because those who experience a security breach do not incur all of the cost of dealing with the breach (for example, ISPs that handle traffic for a retailer).

We identified two primary market failures limiting an organization's ability to determine, and incentives to pursue, a socially optimal cyber security investment strategy. The first is the limited availability of reliable, cost-effective information from which the organization can make an informed investment decision. The second is the cost externalities (that is, negative externalities) that spill over to organizations and consumers throughout the network as a result of security breaches.

With regard to information, it is both difficult and costly for an organization to assess the probability of a security breach, much less to assess all possible related impacts, especially those that are external. These impacts include, but are certainly not limited to the following: assessing the effectiveness of available cyber security technologies that are in-house or available from vendors; determining the implementation and maintenance costs of these technologies once identified; and estimating the overall reputational cost to the organization from experiencing a breach.

Relevant and applicable knowledge is a scarce good. Consortia and trade associations encourage information sharing; however, the lack of economic incentives to participate fully and openly and to share technical information which could provide a competitive advantage to a competitor has limited their success. As a result, private organizations are unable to calculate private benefits correctly. In general, the lack of reliable information to inform analysis may be one of the primary factors limiting the use of traditional economic methods for evaluating the efficiency by which cyber security investments are made.

Regarding the externalities and public-goods nature of cyber security, any investment an organization makes in cyber security, particularly of a proactive nature, will likely generate social benefits in excess of private benefits. That is, an organization will not appropriate all of the benefits it receives from cyber security investments because some of these benefits (also referred to as positive network externalities) spill over to organizations throughout the information system. Thus, from a social perspective, this can lead to an underinvestment in proactive cyber security solutions, which tend to be more expensive. Similarly, if the private costs do not reflect the true social costs of security breaches (negative externalities), it logically follows that organizations may underinvest in cyber security because of its public-goods nature.

GOVERNMENT'S ROLE IN ENHANCING CYBER SECURITY

The theoretical basis for government's role in market activity, cyber security related or otherwise, is based on the concept of market failure. Market failure is typically attributed to market power, imperfect information, externalities and public goods. Government's role, then, is to lessen or remove any barriers associated with market failure and the like. In our case, the proper role for government might be to avoid underinvestment in a proactive strategy toward cyber security.

Governmental tools to accomplish this goal are limited, but the quantitative and qualitative information we collected during our interviews and case studies suggests several areas of potential focus as follows:

1) The government could help fund the collection, analysis and dissemination of both reliable and cost-effective information related to cyber security. This information includes not only data for comparative analyses and internal benchmarking exercises, but also state-of-the-art information on security techniques, software and hardware and best practices in using them. Although many groups attempt to provide such services, the organizations we spoke with (particularly small businesses on the demand side) were interested in more information comparing types of products. Also, experts and organizations identified improved certification of skilled professionals as a key area that would enable more effective and efficient cyber security investing. Evaluating the effectiveness and efficiency of potential cyber security solutions is a complex, costly and often time-intensive activity. In many instances, a relevant taxonomy and metrics do not exist to facilitate comparisons of competing technologies. Government involvement could assist in lowering costs of evaluating and identifying the best technological alternatives (be they proactive or reactive) for individual organizations

2) Government could promote studies that estimate the true cost of cyber breach events while maintaining the confidentiality of the organization providing the data. All the organizations with which we spoke were

interested in continued public sector research focused on estimating the cost of breaches and the probability of future attacks, both of which are extremely difficult to determine. As we discussed in previous chapters, in the absence of accurate projected damage estimates, many investments are based on ancillary productivity impacts.

3) Government needs to promote increased security for small businesses and households. The entities represent the weakest link in the security infrastructure and are increasingly compromised and turned into botnets, from which distributed attacks (an increasing threat) originate. This could be in the form of increased information through trade associations or outreach programs or lowering the cost of security measures through direct or indirect incentives. Government could promote centralized activities such as incentivizing or mandating ISPs to increase security services or supporting the outsourcing of security activities, which facilitate information sharing.

4) Similarly, the government could underwrite the research and implementation costs for larger organizations that are pilot testing new innovations. These endeavors might increase investments in innovative cyber security strategies, shifting investments toward the socially optimal proactive level (as was the case when Congress enacted the Research and Experimentation Tax Credit in 1981). The real question is: How closely can the social and private optimums be aligned? Companies are not in the business of acting in a socially optimal manner, but will certainly do so if they see it as being in their (private) best interests.

5) Related to security breach costs that spill over throughout the network, a potential role for the government is to design mechanisms that redistribute the costs (that is, reduce spillovers and externalities) better to provide incentives for individual organizations to enhance their cyber security. Examples of this type of involvement include regulations that define activities or security thresholds that must be met. The associated threat of litigation from being out of compliance is another way to make private organizations bear the social costs of security breaches. The private sector also engages in similar activities by requiring suppliers and partners to meet cyber security requirements and conduct regular security audits. In both cases, the intent is to internalize cost externalities so that organizations have the proper incentives when evaluating cyber security investments. Placing the responsibility with those who have the control is important; the private sector could be at least as good as the government if it evaluated the risks it was facing.

However, there are mixed opinions regarding whether regulations or business mandates could be an efficient means of enhancing cyber security. Because industries and business operations are unique, one-size-fits-all solutions may not lead to efficient solutions. In most cases, organizations believe that the impact of current regulations has been positive by increasing the overall level of security, although several organizations mentioned a very high compliance cost. Several firms noted that regulations could be more prescriptive, while others noted that the regulations should only be viewed as a baseline, providing organizations with the flexibility to select the lowest-cost solution.

SUGGESTIONS FOR FUTURE PUBLIC SECTOR SUPPORTED RESEARCH

Clearly, more information is needed about factors that influence an organization's investment and implementation strategies before any definitive determination of specific government actions or other tools is made. As such, the following is a list of suggested future policy-related research on cyber security investment activity which we call for the public sector to support.

- Conduct expanded interview- and survey-based studies with the goal of more explicitly understanding how organizations, from their private perspectives, reach what they consider to be an optimal mix of cyber security investment decision strategies.
- Investigate organizations' specific barriers that inhibit their use of external resources – both information resources and tangible resources. We expect that there will be differences among identifiable barriers that apply to the use of hardware, software and cyber security procedures.
- Investigate the flows and magnitudes of cost externalities to determine who actually bears the costs of cyber security breaches. For example, one research question is: When one firm is attacked, are the costs pushed upstream to suppliers, or are costs pushed downstream to final consumers?
- Investigate the applicability of risk management tools and techniques to cyber security optimization. For example, one research question is: Could agent-based models and simulation techniques used for

financial and health modeling help predict cyber security risks more explicitly?

- Investigate empirically whether outsourcing of cyber security activities results in increased security to all users. For example, building on the investigation of externalities proposed above, one research question is: What types of outsourcing activities result in benefits outside the outsourcing firm and of what magnitude?
- Investigate the role ISPs could play in increasing cyber security. For example, one research question is: What incentives would be needed for ISPs to assume greater monitoring, validation and enforcement activities?
- Investigate the infrastructure needed to support litigation related to security breaches. Is the forensics technology available to identify the source of breaches that ripple through the network? And from a legal perspective, what is required to prove negligence as opposed to ineptness?

References

Anderson, R. (2001), 'Why Information Security is Hard: An Economic Perspective', Presented at the Annual Computer Security Applications Conference, New Orleans, LA.

Andersson, M. and J. Bergstrand (1995), 'Formalizing Use Cases with Message Sequence Charts', unpublished Master's thesis, Lund Institute of Technology, Lund, Sweden.

Answers.com (2005), 'Definition for VPN', http://www.answers.com.

Apfelbaum, M. and J. Doyle (1997), 'Model Based Testing', paper presented at the Software Quality Week Conference.

Arora, A., C. Forman, A. Nandkumar and R. Telang (2007), 'Competition and Quality Restoration: An Empirical Analysis of Vendor Response to Software Vulnerabilities', Carnegie Mellon University working paper.

Austin, R. and C. Darby (2003), 'The Myth of Secure Computing', *Harvard Business Review*, June: 120–136.

Baird, J.M. (2004), Interview by RTI, IPv6 Pilot Implementation Manager with the DoD High Performance Computing Modernization Program (HPCMP).

Barkley, J.F. (1995), 'Application Engineering in Health Care', paper presented at the second annual CHIN Summit.

Barkley, John F., Anthony V. Cincotta, David F. Ferraiolo, Serban Gavrila and D. Richard Kuhn. (1997). 'Role-Based Access Control for the World Wide Web's, 20th National Computer Security Conference.

Beizer, B. (1984), *Software System Testing and Quality Assurance*, New York: Van Nostrand Reinhold Company, Inc.

Beizer, B. (1990), *Software Testing Techniques*, Boston, MA: International Thomson Computer Press.

Berinato, S. (2005), 'The Global State of Information Security 2005', http://www.csoonline.com/pdf/091505_survey.pdf.

Black, Paul. (2007), 'The NIST SAMATE and Evaluating Static Analysis Tools', Presented at the 12th International Conference on Reliable Software Technologies: Ada-Europe, Geneva Switzerland, June 2007. Presentation available at http://hissa.nist.gov/~black/Papers/staticAnalyExper%20Ada%20Geneva%20Jun%20007.ppt#344,3,The NIST SAMATE Project.

Bresnahan, T.F. and M. Trajtenberg (1995), 'General Purpose Technologies', *Journal of Econometrics*, **65**, 83–108.

Briney, A. (2000), 'Security Focused', *Information Security*, September, 40–68.

Byrnes, Christian (1997), Vice-President: Services and Systems Management, The META Group, June 13, 1997, 'Security Administration Grows Up' An analyst report produced for Tivoli, an IBM company.

Campbell, K., L.A. Gordon, M.P. Loeb and L. Zhou (2003), 'The Economic Cost of Publicly Announced Information Security Breaches: Empirical Evidence from the Stock Market', *Journal of Computer Security*, **11**, 431–448.

Cashell, B., W.D. Jackson, M. Jickling and B. Webel (2004), 'The Economic Impact of Cyber-Attacks', Congressional Research Service (CRS), CRS Report for Congress.

Charette, R.N. (1991), 'The Risks with Risk Analysis', Inside Risks column, *Communications of the ACM*, **34**(6), 106.

CCID Consulting Company (2007), '2006–2007 Annual Report on the Development of the Global E-Commerce Industry', www.wjef.net/report_sample/english/16.pdf.

Chen, L., T. Longstaff, and K. Carley (2004), 'The Economic Incentives of Providing Network Security Services on the Internet Infrastructure', *Journal of Information Technology Management,* **15**(3–4), 1–13.

Cisco Systems, Inc. (2001), 'The Return on Investment for Network Security', white paper, San Jose, CA: Cisco Systems, http://www.cisco.com/warp/public/cc/so/neso/sqso/roi4_wp.pdf.

Cisco Systems, Inc. (2002). 'Economic Impact of Network Security Threats', white paper, San Jose, CA: Cisco Systems.

CNN (2004), 'Software bug linked to blackout', February 13, 2004, http://www.cnn.com/2004/US/Northeast/02/13/blackout.ap/.

CNN (2007), 'Sources: Staged cyber attack reveals vulnerability in power grid', http://www.cnn.com/2007/US/09/26/power.at.risk/.

Cohen D.M., S.R. Dalal, J. Parclius and G.C. Patton (1996), 'The Combinatorial Design Approach to Automatic Test Generation', *IEEE Software*, **13**, 83–88.

Common Vulnerabilities and Exposures (CVE) (2005), *MITRE CVE*, http://www.cve.mitre.org/compatible.

Computer Security Institute (CSI) (annual), 'CSI/FBI Computer Crime and Security Survey', San Francisco, CA.

Consumers Union (2006), 'Notice of Security Breach State Laws', last updated 21 August 2007, http://www.consumersunion.org/campaigns/Breach_laws_May05.pdf.

Cyber Security Research and Development Act of 2002, Public Law 107-305.

D'Aqostino, D. (2003), 'Insuring Security', *CIO Insight*, http://www.cioinsight.com/article2/0,1397,1216110,00.asp.

Deloitte (2006), '2006 Global Security Survey', http://www.deloitte.com/dtt/research/0,1015,cid%253D121102,00.html.

Dempsey, M. (1996), 'The Development of a Theory of Corporate Investment Decision Marking: An Historical Perspective with Implications for Future Development and Teaching', Leeds: School of Business and Economics Studies, University of Leeds.

Department of Homeland Security (2007), 'Build Security In', Website accessed on October 18, 2007. https://buildsecurityin.us-cert.gov/daisy/bsi/home.html.

E-Crime Watch Survey (2006), www.cert.org/archive/pdf/ecrimersurvey06.pdf.

Evers, Joris. July 19, 2005, 'ISPs versus the Zombies', Cnet News.com.

Federal Trade Commission (FTC) (2004), 'FTC Enforces Gramm-Leach-Bliley Act's Safeguards Rule Against Mortgage Companies', http://www.ftc.gov/opa/2004/11/ns.htm.

Ferraiolo, D.F. and D.R. Kuhn (1992), 'Role Based Access Control', paper presented at the 15th National Computer Security Conference.

Ferraiolo, D.F., D.M. Gilbert and N. Lynch (1992), 'Assessing Federal and Commercial Information Security Needs', NISTIR 4976, Gaithersburg, MD: National Institute of Standards and Technology.

Ferraiolo, D.F., J.A. Cugini and R. Kuhn (1995), 'Role Based Access Control: Features and Motivations', *Proc. Eleventh Annual Computer Security Applications Conference*.

FIRST (2006), http://www.first.org/newsroom/releases/20060625a.html.

Frye, C. (2007), 'The State of Software Quality, Part 1: Problems Remain, But All is Not Doomed', *Software Quality News*, 16 February, 45–46.

Gal-Or, E. and A. Ghose (2005), 'The Economic Incentives for Sharing Security Information', *Information Systems Research*, **16**(2), 186–208.

Gallaher, M.P. and B. Kropp (2002), 'The Economic Impact of Inadequate Infrastructure for Software Testing', Prepared for the National Institute of Standards and Technology.

Gallaher, M.P., A.C. O'Connor, and B.M. Kropp (March 2002), 'The Economic Impact of Role-Based Access Control', Prepared for the National Institute of Standards and Technology.

Gallaher, M.P. and B. Rowe (2005), 'IPv6 Quantitative Economic Impact Assessment', Prepared for the National Telecommunication and Information Administration and the National Institute of Standards and Technology.

Gallaher, M.P. and B.R. Rowe (2006), 'The Costs and Benefits of Transferring Technology Infrastructures Underlying Complex Standards: The Case of IPv6', *Journal of Technology Transfer*, **31**, 519–544.

Gallaher, M.P., B.R. Rowe, A.V. Rogozhin and A. Link (2006), 'Economic Analysis of Cyber Security and Private-Sector Investment Decisions', Final report to the Information Grid Division of the Rome Air Force Research Laboratory and the Homeland Security Advanced Research Projects Agency of the Department of Homeland Security, Research Triangle Park, NC.

Garg, A., J. Curtis and H. Halper (2003), 'The Financial Impact of IT Security Breaches: What Do Investors Think?' *Information Systems Security*, March/April.

Gomolski, B. (October 29, 2004), 'Gartner 2004 IT Spending and Staffing Survey Results.

Gordon, L.A., and M.P. Loeb (2002), 'The Economics of Information Security Investment', *ACM Transactions on Information and System Security*, **5**, 438–457.

Gordon, L.A., and M.P. Loeb (2003), 'Economic Aspects of Information Security', Presentation.

Gordon, L.A. and M.P. Loeb (2006), *Managing Cyber Security Resources: A Cost–Benefit Analysis*, New York: McGraw Hill.

Gordon, L.A. and R. Richardson (2004), 'Infosec Economics: New Approaches to Improve Your Data Defenses', *Network Computing*, April, 67–70.

Gordon, L.A., M.P. Loeb and W. Lucyshyn (2003a), 'Sharing Information on Computer Systems Security: An Economic Analysis', *Journal of Accounting and Public Policy*, **22**, 461–485.

Gordon, L.A., M.P. Loeb and T. Sohail (2003b), 'A Framework for Using Insurance for Cyber-Risk Managements', *Communications of the ACM*, **44**(9), 70–75.

Gordon, L.A. M.P. Loeb, W. Lucyshyn and R. Richardson (2005), *2005 CSI/FBI Computer Crime and Security Survey*, Computer Security Institute.

Hagedoorn, J., A.N. Link and N.S. Vonortas (2000), 'Research Partnerships', *Research Policy*, **29**, 567–586.

Hall, B.H., A.N. Link and J.T. Scott (2003), 'Universities as Research Partners', *Review of Economics and Statistics*, **85**, 485–491.

Hayes, R.H. and W.J. Abernathy (1980), 'Managing Our Way to Economic Decline', *Harvard Business Review*, July–August, 67–78.

Hilchenbach, B. (1997), 'Observations on the Real-World Implementation of Role-Based Access Control', 20th NISSC Proceedings, Baltimore, MD.

Hodder, J. (1986), 'Evaluation of Manufacturing Investments: A Comparison of US and Japanese Practices', *Financial Management*, Spring, 17–24.

Hodder, J. and H. Riggs (1985), 'Pitfalls in Evaluating Risky Projects', *Harvard Business Review*, January–February, 128–135.

Hovav, A. and J. D'Arcy (2003), 'The Impact of Denial-of-Service Attack Announcements on the Market Value of Firms', *Risk Management and Insurance Review*, **6**, 97–121.

Huston, G. (2003), 'Waiting for IP version 6', *The ISP Column*, http://www.potaroo.net/papers/isoc/2003-01/Waiting.html.

ICSA Labs (2005), 'The Security Device Event Exchange (SDEE)', http://www.icsalabs.com/icsa/topic.php?tid+b2b4$52d6a7ef-1ea5803f$4c 69-ff36f9b5.

IDC Research (2002), *Internet Usage and Commerce in Western Europe: 2001–2006*, www.idc.com/get-doc.jhtml?containerId= fr2002_04_19_ 115126.

InformationWeek (2004), 'Study: Spammers, Virus Writers Getting Chummy', http://www.informationweek.com/story/showArticle.jhtml? articleID=29101653.

Infosecurity Magazine (annual), http://www.infosecuritymag.com.

Institute for Electrical and Electronics Engineers (IEEE) (1988), *IEEE Guide for the Use of IEEE Standard Dictionary of Measures to Produce Reliable Software*, New York: Institute of Electrical and Electronics Engineers.

Institute for Electrical and Electronics Engineers (IEEE) (1996), *IEEE Software Engineering Collection: Standard Dictionary of Measures to Produce Reliable Software*, New York: Institute of Electrical and Electronics Engineers.

International Business Machines (IBM) (2005), 'IBM Report: Government, Financial Services and Manufacturing Sectors Top Targets of Security Attacks in First Half of 2005', http://www-03.ibm.com/industries/ financialservices/doc/content/news/pressrelease/1368585103.html.

International Organization for Standardization (ISO) (1991), *Information Technology Software Product Evaluation: Quality Characteristics and Guidelines for their Use, ISO-9126*, Geneva: International Organization for Standardization.

Internet Engineering Task Force (IETF) (2005), 'The Intrusion Detective Message Exchange Format', http://www.ietf.org/internet-drafts/draft-ietf-idwg-idmef-xml-14.txt.

ITToolbox (1999), 'ITToolbox Knowledge Bank Forums, SAP 4.5B Test Scripts', http://www.sapassist.com.

Jackson, W. (2001), 'CERT's Full-Disclosure Is Responsible, but Mistrust Remains', *Government Computing News*.

Jaffe, A.B. (1998), 'The Importance of "Spillovers" in the Policy Mission of the Advanced Technology Program', *Journal of Technology Transfer*, **23**, 11–19.

Joshi, J., A. Ghafoor, W.G. Aref and E.H. Spafford (2001), 'Digital Government Security Infrastructure Design Challenges', *Computer*, **34**(2), 66–72.

Keizer, G. (2005), 'AOL: We're Not Zombie Haven', *Information Week*, http://www.informationweek.com/story/showArticle.jhtml?articleID=164 303641.

Krebs, B. (2002), 'White House Pushing Cybersecurity Insurance', *Washington Post*, June 27.

Leech, D.P. and M.W. Chinworth (2001), 'The Economic Impacts of NIST's Data Encryption Standard (DES) Program', Prepared for the National Institute of Standards and Technology, October 2001.

Lemos, R. (2002), 'Data on Internet Threats Still Out Cold', http://news.com.com/Data+on+Internet+threats+still+out+cold/2100-100 1_3-819521.html.

Lichtman, Doug and Eric Posner (2004), 'Holding Internet Service Providers Accountable', University of Chicago John M. Olin Law & Economist Working Paper No. 217.

Link, A.N. and J.T. Scott (2001), 'Public/Private Partnerships: Stimulating Competition in a Dynamic Market', *International Journal of Industrial Organization*, **19**, 763–794.

Link, A.N. and D.S. Siegel (forthcoming), *Innovation, Entrepreneurship, and Technological Change*, Oxford: Oxford University Press.

Litan, Robert E. and Alice M. Rivlin (2001), *The Economic Payoff from the Internet Revolution*, Brookings Institution Press, Washington, DC.

Markoff, J. (2005), 'Early Look at Research Project to Re-Engineer the Internet', *New York Times*, 29 August.

Marsan, C.D. (2004), 'Verio First to Offer Commercial IPv6 Service', *Network World*, 5 January.

Martin, S. and J.T. Scott (2000), 'The Nature of Innovation Market Failure and the Design of Public Support for Private Innovation', *Research Policy*, **29**, 437–448.

McCall, J., P. Richards and G. Walters (1977), 'Factors in Software Quality', NTIS AD-A049-014, -015, -055.

McCullagh, Declan (May 23, 2005), 'Feds to Fight the Zombies', Cnet News.com.

Mi2g (2005a), 'SIPS Report (January)', http://www.mi2g.com/cgi/mi2g/press/ged2004.pdf.

Mi2g (2005b), 'Frequently Asked Questions–SIPS & EVEDA–v1.00', http://www.mi2g.com/cgi/mi2g/press/faq.pdf.

Modigliani, F. and M.H. Miller (1958), 'The Cost of Capital, Corporation, Finance, and the Theory of Investment', *American Economic Review*, **48**, 261–297.

Mowery, D. and T. Simcoe (2002), 'Is the Internet a US Invention? An Economic and Technological History of Computer Networking', *Research Policy*, **31**, 1369–1387.

National Institute of Standards and Technology (NIST) (1997), 'Metrology for Information Technology', http://www.nist.gov/itl/lab/nistirs/ir6025.htm.

National Science Foundation (NSF) (2002), Research and Development in Industry: 2000, Arlington, VA: National Science Foundation.

National Science Foundation (NSF) (2003), Table E-2, 'Research and Development in Industry: 2000', http://www.nsf.gov/statistics/srs02403 (accessed March 12, 2006).

National Science and Technology Council (2006), *Federal Plan for Cyber Security and Information Assurance Research and Development*, Washington, DC: Office of the President.

Neumann, P. (2004), 'Optimistic Optimization', *Communications of the ACM*, **47**: 6.

O'Brien, T.L. (2005), 'Gone Spear-Phishin', *New York Times*, December 4, 2005, http://www.nytimes.com/2005/12/04/business/yourmoney/04spear.html.

Office of Technology Assessment (OTA) (1987), *Defending Secrets, Sharing Data: New Locks and Keys for Electronic Information*, OTA-CIT-3310, Washington, DC: US Government Printing Office.

Ogut, H., M. Nirup and S. Raghunathan (2005), 'Cyber Insurance and IT Security Investment: Impact of Interdependent Risk', presented at the 2005 Workshop on the Economics of Information Security at Harvard University.

Parameswaran, M., X. Zhao, A. Whinston, and F. Fang (2007), 'Reengineering the Internet for Better Security', *IEEE Computer Magazine* **40**(1), 40-44.

President's Information Technology Advisory Committee (2005), *Cyber Security: A Crisis of Prioritization*, Washington, DC: National Coordination Office for Information Technology Research and Development.

Richards, J. (2007), 'Make Firms Bear the Cost to Improve Information Security, says Schneier', Computer Weekly.com, http://www.computer weekly.com/Articles/2007/05/22/223959/make-firms-bear-the-cost-to-im prove-information-security-says-schneier.htm.

Rivers, A.T. and M.A. Vouk (1998), 'Resource, Constrained Non-operational Testing of Software', paper presented at the Ninth International Symposium on Software Reliability Engineering, Paderborn, Germany.

Ross, S.A. (1978), 'The Current Status of the Capital Asset Pricing Model', *Journal of Finance*, **33**, 885–901.

Rowe, B.R. (2007), 'Will IT Security Outsourcing Increase the Social Level of Security?' Presented at *2007 Workshop on the Economics of Information Security*, Pittsburgh, Pennsylvania, June 6–8, 2007.

Rowe, B.R. and M.P. Gallaher (2006), 'Could IPv6 Improve Network Security? And If So, at What Cost?' *I/S: A Journal of Law and Policy for the Information Society*, **2**(2), 231–267.

Ryan, R.J. (1982), 'Capital Market Theory: A Case Study of Methodological Conflict', *Journal of Business Finance and Accounting*, **9**, 443–458.

Sandhu, R.E. and P. Samarati (1994), 'Access Control Principles and Practice', *IEEE Communications*, **32**, 8–15.

Sandhu, R.E., E. Covne, H. Feinstein and C. Youman (1997), 'Role-Based Access Control Models', *IEEE Computer*, **29**, 38–47.

Schechter, S. (2004), 'Computer Security Strength and Risk: A Quantitative Approach', PhD thesis, Harvard University. Boston.

Schneier, B. (May 2007), 'Schneier on Security', http://www.schneier.com/blog/archives/2007/05/do_we_really_ne.html.

Scholtz, T., J. Heiser, J. Pescatore and R. Mogull (2005), 'Use a Cost–Benefit Approach to Justify Security Spending', Gartner Report.

Scott, J.T. (1999), 'The Service Sector's Acquisition and Development of Information Technology: Infrastructure and Productivity', *Journal of Technology Transfer*, **24**, 37–54.

Shaikh, K. (2005), 'IPv6: The Path to Secure Converged Networks', *Sixth Sense Newsletter*, **2**, 34–39.

Smith, L.M. and J. Smith (2006), 'Cyber Crimes Aimed at Publicly Traded Companies: Is Stock Price Affected?' presented at the American Accounting Association Southeast Region Conference.

Soo Hoo, K.J. (2000), 'How Much is Enough? A Risk-Management Approach to Computer Security', PhD thesis, Stanford University, CA.

Sophos (2005), 'Sophos Virus Analyses', http://www.sophos.com/virusinfo/analyses/w32blastera.html.

Stallings, Bill (2008), 'Role-Based Access Control in Computer Security', in *Computer Security: Principles and Practice*, Upper Saddle River, NJ: Prentice Hall.

Stanton, J. (2007), 'Best Practice from the Practitioner', *IT Compliance Magazine*, http://www.itcompliancemagazine.com/best-practice-from-the-practitioner-8.html.

Stenbit, J. (2003), 'Internet Protocol Version 6 (IPv6)', US Department of Defense memorandum of intent dated 9 June.

Stigliz, J. (1988), *Economics of the Public Sector*, New York: W.W. Norton & Company.

Symantec (2005), 'Symantec Internet Security Threat Report: Trends for July 04–December 04', 7.

Tai, K.C. and R.H. Carver (1995), 'A Specification-Based Methodology for Testing Concurrent Programs', in W. Schafer and P. Botella *(eds.), 1995 Europe Software Engineering Conference, Lecture Notes in Computer Science*, Boston, MA: Springer.

Tassey, G. (1997), *The Economics of R&D Policy*, Westport, CT: Quorum Books.

Tassey, G., M. Gallaher and B. Rowe (forthcoming), 'Complex Standards and Sustained Innovation: The Internet Protocol', *International Journal of Technology Management*.

UK Department of Trade and Industry and PriceWaterhouseCoopers (2004), 'Information Security Breaches Survey 2004', http://www.dti.gov.uk/industry_files/pdf/isbs_2004v.3.pdf.

US Census Bureau (2002), '2002 Economic Census: Table 1. Advance Summary Statistics for the United States–2002 NAICS Basis', Available at http://www.census.gov/econ/census02/advance/TABLE1.HTM.

US Census Bureau (2006), *Information and Communication Technology, 2004* (ICT/04), Washington, DC: US Census Bureau.

US Department of Commerce, National Institute of Standards and Technology (NIST) and National Telecommunications and Information Administration (NTIA) (January 21, 2004), 'Request for Comments on Deployment of Internet Protocol Version 6', *Federal Register*, 69 Fed. Reg. 2,890. Copies of those comments are available at http://www.ntia.doc.gov/ntiahome/ntiageneral/ipv6/index.html.

US Department of Commerce (DoC) Task Force on IPv6 (2006), *Technical and Economic Impact Assessment of Internet Protocol Version 6 (IPv6)*.

US Department of Labor, Bureau of Labor Statistics (BLS) (2003), 'National Occupational Employment and Wage Estimates', http://www.bls.gov/oes/2003/may/oes_15Co.htm.

USA Patriot Act (2001), Public Law 107-56.

Varian, H. (2000), 'Managing Online Security Risk', *New York Times*.

Villano, M. (2005), 'Seeing No Evil', *CIO Magazine*.

Vouk, M.A. (1992), 'Using Reliability Models During Testing with Non-Operational Profiles', Presented at the Second Workshop on Issues in Software Reliability Estimation, Livingston, NJ, October 12–13.

Wessner, C.W. (2005), *Partnering Against Terrorism*, Washington, DC: National Academies Press.

White House (2003), 'The National Strategy to Secure Cyberspace', Washington, DC: White House.

Wikipedia (2007), http://en.wikipedia.org/wiki/Network_address_translation.

Index